Employment and Work Relations in Context Series

Series Editors

Tony Elger and Peter Fairbrother

Centre for Comparative Labour Studies,

Department of Sociology,

University of Warwick

The aim of the Employment and Work Relations in Context series is to address questions relating to the evolving patterns of work, employment and industrial relations in specific workplaces, localities and regions. This focus arises primarily from a concern to trace out the ways in which wider policy making, especially by national governments and transnational corporations, impinges upon specific workplaces, labour markets and localities in distinctive ways. A particular feature of the series is the consideration of forms of worker and citizen organization and mobilization in these circumstances. Thus the studies will address major analytical and policy issues through case-study and comparative research.

RESTRUCTURING KRAKOW

Desperately Seeking Capitalism

Jane Hardy and Al Rainnie

MANSELL

First published 1996 by
Mansell Publishing Limited, *A Cassell Imprint*
Wellington House, 125 Strand, London WC2R 0BB
215 Park Avenue South, New York, NY 10003

British Library Cataloguing in Publication Data
A catalogue record for this book is available from the British Library.

Library of Congress Cataloging-in-Publication Data
Hardy, Jane.
   Restructuring Krakow: desperately seeking capitalism / Jane Hardy and Al Rainnie.
      p.   cm. — (Employment and work relations in context)
   Includes bibliographical references (p.   ) and index.
   ISBN 0–7201–2231–7
   1. Poland – Economic policy — 1990 –   2. Krakow Region (Poland) – Economic policy.
3. Poland – Economic conditions — 1990 –   4. Krakow Region (Poland) – Economic
conditions. I. Rainnie, Al. II. Title. III. Series.
HC340.3.H37 1996
338.9438 ' 6 – dc20   95–48 979
                                                                              CIP

Typeset by York House Typographic, London
Printed and bound in Great Britain by
Biddles Ltd, Guildford and King's Lynn

CONTENTS

Acknowledgements

Financial support for the research on which this book is based came from a number of sources, including TEMPUS, the University of Hertfordshire, and the Nuffield Trust.

Without the organizational, translating and personal support of our colleagues at the Krakow Academy of Economics, as well as their friendship, this book could never have been written. We are particularly grateful to Janusz Jaworski, Janusz Kot, Ewa Piasecka, Marek Dziura and Malgorzata Bednarczyk.

We owe an enormous debt to the series editors, Tony Elger and Peter Fairbrother. Their comments, though critical and painful at the time, were enormously helpful. We would also like to thank Mike Haynes and Hugo Radice, who read and made helpful comments on early drafts of various chapters.

We do not expect that our friends and colleagues mentioned above will agree with our argument, but we are grateful for all their help and support.

Jane Hardy
Al Rainnie

Hertford, August 1995

Abbreviations

CMEA	Committee for Mutual Economic Assistance
CRZZ	Official Trade Union Federation, reformed in early 1980s
EBRD	European Bank for Reconstruction and Development
FDI	Foreign direct investment
GATT	General Agreement on Tariffs and Trade
GDP	Gross domestic product
GNP	Gross national product
GUS	Polish Central Statistical Office
HTS	Huta Tadeusz Sendzimira – the Krakow Steelworks
IMF	International Monetary Fund
JVC	Joint venture company
NAFTA	North American Free Trade Area
NIC	Newly Industrialized Country
NIF	National Investment Fund
NSZZ	Solidarity Solidarnosc
OPZZ	Replaced CRZZ in early 1980s
PAIZ	Polish State Agency for Foreign Investment
PIT	Partners in Transition (Poland, Czech Republic, Slovakia and Hungary)
Popiwek	Tax-based incomes policy
PSL	Peasant Party
PZPR	Polish Communist Party
Sejm	Polish parliament

SMEs	Small and medium-sized enterprises
SdRP	Social Democracy of the Polish Republic (reformed Communist Party)
SLD	Coalition dominated by SdRP
SOE	State owned enterprise
Solidarity 80	Radical offshoot from Solidarity
TNC	Transnational corporation
Zl.	Polish zloty (£1$\simeq$ 21.37 000 in 1994)
ZPT	Tobacco factory

INTRODUCTION

This book is about Poland and its people, particularly those in the Krakow region, in the aftermath of the transformation of 1989. Our book joins a rapidly growing library of texts devoted to the economies of Central and Eastern Europe in the wake of the collapse of the old regimes, but attempts to develop a framework that sets us apart from most orthodox analyses of the past, present and future of countries such as Poland.

In the aftermath of the collapse of the Berlin Wall the prevailing mood in the West, amongst political leaders at least, appeared to be self-righteousness born out of apparent victory. Capitalism was seen as the inevitable victor over a sclerotic, repressive and hopelessly inefficient mode of production – the centrally planned so-called socialist economy. Furthermore, the lesson we were being asked to learn was that it was a particular version of capitalism that had triumphed, one based on competition, free markets and minimal state intervention. The lesson for the transforming economies of Central and Eastern Europe was obvious; adopting a set of blue prints based on the economics of the New Right meant that transformation would rapidly and unproblematically bring wealth and freedom. Viewed from Britain in the mid-1990s after sixteen years of free-market rhetoric, with a seemingly intractable unemployment problem, growing homelessness and a widening gap between rich and poor, there are obvious and serious questions regarding the kind of society that might emerge in Poland from the process of transformation. However, initially at least, the medicine was enthusiastically administered and was underpinned by an unquestioning faith in what markets could deliver.

There is a whole series of theoretical and empirical problems with the popular prescriptions, but at least two are worth mentioning here. The first was that analyses of the process and pattern of transformation appeared to be developing in glorious isolation from a wider analysis of the changes taking place in global capitalism. Little attempt was made to place Poland in the context of an emerging international division of labour. Secondly, and surprisingly for a country that had produced Solidarity, one of the most important independent trade-union movements the world has ever seen, workers were either absent from the analysis, or in the case of neoclassical economics, unions appeared simply as a blot on the free-market landscape.

Our problems with orthodox (not just neoclassical) economics and its various attempts to construct accounts of the process and outcomes of transformation were reinforced by a short visit to Krakow in 1993. Unemployment was high and rising while poverty was affecting a growing proportion of the population. There was an obvious disparity between the rhetoric and the reality of transformation in terms not only of levels of foreign investment and speed of growth of the private sector, but also of the effects of transformation on people's lives. The picture of Poland as a success story could only have been produced by academics who studied the statistics emerging from the ministry of ownership transformation and certainly never set foot outside the government buildings of Warsaw. Nothing that we had read captured the complexities of the changes that we were witnessing at workplace level. Initial euphoria was being replaced by uncertainty and a questioning of the simplistic nostrums of the first wave of American free marketeers, who by 1993 had long since departed. In general, Poles were becoming increasingly critical of 'seagulls', both academics and advisers, who arrived, made a great noise, crapped on people from a great height and then flew away.

This book then is about change in Poland in general, and Krakow in particular. However, it is not a book that celebrates the changes that are taking place, as so many do, as the inevitable and welcome victory of the free market over a satellite of the 'evil empire'. As socialists, we celebrated the victory of Solidarity and the collapse of the Soviet empire, but for very different reasons from most commentators. The new society will bring new possibilities, but also a new kind of fear. On the one hand, we explore the fears generated by poverty and unemployment, driven by increasing integration into the world economy. On the other hand, independent trade unions and independent political parties, freed from the dead hand of Stalinized versions of socialism, open up avenues of organization and resistance that have been effectively closed for half a century. It is in this light that we welcome the changes that have taken place.

It should be clear, therefore, that anyone searching in this book for an argument that justifies some rose-tinted view of a supposedly socialist past will be sadly disappointed. Our approach is predicated on the assumption that Poland was never a socialist society. If, as we believe, socialism is concerned with working people taking control of their workplaces and communities, then a society that systematically and repeatedly repressed workers demanding precisely these things forfeited any claims to being socialist.

Our purpose then in writing this book is to attempt to fulfil a number of tasks: firstly, to develop a Marxist analysis of the decline and collapse of the economies of Central and Eastern Europe in general, and Poland in particular; secondly, to develop a critique of orthodox (and some radical) analyses of, and prescriptions for, the process of transformation; and thirdly, to develop an analysis of the way that the process of transformation is affecting the economies and people of regions such as Krakow.

We move from a fairly abstract and theoretical discussion of approaches to transformation to a detailed analysis of the changes that are taking place in people's working lives in factories in Krakow. Concretely, we look at the way that decisions taken by transnationals will affect the jobs and conditions of workers in Krakow, particularly women, who have borne the brunt of the costs of transformation. We do not see an unproblematic transmission from the global to the local, and we develop an analysis of the way that the changing role of the local and national state intervenes in this process.

A Note on Method

This book is based on seven visits to Poland, principally to Krakow, but also to Warsaw, that we undertook between 1993 and the end of 1994. The research was not based on a predetermined plan of action, but developed as time went on and sources of finance and access to individuals and organizations occurred. This was a rapidly developing piece of work taking place in rapidly changing circumstances. Access and analysis developed alongside each other, and we had to seize opportunities to gain access to significant individuals or organizations as they arose or (more likely) as often as we could construct them.

Our first visit provided two invaluable sources. The first was access to key officials in the ministries in Warsaw which was arranged by a contact from KPMG Peat Marwick in Poland. In the early 1990s we were surprised at how easy it appeared to be to arrange access to senior officials in various ministries who were willing to discuss issues ranging from privatization to small firm formation and industrial relations with us at great length. We continue to have access in a way that we could not expect in Britain. The second source was a group in the Krakow Academy of Economics with whom we came into contact during our first, TEMPUS-funded visit. Dr Janus Jaworski and his colleagues at the Centre for International Enterprise Development have provided us with a base upon which all our work has been built. Crucially, our colleague at the Centre, Janusz Kot, turned out to be the Solidarity representative for the Academy. Nearly all our subsequent access to individuals and organizations in and around Krakow was arranged by Janusz through the Solidarity network. Furthermore, two days spent interviewing senior national Solidarity officials in Gdansk were organized through the same contact network. Orthodox approaches to access, learnt from research in Britain, would simply not have yielded the same depth and breadth of information, and indeed might not have gained us access at all.

The outcome was an astonishing degree of generosity and openness on the part of the individuals and organizations we visited. Workplace visits would last anything up to four hours, and yielded an enormous amount of detail. However, it is worth mentioning one or two points about the process of information gathering. The first problem arises with reference to the nature of statistical data. There are well-attested problems of reliability with statistical data from state sources in former centrally planned economies, but the problems do not stop there. We were warned at a very early stage about putting too much reliance on the information that organizations gave us concerning their financial position, firstly because technical accounting skills were still relatively scarce, and secondly because there were still a whole series of good reasons why organizations might wish to conceal their financial status. There is no easy method of confronting these problems.

A further methodological issue arose from our heavy reliance on semi-structured interviews as a research method. Beyond the issues that arose that are covered in most text books, such as the reliability of memory, the effects of class and gender on interviewer–interviewee relations, and comparability of data, problems arose from working in Poland; specifically, neither of us speaks Polish, so we have been totally reliant on translators at all times. We have been astonishingly fortunate in so far as our colleagues have translated at most interviews. It makes an enormous difference having a translator who is familiar with the academic substance of the interview, as we noticed on the few occasions when we had to use specialist but non-technical translators. In one interview 'Total Quality Management (TQM)', we found out subsequently, was being translated as 'Total Management Control'. This may be accurate as a statement of the underlying managerialist philosophy of TQM, but it did not aid the interview process.

No matter how competent the translator, it is still the case that our questions and our respondents' answers are both being filtered through the translation process. We have no idea to what extent our questions and any responses were being interpreted, rather than reported. Researching change in Poland is a highly political issue and this may have an effect on the data and its interpretations. For example, our colleagues at the Academy are all supporters of Solidarity, which may not appear to be a problem, but there appeared to be a tension in the atmosphere when we interviewed representatives from the old Stalinist union confederation, OPZZ. There is no love lost between OPZZ and Solidarity.

Furthermore, we made no attempt to record interviews on tapes. This was partly because of the language issue, but also because Poland is a society only recently emerging from forty years of repression, and we felt that putting a tape deck in the middle of the table at the start of an interview might be unnecessarily intimidatory. We relied on taking field notes. This accounts for the lack of any directly reported speech in a text that relies heavily on interviews as a research method.

Structure of the Book

The book comprises of four sections.

Section I consists of Chapter 1 only and examines the nature of the debate around the transformation of the economies of Central and Eastern Europe. A critique of neoclassical, evolutionary and institutionalist approaches is outlined. The second half of the chapter, after criticizing analyses that are based on 'exceptionalist' approaches to countries such as Poland, concludes by outlining an approach that sees the autarchic development of the Visegrad countries as an extreme form of capitalist development that characterized a particular period in the development of global capitalism. It is important to emphasize that we are not engaged in some dry abstract academic debate. The theories that we criticize have underpinned prescriptions that have had a dramatic impact on real people's lives. It is with this in mind that we develop our particular approach which has implications for the way that people conduct their lives, just as much as for the possibilities of radical change.

Section II, consisting of four chapters, applies the framework of analysis developed in Chapter 1 to the experience of Poland. Chapter 2 provides an overview of the development of the Polish economy from 1948 to 1994. The following three chapters deal with industrial relations, foreign direct investment (FDI) and privatization, respectively. Three themes are developed: firstly, that continuity as well as change is important in analysing post-1989 developments; secondly, an emphasis on the centrality of the role of organized labour to the process and pattern of development of Poland throughout the whole of our period; and thirdly, that foreign direct investment and privatization are both central to the process of transformation and inextricably linked. Rather than emphasizing the uniqueness of the process of transformation, we emphasize the way that FDI and privatization must be put into the context of tendencies towards internationalization and deregulation in the restructuring of the global economy.

Section III comprises four chapters which examine in detail the process and outcomes of the transformation of the Krakow regional economy. Previous sections have taken us from abstract theoretical debate to an analysis of the forces that are driving the process of transformation of regions such as Krakow. Essentially, the analysis has taken us to the gates of particular workplaces. We now enter workplaces in the Krakow region and examine changes taking place in both organizational structure and labour-process characteristics. In so doing we counter any threat of economic determinism, by suggesting that organizations and individuals have their freedom of manœuvre constrained by the forces that bear down on particular workplaces. However, by organizing and taking action, individuals change not only their workplaces but also the nature of the forces at play, and indeed themselves.

In Chapter 6 we outline the development of the Krakow regional economy, stressing the region's dependence on Huta T. Sendzimira, HTS (the steel works). The next chapter critically examines Western models of local economic development that are either being applied in Krakow or recommended for the region. All these models assume, mistakenly we believe, that there is a total institutional void in regions such as Krakow. In Chapters 8 and 9, we examine in detail the sectoral trajectories of development of steel, confectionery and cigarette production, using three Krakow factories as case studies. The tension between Solidarity's role as agent of restructuring and as workplace trade union runs through all our case studies.

Section IV concludes the book by bringing together all the elements of our analysis in Chapter 10, together with an exploration of how the future of the Krakow economy might unfold. Our conclusions might appear to be bleak, in so far as we see Poland generally developing the characteristics of a peripheral economy, with the process of combined and uneven development producing small islands of advanced development. However, we see nothing inevitable in this process and, in particular, suggest that the process of development is creating conditions that foster the emergence of a new independent labour movement.

SECTION I Theories of Transition

1 PROPHETS AND PROFITS

There is an emerging consensus in the West that views the events of 1989 in Central and Eastern Europe as a watershed, demonstrating the inevitable failure of a Soviet-style economy and the equally inevitable victory of the market. Emerging from this view is the belief that the change is revolutionary and will, in the fullness of time, bring social, political and material gains for most, if not all, the people of the formerly planned economies. Furthermore, it posits the idea that the motor of change is endogenous, the impetus being rooted in the failure of a particular mode of production, the planned economy. What unites most accounts of this process of transformation is a belief that Poland in particular and Soviet style economies in general were somehow exceptional. The internal dynamic of these economies was taken to be separate from, and different to, the dynamics of capitalism in general, from which these economies were taken to be almost hermetically sealed. The logic of this is that the development of, and subsequent crises in these economies, it is argued, emanated from within. It is held that there was a peculiar internal dynamic to these systems that led inevitably to stagnation and ultimate collapse. What follows from this approach is a belief that these economies could be analysed in isolation from the developments within the world economy. Although there are degrees of difference between the various strands that comprise this dominant ideology, they can all be grouped under the heading of exceptionalism, that is the idea that Central and East European economies were somehow a different species from the capitalist animals of the West.

A further consequence of the exceptionalist approach is the view that free markets and centrally planned economies are inevitably juxtaposed. Rather than being viewed as lying at different ends of a spectrum, economies are grouped into two broadly defined but mutually exclusive camps, each with its own distinct features and dynamics. Change is then seen as the movement between two discrete and unconnected end points, two clearly defined ways of organizing production and distribution. Once this view is accepted, the task in hand becomes clear; it is one of generating a transition from a planned to a market economy. As a result, there was little disagreement between policy-makers, academics and the leadership of Solidarity about the desirability of a Western-style market economy as the end result of the process of transformation. There was, however, sharp disagreement regarding the sequencing and speed of reforms and the appropriate institutional frameworks of transition (Brada 1993, Murrell 1993).

This chapter starts by examining the theoretical background to and prescriptions emerging from the three main schools of economic thought that have dominated the debate on transformation. The approaches can be classified as neoclassical, evolutionary and institutionalist. All three fall under the heading of exceptionalism because they share a view of the internal collapse of what they take to be non-capitalist Central and Eastern Europe, but they differ in their conceptions of the character of the appropriate capitalist end state and in their related analyses of the process of transition itself. Our critical assessment will identify both the similarities and the differences between them, and in so doing lay the basis for our own alternative analysis.

In the second half of the chapter we develop a Marxist approach which informs our analysis of transformation both at a general level and specifically in the case of Krakow. In doing so, we go back to the basics and stress that the dynamics of capitalism are rooted in two fundamental forces: firstly, competition, that is the clash between competing blocs of capital; and secondly, accumulation, that is the conflict between capital and labour over the drive to extract surplus value successfully. The forces of competition, furthermore, make the drive to accumulate appear to be an externally imposed necessity. However, the development of capitalism cannot simply be explained by the unfolding of a series of determinate laws, nor simply as the outcome of a series of strikes or struggles. The outcome of such struggles, as Clarke (1991: 1) points out, will not be determined merely by the will or determination of the forces at play, but would also be circumscribed by the economic, social, political and ideological framework within which they are fought out. People take action in a world within which the room for manœuvre is restricted to a degree by the forces which drive capitalist development. However, in taking action, people not only change the nature of those forces, but in so doing change themselves (Callinicos 1989).

On this reading, industrial restructuring is a necessary element in the dynamic of capital accumulation, involving a process of creative destruction that reallocates capital between industries, sectors and locations. As Hudson (1992) argues, within the framework of a capitalist economy, with commodity production at its centre, that is production for exchange and the pursuit of profit, restructuring is a social process driven by the imperative of competition. This involves the main social actors involved in the production process – capital, labour and the state. We argue, therefore, that the state in Central and Eastern Europe was and indeed remains a capitalist state, and cannot, as in many current forms of analysis, be seen as a neutral arbiter of the national interest. We start, though, with more orthodox analyses of the transformation of Central and Eastern Europe.

Capitalist Triumphalism?

By 1989, as we shall see, there was a general consensus amongst academics, politicians and union leaders in Poland that piecemeal reform was no longer on the agenda. Fundamental reform was thought to be necessary, and there was no shortage of Western advisers and academics who were willing to preach the virtues of capitalism. The cure for the disease inherent in the body politic of the previous regime required drastic and painful surgery. Specifically, the neoclassical prescription in the case of Poland manifested itself in the shape of the Balcerowicz Programme (1990), which had two main elements. The first was a draconian stabilization programme along standard International Monetary Fund (IMF) lines, to deal with hyperinflation. The second was liberalization, aimed at creating the conditions for the emergence of competitive markets. In other words, an attempt to jump start a market economy. This involved measures which were supposed to free up entrepreneurship, abolish barriers to entry and exit to the market, and abolish central price controls, with privatization lying at the core of the policy. What was distinctive about the Balcerowicz Programme was that it stressed the necessity of the immediacy, comprehensiveness and simultaneity of reforms (see Lipton and Sachs 1990: 99):

> The transition process is a seamless web. Structural reforms cannot work without a price system: a steady working price system cannot be put in place without ending the excess demand and creating a convertible currency: and a credit squeeze and tight macroeconomic policy cannot be sustained unless prices are realistic, so that there is a rational basis for deciding which firms should close. At the same time, for real structural adjustment to take place under the pressure of tight demand, the macroeconomic shock must be accompanied by other measures, including the selling off of state assets, freeing up of the private sector, establishing provision for bankruptcy, preparing a social safety net and undertaking tax reform. Clearly the reform process must be comprehensive.

If a new system is to be established a critical mass of market institutions is necessary for its functioning (comprehensiveness). The transition is necessarily painful in terms of unemployment and other social costs, but there is no reason to delay the inevitable, since this would allow enemies of reform to subvert the process (speed). Finally, a market system cannot be installed in a piecemeal fashion because of the interconnectedness of the system (simultaneity).

In the neoclassical view the engine of development, in the case of either economies in transition or developing economies, is efficient resource allocation, which reduces the task of policy-makers to little more than setting the framework for the pursuit of equilibrium and 'getting the price right'. Once the appropriate institutional arrangements are in place to generate efficient resource allocation, growth will automatically follow. The necessary institutional arrangements are, unsurprisingly, competitive markets, in both the domestic economy and international trade. Ultimately the government should leave private producers operating through the market mechanism to supply all but a few public goods. The role of the government should be confined to that of providing the physical and institutional infrastructure of a market economy. Kornai (1990a: 38) argues that 'unambiguous and emphatic statutory force (should be given) to the principle that the private sector has unrestricted scope in the economy'. Not only does the neoclassical view, exemplified by Lipton and Sachs (1990), emphasize the market as an allocative mechanism, but it is also invoked as a Darwinian selector, suggesting that the market will bring forth the necessary structural changes as price signals indicate which industries should close and which survive.

This approach emanates from the view that the market and market economies are some sort of self-evident and natural mechanism from which societies can only deviate for a short time and at their peril. For example, Kornai (1990a) suggests that units of the private sector need no stimulation, agitation or direction to act along the lines of the market, as this is their natural mode of existence. Furthermore, he claims that the first engines of capitalist development are individual entrepreneurs and this can be generalized throughout all epochs and all societies. This view ignores the formidable evidence suggesting that market forms have been a peripheral force in determining production and human development (Polanyi 1944). Rather than relying on market forces during their initial stages of development, emerging industrial capitalist economies were nurtured by mercantilist policies of the state, which provided the necessary institutions and infrastructure and, in particular, protection to support private initiative. Thus, it was states that preceded markets rather than the other way round. To suggest that on the eighth day markets were created and states simply appeared to rectify market failure ignores the whole history of capitalist development, whether it be seventeenth-century Britain or the East Asian Newly Industrialized Countries (NICs) after 1945.

The intervention of the state in the process of transformation is only deemed to be appropriate in cases of market failure. Past experience of 'excessive' state intervention dictates that enterprises are largely left the task of reorganizing their own activities, with the idea of formulating an active industrial policy being rejected (Gomulka 1992: 361). Lipton and Sachs (1990: 88) go further, suggesting that the legacy of communist bureaucracy makes the state incapable of intervening in cases of market failure, even where theory suggests a more nuanced policy: 'the existing bureaucracy as equipped, professionally or temperamentally cannot be relied upon to implement sophisticated policies, based on Western style theories of welfare economics of the second-best. The bureaucracy cannot be relied upon for efficiency in regulating monopoly prices, promoting infant industries or implementing industrial policy.' Existing institutions and structures must be either bypassed or circumvented, if not abolished altogether. Whilst it is acknowledged that a *nomenklatura* exists, the analysis remains at a simplistic level, viewing this strata as a homogeneous mass, uniformly wedded to power within a communist system that is implacably opposed to any process of marketization. However, far from the *nomenklatura* ruling class resisting change, partial reforms in the previous decade allowed some sections of this group the opportunity to transform themselves into management and entrepreneurs. Thus sections of the *nomenklatura* had gradually accommodated to the idea of the market economy in the period of reforms aimed at instituting market socialism in the 1980s. For example, in the years before 1989 many companies were bought, often by senior members of the Communist Party using imprecise regulations to take over factories at a nominal price. Thus the *nomenklatura* began to distribute the benefits of the development of the market economy well before 1989 (Cieochinska 1992). Therefore, contrary to the idea that the state will be circumvented, it is rather the case that certain sections of the old bureaucracy constitute a significant element of the embryonic entrepreneurial class.

This does not sit comfortably with the dichotomy of market and state assumed by Lipton and Sachs (1990), which suggests that jump starting a market economy will shift decision making to the anonymous market and undermine the bureaucratically and economically dominant elite. Thus an understanding of the recent past is critical in terms of explaining the present, in that power relations and class interests are not only more complicated than has been suggested, but also that these tensions will manifest themselves in the processes and outcomes of restructuring. This is an important point to which we shall return.

The neoclassical approach is essentially ahistorical and depends on a massive myth concerning the operation of markets. It is reliant on a myth in so far as it depends upon a conception of the existence of and operation of markets that has not and never will correspond to anything like reality. We understand that theory is based on abstraction from the 'real', but to suggest that the dynamic of capitalist economies depends on decisions of atomized economic actors in general and entrepreneurs in particular is simply a false abstraction. The global economy into which Poland is inextricably bound is riven by contradictory tendencies determined by globalization, balkanization and the role of increasingly powerful transnational corporations. To suggest, in these circumstances, that liberalization is about liberating latent entrepreneurialism is simply disingenuous. The reality is opening Poland and its people up to the machinations of international monopoly capitalism. Poland has already had some experience of what this might entail, in that the initial impact of the Balcerowicz Programme was more shock than therapy, and far more brutal than its proponents had predicted. The reform programme assumed a fall in national product of 1 per cent, a fall of production in the socialized economy by about 5 per cent, 20 per cent inflation and 2 per cent unemployment (Ksiezopolski 1992: 231). In reality, employment in the state sector fell by more than 14 per cent in 1989–90, and output in the socialized sector fell by 24 per cent. Unemployment rose from 0.05 per cent in December 1989 to 8.4 per cent (more than 1.5 million people) by June 1991. Inflation reached levels of around 250 per cent. Real wage levels fell in the state sector in 1990, and real household incomes fell by over 30 per cent for pensioners and more than 50 per cent for peasant households in the first quarter of 1990 (Ksiezopolski 1991, Gora *et al.* 1993).

The outcome was, at least in some circles, a growing disillusionment with the simple (and simplistic) nostrums of the free marketeers. The image of capitalist life to be derived from the media clashed horribly with growing unemployment and poverty. The disillusionment was enhanced by the here today and gone tomorrow attitude of the free-market gurus. Capitalism *per se* was not rejected, however, but the red in tooth and claw variety had not only failed to deliver but was also seen to be creating fundamental problems. Instead of a quick fix, what was offered was a slower transition towards a market economy with a human face.

Evolutionary Counterattack? Same Destination, Different Route

The door was therefore open for prescriptions based on the evolutionary paradigm (Murrell 1992, Pickel 1992, Stark 1990, 1993). This perspective provides a critique of the neoclassical school, and offers an explanation as to why shock therapy failed, by suggesting that the focus on allocative efficiency and competition within a general equilibrium framework is misleading. The evolutionists are highly critical of the predictive and prescriptive capacity of economic theory for being reliant on a set of theoretical propositions known to be true only under highly stylized circumstances. Further, policy-makers, such as Lipton and Sachs (1990), are criticized for seeing themselves as technocrats with 'correct answers' standing outside of society, untainted by historical prejudices and present commitments. Policy recommendations are thus oblivious to history and the specific local conditions in which these prescriptions are applied.

Whilst this perspective is not strictly homogeneous and encompasses a spectrum of views, broadly the central arguments can be summarized as follows: firstly, it is argued that the centre of attention should be on processes and mechanisms producing growth and change, focusing particularly on innovation at the level both of technology and institutions, rather than equilibrium processes; and, secondly, that economic theorizing should begin with a satisfactory description of economic agents.

According to the evolutionists, the behaviour of economic agents is a product of both present incentives and historical and social processes. Thus reformers are criticized for taking as their starting point what they assume to be current incentives, rather than taking account of the way that historical processes and past behaviour have shaped economic institutions and the behaviour of economic agents. Evolutionists are highly critical of any notion of a blueprint of a market economy or of the market institutions which comprise it. They point to the irrelevance of textbook economic theory when compared to the vividness and variety of arrangements present in functioning capitalist economies, where the institutional matrix produced is idiosyncratic and contingent.

Specifically, the evolutionists purport to make a contribution to understanding the behaviour of firms, in that by arguing that markets and institutions are embedded, they are able to explain the slow adjustment of state owned enterprises (SOEs) to the hard budget constraint (limited subsidies). They suggest that the use of routines and search reflect the historical experience of an organization, and argue that it follows that persistence in organizational behaviour is to be expected. Thus, in the short term, the stock of existing routines, behavioural patterns and expectations may not be suitable for the new environment. These continuing patterns of behaviour may have been entirely appropriate for the old world, but do not match the new conditions that are to be faced. Indeed, this point is made more concrete by Winieckie (1992) when he discusses the perverse behaviour of SOEs in response to the hard budget constraint. Old patterns of behaviour carried over, with the result that large firms possessing the strongest political clout encountered no problems in borrowing. So the list of 523 enterprises that had lost their creditworthiness by January 1991 did not include any large enterprises, whilst at the same time firms that may have had potential, but no influence, were declared bankrupt. Thus the high survival rate of industries that were assumed to fail under the new market conditions reflected special side deals carried over from the previous regime, rather than effective adaptation to market conditions. The extensive use of inter company credit to circumvent the (slightly harder) budget constraint provides an example of the unanticipated adaptive behaviour of economic agents.

Whilst the evolutionary paradigm makes a contribution in that it provides a powerful attack on the neoclassical case where markets are exogenous and institutions peripheral, the difference between the two views should not be overstated. Central to the evolutionists' case for gradualism is the argument that economic agents adapt their behaviour slowly. However, the short-term failure of economic agents to adjust may have been very short term indeed, according to research by the World Bank. Whereas much literature on Eastern Europe assumes that existing managers are incapable of restructuring firms to adapt to the market economy, the World Bank Study (Pinot 1992) showed substantial differences in the profitability of firms, even though companies in the same branch of industry faced similar external circumstances. The assumption that the lack of entrepreneurial skills accounts in a significant way for the lack of restructuring by firms should be treated with some caution. In the following chapter we discuss the way in which both the operation of the informal economy and increased contact with Western firms increased the entrepreneurial opportunism of sections of Polish management and bureaucracy before 1989.

Despite the fact that the main task of the evolutionist literature on Central and Eastern Europe is to criticize shock therapy and the neoclassical assumptions that underpin it, both their prescriptions and their vision of the end state of transformation are remarkably similar. On the basis of developments in the Chinese economy, Murrell (1992) advocates a dualist approach, whereby the state and private sectors are subject to different institutional arrangements and macroeconomic policy, reflecting different requirements determined by the different historical development of these sectors. Resources, he argues, should be concentrated initially in the private sector, which will be the engine of growth, eventually displacing an undynamic and inefficient state sector. Therefore, their disagreement lies in the speed of reform, which, the evolutionists suggest, should be more gradual, and the sequencing of reforms whereby the private sector is encouraged before reform of the state sector is undertaken. For evolutionists, the growth of markets is ultimately a desirable outcome.

Whilst the evolutionary paradigm stresses the importance of institutions, innovation and economic development, it fails to provide a coherent framework in which these elements interact. The end state, the particular combination of market and hierarchy, will ultimately be determined by the market, with the most efficient institutions gradually emerging. This reduces the debate between the shock therapists and the evolutionary perspective to one in which the former emphasize the immediacy, speed and simultaneity of reform, and the latter ultimately argue for gradualism, seeing the seeds of change coming from within existing institutions and prepared to tolerate a wider number of configurations of state and market. Whilst we acknowledge that institutions limit the field of action, precluding some directions and constraining certain courses (Stark 1993), the evolutionists fail to provide a framework of analysis that offers any explanation of the constraints and limitations in which states and markets operate. Their approach is essentially pluralist and devoid of class analysis, seeing no inherent contradiction between workers and the demands of capital.

The Institutionalists: 'The Wrong Type of Capitalism'

There is another school of thought which has influence in Central and Eastern Europe and can broadly be described as 'institutionalist'. It includes Lo (1995) and Chang (1995) but finds its clearest expression in the work of Amsden *et al.* (1994). The aim of this approach is to encourage the development of a 'Western-style corporatist social order' (Amsden *et al.* 1994: 209). The major point of departure from the evolutionary approach is that the institutionalists do not believe that this will happen either spontaneously, or as a response to the forces of supply and demand. Planning has to be reinvented and capitalism embedded in societies in which, it is argued, for decades it has been unable to fit.

All of these writers draw on notions of 'late industrialization' and in particular the experience of the East Asian NICs. Chang (1995) argues that these countries are not a special case and further that the lessons of adopting a long-term industrial strategy are not only desirable for the economies of Central and Eastern Europe, but also transferable to them. In the case of South Korea, the role of the state involved nurturing an effective domestic capitalist class and compelling foreign capital to conform to a national development strategy, through appropriate ownership, pricing, financial and exchange rate policies. In South Korea and Japan, the strength of the state relied heavily on the interdependence of firms being recognized and built into strategic decision-making in the business sector. Late industrialization involves a number of essential elements; firstly, that large firms are bred by deliberate government policy in order to compete internationally against the oligopolies of industrialized countries; and secondly, that this process is mediated by the state, in particular by an autonomous bureaucracy embedded in the society at large. The outcome is semi-autarchic development, state driven, with a high degree of protection from international competition playing a pivotal role in restructuring (Chang 1995: 342).

For the institutionalists, the lessons of late industrialization are that backward economies can only instigate a catching up process if such actions are mediated by the state and the institutions of an autonomous bureaucracy. State owned enterprises (SOEs) it is argued, for example, could not be expected to restructure themselves unaided. Amsden *et al.* (1994) argue that, for the economies of Central and Eastern Europe of the mid-1990s, common sense dictates the following course of action; creating conditions under which viable state enterprises can be self-selected into growth; giving these state enterprises (as they turn into privately owned enterprises) adequate institutional support to generate saving, aid investment, and further technical advance; and empowering a government bureaucracy that can harmonize political democracy with the degree of economic governance that modern capitalism requires (Amsden *et al.* 1994: 206). On this reading, shock therapy may have had a role to play in signalling a shift in the trajectory of the economy, but it was entirely unsuited to the task of capitalist construction. Indeed, Amsden *et al.* (1994: 4) argue that this was quite simply the wrong capitalist model. They conclude that the activities and prescriptions of the Bretton Woods institutions, such as the World Bank and the IMF, allied to a mistaken commitment to the free market based on simplistic eighteenth-century liberalism, have been little short of disastrous in places such as Poland. If these economies had reinvented planning and put into place appropriate institutional structures, recognizing the centrality of the state in any process of restructuring, then outcomes could have been different. Radice (1994a) is pessimistic regarding the transferability of the late industrialization model and concludes that, in the absence of the East Asian model, the future for Central and East European economies is to be situated in a dependent and semi-peripheral position within the new international division of labour. This will yield a tolerable standard of living for most citizens, but with permanent high unemployment and inequalities typical of the semi-periphery.

There are a number of problems with this approach, not least of which is the analysis of the state. The pluralist analysis of the state adopted by Amsden *et al.* views the state as an independent, honest broker that not only mediates between competing interest groups but also has power and influence in negotiating with nation states, trading blocs and transnational corporations. In contrast, as we shall see, we view the relationship between the state and capital as far more intimate than Amsden *et al.* acknowledge. The relationship between the two is complex and ever changing; however, the two grow up side by side and are inextricably linked. The major role of the state is to guarantee the conditions for successful capital accumulation within its own borders and the state cannot be viewed as an independent arbiter of some reified notion of the national interest. A particularly thorny issue, as Amsden herself admits, is that it is unclear whether the spectacular growth of the East Asian NICs could have been achieved under conditions of democracy.

Amsden acknowledges that the conditions that allowed semi-autarchic development of the type followed by Latin American countries between the 1930s and 1960s, or, in an extreme sense, by the Central and East European countries after 1948 no longer exist. It is argued that these economies must follow a path of increasing involvement in the international economy and, therefore, must produce goods that are competitive on world markets. Radice (1994a) takes this point further, stressing the dynamics of capitalist development through internationalization of production, and in particular foreign direct investment (FDI) as a way of locking countries and regions into the emerging international division of labour. Neither Radice nor Amsden *et al.* follow the logic of their argument by acknowledging that the changing relationship between the state and capital at a general level fatally undermines late industrialization as a model of development. In essence, Radice overestimates the power of individual states, particularly those in peripheral economies, to intervene in this process to attract and secure elements of mobile capital.

The integration of Poland into the world economy is going to be largely determined by its relationship firstly with the European Union (EU), and secondly with FDI. In both cases, the relationship is complex but the Polish state finds itself in a weak, if not subservient, position. The institutionalist analysis understates the fact that given the disintegration of the Committee for Mutual Economic Assistance (CMEA) in 1991, the Visegrad countries (Poland, Hungary, Czech Republic, the Slovak Republic) are increasingly locked into the EU as peripheral and unequal partners. FDI is simply seen in the Amsden *et al.* analysis as an ingredient in transformation, rather than a powerful force, driven by transnational corporations (TNCs). Against this we suggest that states retain a considerable amount of negative power to disrupt, manage or distort trade, but they cannot easily control production aimed at the world market. In other words, the states' positive power to harness internal resources is decidedly constrained when they try and influence where and how international production takes place (see Stopford and Strange 1991). We develop these arguments in more detail in Chapter 4.

Flexible Specialization

Chang, Amsden *et al.* and Lo all concentrate on the role of the state at a national level for the restructuring of the Central and East European economies. However, there is a variant on the institutionalist theme that makes a specific link between restructuring at a global level and the re-emergence on to the economic stage of local economies. Coalescing around the concept of flexible specialization, this claims to have important and radical prescriptive implications for the restructuring of regions of Central and Eastern Europe. We would emphasize that

15

differences with the broad institutionalist school outlined above are a matter of degree rather than a matter of kind, but we deal with this approach separately, largely because it has important policy prescriptions for regional development in countries such as Poland. Associated in Britain with the work of Hirst and Zeitlin (1989, 1991), the approach is being adopted, albeit in a modified form, by economists such as Cowling and Sugden (1994).

In reviewing the crisis in the world economy, Cowling and Sugden reject both free-market solutions and bureaucratic state planning as viable options. Pointing to the success of areas such as Emilia Romagna and the Asian Dragons, they argue that 'star performers' are guided rather than free markets, depending on a deep intrusion by the state, representing the broader polity, within the inner workings of the capitalist economy. Echoing Amsden *et al.*, they conclude that, as far as the countries of Central and Eastern Europe are concerned, the current chaos could have been avoided if a more strategic integration into the world capitalist economy along Japanese lines had been followed (Cowling and Sugden 1994: 20–1).

Examining trends towards the globalization of the world economy, Hirst and Thompson (1992) suggest that what is actually emerging is a newly regionalized international economy, possibly dominated by a trilateralism of the United States or North American Free Trade Area (NAFTA), an expanded EU and Japan (with or without Pacific rim allies). The upshot of these developments has been progressively to limit the effectiveness of strategies of national economic management, be they Keynesian or monetarist. Whilst the state may no longer be a sovereign economic regulator in the traditional sense, it retains extensive powers to influence and sustain economic activity and actors within its territory. In these new times, the key functions of the state are taken to be, firstly, constructing a distributional coalition, that is winning the acceptance of key economic actors and organized social interests. Following from this is the need to orchestrate a social consensus on the basis of a collaborative political culture. Finally, the national state must promote regional government, following the examples of Baden Wurttemburg and Emilia Romagna.

The theoretical underpinning for the promotion of a form of microcorporatism (the new localism) at a regional level lies in the changes supposedly taking place in a world previously dominated by mass production, but now adopting and adapting to flexible specialization (Hirst and

Zeitlin 1991). Fordism – that is, a world defined by the manufacture of standardized goods in high volumes using dedicated machinery and predominantly unskilled labour – is transforming into the manufacture of customized products in short runs using flexible, general purpose machinery and skilled, adaptable workers.

The approach draws on regulationist theory, institutionalist and evolutionary economics and the new economic geography (Scott and Storper 1991: 5–6). Regulationist theory provides a view of economic history as a chain of distinctive periods. These periods are defined by dominant sets of production relations complemented by different political arrangements which co-ordinate the economy. Institutional economics indicates that socio-political organizations are essential underpinnings of any efficient capitalist economy. Evolutionary economics conceives of the development of technologies, markets and institutions as pathways whose trajectories of development are governed by the interplay between prevailing rules of social order and experimental behaviour in the context of prior states of the system. Economic geography argues that each period of capitalist history tends to be marked by its own peculiar spatial characteristics, so with the rise of new flexible production systems some sectors broke away from the old core regions and formed new locational domains. In these domains, new institutions, technologies and labour relations are being generated. New flexible production systems are characterized by progressive vertical disintegration of production with producers of various sizes bound up in network structures. Two major institutional frameworks fulfil this function; firstly, the re-emerging Marshallian Industrial District; and secondly, the decentralization of large firms. The former comprise networks of small firms, and the latter comprise networks of quasi small firms, with new subcontracting relationships linking the two phenomena. Within these networks, units tend to cluster close together, fostering dense interrelationships. Three groups of contemporary region can be identified: craft based, design intensive; high technology industry; and advanced producer and financial service agglomerations (Scott and Storper 1991: 7–8).

What emerges is a double faceted view of regional economic development in the new global context. The global economy into which the regions of Central and Eastern Europe must now fit is taken as being made up of a series of specialized regional production systems entwined in a worldwide web of interindustrial linkages, investment flows and labour migrations. At a global level, TNCs, international subcontracting, strategic alliances and international agreements have an important mediating effect. The conclusion is that the economic geography of the contemporary world is viewed not so much as core-periphery, or even an aggregation of nation states, but a global mosaic of regional economies (Scott and Storper 1991: 11). At the intervention level, what emerges is a politics of place that requires the construction of a local regulatory framework. The viability of flexible production agglomerations depends on effective institution-building and policy-making at the regional level. Public policy then becomes limited to providing support for sectoral and regional initiatives aimed at building regional institutions for economic co-operation. Regional economic policy is now taken to offer the best way of compensating for the lessened effectiveness of national economic policy.

The flexible specialization approach has been criticized for being both simplistic and deterministic, reducing capitalist development to little more than a never-ending transition from one dominant mode of production (mass production) to another (flexible specialization) (Williams *et al.* 1987, Callinicos 1989, Rainnie 1991b). Furthermore, any notion of combined and uneven development is doomed in so far as each dominant mode is taken to consist of a simple dualistic structure. Under mass production the relationships between large firms and their small suppliers are taken to be competitive and dependent, whilst under flexible specialization relations become symbiotic and co-operative. Equally, competition between capital and labour is replaced by co-operation in the transition to flexible specialization. As we shall see in Chapter 7, crude dualisms do not assist in the task of analysing the form and function of small and medium-sized enterprises (SMEs) in the process of restructuring. Furthermore, there is little evidence to suggest that the exploitation that lies at the heart of capitalism has undergone any radical metamorphosis.

The simplistic approach adopted means that a number of quite different phenomena are lumped together under the title of Marshallian industrial districts. Thus, Emilia Romagna, Silicon Valley and Baden Wurttemburg are taken as examples of successful localities driven by the same internal dynamic. This dynamic is taken to include the actions of significant local actors, in particular large firms and the local state. This error is partly attributable to the same naive analysis of the state that all institutionalist approaches exhibit, but also to a failure adequately to analyse the relationships between large firms and the state. As we shall see in Chapters 7 and 8, an analysis which suggests that localities can now determine their own future and successfully confront the power of TNCs flies in the face of the realities of the emerging international economic order. In essence we agree with Ash Amin (1988: 1), when he concluded that flexible specialization is a Utopian myth, hinged upon partial truths, obscured realities, discontinuities with the past and unattainable panaceas. Although dressed up in a radical rhetoric, as we shall see, flexible specialization in practice reduces to little more than a conservative agenda for local economic development.

The Marxist Alternatives

The institutionalists are driven by an abhorrence of the effects of unfettered market forces on the lives of working people and a desire to substitute a system that they believe can deliver growth and prosperity for the majority of the population. Whilst they describe themselves as being 'against the mainstream', their ideas centre on the possibility of taming and directing capitalism to benign ends. This, we suggest, is a Utopian dream which fails to grasp the dialectical nature of the process of change and how it has manifested itself in Central and Eastern Europe. The collapse of the economies of Central and Eastern Europe has not led to the inevitable demise of Marxism, despite the hopes of commentators such as Francis Fukuyama. For many analysts the political organization of these economies was never more than what Amsden has described as pseudo-socialism. However, it has been important for Western Marxists to analyse the demise of the bureaucratic regimes in countries such as Poland, not least because of the necessity of rescuing the theory and practice of socialist organization from the distortions of Stalinism.

A Marxist approach stresses two elements that are largely absent from the forms of analysis examined so far: the first is the idea that one cannot examine economies such as Poland's in isolation from developments in the world economy at large; the second is a recognition that the working class, organized or otherwise, has a central role to play in determining the pattern of economic development. In many forms of radical analysis the working class is a passive inert mass of workers who have things done to them and suffer from low pay and unemployment, rather than acting for themselves. Workers are the object, not the subject of history, peripheral to the central drive of the analytical framework, existing only as a factor of production and important only as a locational determinant. Thus any claim that only the re-emergence of the active workers' movement offers any possibility of an alternative to peripheral dependent status ranks only as wishful thinking, since there is no means of determining how this might come about. However, Clarke *et al.* (1993), in a book entitled *What About the Workers?*, provides a detailed analysis of the Soviet system that counteracts this tendency.

A major strength of the Clarke thesis is the acceptance that the nature of the crisis facing Russia (and by extension Poland) is that the system was no longer able to continue to reproduce the conditions of rule of the exploiting class (Clarke *et al.* 1993: 7). Furthermore, the book provides a detailed description of the organization of the labour process within Soviet-style economies. The analysis is important because it takes us, in the case of trade unions, beyond the formal appearance of Stalinist trade-union federations, on the one hand, and the simplistic nostrums of some Western commentators, on the other, who viewed Soviet trade unions simply as organs of repression. The main role of Soviet-style trade unions was to increase productivity, but most time was spent on the welfare function (Clarke *et al.* 1993: 103). The system, for most of the time, successfully suppressed collective conflict at the enterprise level. Alienation and resistance manifested themselves in individual responses such as absenteeism and alcoholism. However, spontaneous strikes did happen, and strike waves did erupt, the most important and dramatic being provoked by price increases (Clarke *et al.* 1993: 110). This last point will assume great importance when we examine the role of working-class resistance in patterning the dialectic of change in Poland.

The working class is central to the analysis, and the nuances and complexities of control and compliance in the Soviet factory are beautifully portrayed in this book. There are, however, problems with the analysis, most of which emanate from the authors' adoption of a particular brand of exceptionalist analysis, preferring to remain within a school that identifies capitalism strictly with the emergence of private property. Although Clarke *et al.* acknowledge that the Soviet economy was locked into the world economy long before 1989, and point to the existence of both a ruling class and a working class in Russia, they do not acknowledge that the Soviet system was a form of capitalism. This leads them to some strange conclusions, for example the suggestion that there is only the 'appearance' of the re-emergence of capitalism in Russia.

Privatization has led to the formation of independent production units and the disintegration of the administrative or command system, but this does not herald the emergence of a new social form of production and reproduction. Privatization has taken a purely juridical form, there is no content to it, in that private property is not yet constituted as capital. Capitalist elements have emerged, but only in the niches, in the interstices of the administrative or command system. Furthermore, the disintegration of that system has not led to a transformation of production relations. Therefore, they conclude that, as Russia was not capitalist prior to 1989 and production relations have not fundamentally altered, there is no evidence to support the contention that Russia is in a transition to capitalism. The growth of the market has not been associated with the development of competition through which enterprises would be subjected to the law of value (Clarke *et al.* 1993: 200–1). Because we disagree with the contention that a necessary defining characteristic of capitalism is private ownership of the whole means of production, we start to develop an alternative to the Clarke *et al.* thesis with an examination of the relationship between capital and the state.

Capital and the State

So far we have talked about state formations in Central and Eastern Europe as though they were an undifferentiated mass. Despite the emphasis that we have placed on the role of organized labour in determining patterns of development, our discussion of state formation so far is in danger of slipping into a form of economic determinism, implying no national differences and, at best, a marginal role for politics. As a counterbalance, we suggest that though there are underlying dynamics to the process of state formation, capitalist development has produced a system of nation states, each having its own particular imprint.

Reflecting our concentration on both the capital-capital and capital-labour relations, and following Barker (1991), we argue that social relations of capital have a dual form: anarchy and despotism. Capitalist competition is essentially anarchic, and despotism characterizes relations within production, furthermore the two essential characteristics mutually condition each other. Reflecting this duality, the capitalist state then becomes both a structure of competition and a structure of despotism, part of, rather than separated from, the relations of production. The state is, therefore, both an apparatus of class domination and an apparatus of competition between segments of the bourgeoisie (Barker 1991: 204). However, the hostility between capitals not only manifests itself within states, depending on the dominant fractions of capital, but also between states. The nation state's ability to compete depends on the relative size of the sections of capital that fall within its orbit. Three important conclusions flow from this brief analysis: the first is that the pattern of any particular state formation will depend on the balance of forces between capital and labour, and between fragments of the bourgeoisie; secondly, relatively backward states experience the law of value as a coercive force dictating methods of catching up (primarily through state intervention) that differ from more advanced nations; thirdly, and following from the second point, there is no necessary separation between capital and state, they are not mutually exclusive terms. In terms of catching up, the state and capital can become a unity without abolishing capitalist production relations, nor resolving its inherent contradictions. However, for precisely the reasons outlined above, the emergence of state capitalism would be as uneven as the nature of capitalist development itself.

Haynes (1987) and Harman (1991) argue, therefore, that the Polish system is not a qualitatively distinctive mode of production. The qualitative difference assumed in the exceptionalist literature derives from the assumption that capitalism is to be identified with the market and, to a lesser extent, private property, and therefore the suppression of these in Eastern Europe is a negation of capitalism. Against this it is suggested: firstly, that although Poland and Soviet-type economies may be more inefficient and wasteful than Western economies these differences are a matter of degree and the degree may be exaggerated. Secondly, that these problems do not derive from any unique set of characteristics peculiar to the Polish economy or economies of its type, rather they are a product of factors common to both East and West, but which appear in a more intense form in the more state-controlled economies. Thus, the economies of Central and Eastern Europe could be viewed as extremes of the dominant form of late industrialization – autarchic, protectionist, state-led development. Defining these economies as exceptionalist creates problems in so far as such a characterization demands a delineation of the precise point at which 'socialism' ceases and 'capitalism' begins, or when the 'plan' becomes the 'market'.

Once it is recognized, as indeed Clarke *et al.* do, that the Soviet economies were integrated into the world economy at a number of different levels, it then becomes possible to explain both how a dynamic of development arises and why, through varying degrees of protection from competition, the system was able to exist with a degree of slack (Haynes 1987: 25). In the Polish case two distinct forces can be isolated whereby the country was integrated into the world economy and thus into the exigencies of accumulation: foreign trade and military competition. These operated with a varying force at different times, but, as Clarke *et al.* (1993: 9) argue, in the Soviet case the role of foreign trade was vital:

> This did not, of course, mean that the Soviet economy as a whole was thereby insulated from the world economy, for Soviet foreign trade could only be conducted at world market prices, with settlements in gold or convertible currencies. This meant, at the very least, that the international operation of the law of value impinged on the Soviet economy at the level of the macroeconomic balance, and so had to be taken into account in drawing up the plan ...

The second element was linked to the first in that, as Tittenbrun (1993: 22) argues, a considerable part of foreign exchange gained from foreign trade was earmarked for heavy industrial expansion, due to submission to pressure exerted by the industrial-military complex. In fact, Tittenbrun describes the period of extensive accumulation in Poland as 'socialist primitive accumulation', that is forced industrialization conditioned by underdevelopment and defence considerations.

Haynes links these two phenomena together, alongside the drive to accumulate. In so doing, he links the concentration on heavy industrial development with both economic and military competition at a world level, and thus demonstrates why forced industrialization appears not only as an externally imposed necessity, but also as one means of locking Poland into the ebb and flow of the world economy (see Haynes 1992a: 49):

> The industrialisation drives ... had been based on attempts to compete in a world dominated by the imperatives of accumulation and commodity production. To compete here economies had to be built whose structures were in direct competition (both militarily and economically) with the states of the advanced West. Army was set against army, nuclear missile against nuclear missile, steel industry against steel industry and so on. In the Soviet Union in the 1930s the impact of the world crisis forced the economy to turn inward, reducing the importance of foreign trade and therefore of direct commodity production. The main competitive drive came indirectly through the military sector. This continued to be a major axis of competition forcing the process of accumulation ever onward, but over time it was supplemented more and more by the pressure of competition through trade. In the case of Eastern Europe this latter form of competition has always been important. But in both instances trade relations were controlled to some degree in order to be better able to build the economic base in the face of superior Western competition. In other words, in order to better compete with the most advanced military and economic powers in the world economy, the integration of these weaker economies into the world market had to be limited.

As we shall see, although integration into the world economy could only be limited, it was also impossible to seal Poland or any of the CMEA economies hermetically from competition either direct or indirect. Secondly, partial insulation would provide only partial protection for a limited period of time. As we have already seen, by the 1970s extensive accumulation was exhibiting signs of terminal illness, just at a time when a turn to the international economy was undermined by the onset of chronic crisis in the world economy. However, it was not just economic crisis that doomed the CMEA economies, it was also the fact that the nature of the world economy had undergone a fundamental change. In contrast to the exceptionalist school, this form of analysis does not view the transformation of Poland as being from not-capitalism to capitalism. Instead it locates the demise of an extreme form of late industrialization in the changing nature of the world economy.

The Decline of Late Industrialization

Harman (1991) argues that for forty years after the 1930s the process of statification appeared to be inevitable across both the developed and the developing world, as initially the private sector appeared to be incapable of recovering from economic crisis without state intervention. Subsequently, state ownership or control of basic industries appeared to grow remorselessly, accompanied by state sponsorship of advanced technological sectors, and underpinned by Keynesian demand management. In this light, Poland and other Central and East European economies represented simply an extreme form of this dominant pattern of development.

Whilst there was political discontinuity after 1948 with a new regime of Soviet plar ˙ng, there was not the fundamental break with the past implied in n 1y accounts of the Polish economy. On the contrary, before Work Nar II the state had played a key role in industrialization and develop 1ent in response to Poland's relative backwardness. For example, by 1926 the state sector included salt and coal mines, banks, transport ar.d communications, office building and forests. In addition, the state had developed an extensive system of treasury monopolies of tobacco, liquor and matches (Roszkovski 1992). Therefore, we should not view the extension of state control after 1948 as a qualitatively new force but rather as a hyperextension of the old trends through the political rhetoric and economic policy of the Stalinist regimes and their successors (Haynes 1992b).

From the 1960s onwards, the nature of the world capitalist system was changing, as we shall see in more detail in following chapters, with the dominant pattern of economic activity metamorphosing towards a system wherein increasingly large private capital and state capitals traded with each other, laying the basis for an accelerated internationalization of production. However, this trade increasingly took place between the advanced industrial nations of the West, with the outcome being the increasing integration of the economies of the advanced world with each other and, to a lesser extent, those of the Pacific NICs. Increased economic activity in general and internationalization in particular, focused on the Western economies, was also reflected in the merger and acquisition boom of the 1980s, as well as the increasing incidence of joint venture activity (Rainnie 1993). To some extent, successful state-promoted development held within it the seeds of its own destruction in so far as it promoted and accelerated the processes of integration and internationalization that would eventually undermine its efficacy as a mode of development.

However, we are not suggesting that there was a simple march towards internationalization or globalization of the world economy. Balkanization, the emergence of competing blocks such as the EU and NAFTA, is witness to the complexity and contradictions apparent in current trends. In general, Harman argues that there emerged a threefold split in the pattern of capital concentration; towards bigger nationally based firms; towards European firms and partnerships; and towards mergers and links between firms in individual European countries and those in the Pacific and North America. This threefold split is echoed in the different directions in which the capitalist state is being simultaneously pulled: firstly, stressing the consolidation of national blocks of capital; secondly, promoting the formation of European blocs of capital; and, thirdly, the striving for an 'ideal' world in which multinational firms compete without the impediment of national state barriers (Harman 1991: 46). This analytical structure helps us to explore the complexity of the interaction of states and capital, the relevance of which we explore in some detail in an examination of the experience of the restructuring of firms within several sectors in Poland in Chapters 8 and 9.

Commentators as diverse as Amsden *et al.* (1994), Harman (1991) and Clarke *et al.* (1993) agree that these developments, coupled with generalized crisis after the mid-1970s, signalled the end of semi-autarchic, protectionist forms of development as either a dominant or indeed viable model of development. The same developments that sounded the death knell for late industrialization hastened the death throes of the regimes of Central and Eastern Europe. Despite attempts to insulate the Soviet economies from the world, a degree of integration had always existed, so development was always subject to the contradictions of the dynamics of capital accumulation on a world scale. As the inadequacies of extensive accumulation became obvious in the 1960s, there developed a generalized turn towards world markets in an attempt to counterbalance chronic uneven development, which only served to accentuate and exacerbate the inadequacies of the system. Attempts at decentralization simply fuelled planning failure, so this was followed by desperate and futile attempts to recentralize. Systemic decrepitude was turned into disaster by the fact that the turn towards integration into world markets took place, not in the boom conditions of the 1960s, but the slump of the 1980s. As Clarke *et al.* (1993: 37) conclude, the cost of further integration was ultimately the destruction of the system itself; the system had reached a stage where it was no longer capable of continuing the reproduction of the conditions of rule of an exploiting class. A detailed analysis of the interrelationship between internal and external factors which brought about increasingly frequent and severe economic and political crises in Poland will be the subject of the next chapter.

Towards Trans-state Capitalism

Before we examine the changing role of the state in the new conditions facing the world economy, it is important to realize that limitations on state action and questions of legitimacy of intervention were also undergoing a fundamental reappraisal in the West as the certainties of the social democratic consensus, engendered by the long boom, collapsed in the face of systemic crisis from the 1960s onwards. Specifically, the legitimacy and efficacy of state intervention in general and Keynesian demand management in particular were increasingly called into question. State intervention now became part of the problem rather than part of the solution, as followers of the Chicago school acquired places of eminence in policy making. It is important to note that we are not suggesting that the new conditions imply a diminishing role for the state in economic development, rather that a different role emerges. The internationalization of production has forced a different role upon the state in two ways: firstly, the increasing importance of foreign direct investment makes it crucially important to provide the necessary infrastructure to attract and retain mobile capital ('Infrastructure' can be taken loosely to mean 'communications and transport' as well as increasingly human capital, particularly educated labour); secondly, internationalization has driven what is loosely termed 'privatization' and 'deregulation'.

The same ideological and material forces that have underpinned the changing role of the state have also driven the emergence of privatization as a global phenomenon. Growing disillusionment with state intervention as a crisis-solving policy was driven by theorists of the new right to the point where privatization *per se* became a central policy goal.

Equally, growing internationalization, particularly in fields such as finance and telecommunications led to pressures on states to divest themselves of their nationalized sectors. The panacea of privatization, a myth that has been given a hard sell in developing countries, is supposedly associated with demonopolization and increased competition. We are told a story of a shift from state monoliths to popular capitalism, with opportunities for small firms, and a wider distribution of assets through share ownership. On the contrary, we would argue that privatization has been driven, at least partly, by the demands of large capital which needs to compete on global markets without impediment. It is driven by the growing internationalization of important and powerful sectors of the global economy. Henrietta Holsman, in charge of the global privatization promotion activities of the US Agency for International Development, emphasizes the point (see Martin 1993: 9): 'Industries such as telecommunications, finance and energy are being restructured to respond to the needs of the integrated world economy. The globalization of these industries demands their participation in the privatisation process.' Thus demands from global business for a reorientation of utilities to meet their needs has been one of the major pressures on governments to divest or deregulate those services. In its most extreme form, this has manifested itself as large TNCs lobbying directly, and indirectly through political contributions, for contracting out and then seeking their share of the new markets.

The picture we have painted hitherto would seem to suggest a simple unwinding of a series of tendencies – internationalization of production, growing pre-eminence of transnational corporations, balkanization – that lead simply and unproblematically to a redefinition of the role of the state in the process of economic development. However, if we bear in mind the three interweaving complex and contradictory forces isolated by Harman, a more complex picture emerges. To reiterate, Harman suggests a three-fold split in capital concentration – national, regional and global – reflected in different policies at the level of the nation state: consolidation of national capital; regional blocs; and increased internationalization of production.

These tensions are in evidence in the contradictions inherent, on the one hand, in demands for free trade exemplified in the lowering of tariffs through the General Agreement on Tariffs and Trade (GATT), and on the other, an observable increase in the use of covert protectionism. In particular, anti-dumping clauses have been used to protect what are regarded as vulnerable sections of domestic capital. These contradictory tendencies are also clearly reflected in the merger boom of the 1980s, which witnessed a rapid increase in merger and acquisition activity, particularly in mergers based in Europe. However, the lion's share of activity continues to be national mergers, as firms consolidate their position in home markets, before competing within the regional or global economy. In addition, there are those firms whose interests lie in a world with no restrictions, as they need to compete in a world with few impediments. Thus economic complexity is reflected in political complexity, as firms and representatives of various fractions of capital jostle and lobby for policies that best reflect their perceived interests.

These complex and contradictory tendencies have important ramifications as far as the pattern of transformation of Poland is concerned, and in particular, its integration into the world economy. We have already argued that, by the late 1980s, autarchic development, in the late industrialization model, was no longer a viable option. The 1970s and 1980s witnessed an acceleration of the process of integration of the Committee for Mutual Economic Assistance (CMEA) countries, particularly Poland, Hungary and (the former) Czechoslovakia, into the world economy through increased trade and a limited amount of FDI. The interplay between endemic and ever deepening crisis, political opposition and increasing integration fragmented the ruling class, and as we shall see ever more significant fractions, through the 1980s, saw their best interests allied to full-blooded marketization of the sclerotic Polish economy. A similar process of disillusionment with the old system affected the opposition Solidarity movement, who by 1989 were in the forefront of demands for the introduction of a free market.

In 1989, therefore, this pattern of slow integration was massively accelerated, However, the point of development (or underdevelopment) reached by 1989 would crucially affect the pace, scale and form of integration into a global economy exhibiting the complex and contradictory forces already outlined. Lack of domestic capital, coupled with obsolete or outdated processes, led to a heavy reliance on FDI. The complexities of oligopolistic competition (accessing cheap labour, market domination) would crucially influence the conditions and prospects of particular firms and sectors in countries such as Poland. The state would, however, remain a significant owner of capital not only by default, but also as a vital actor in successful privatizations or transformations. Furthermore, the process and outcomes of the privatization programme as a whole, as well as that of individual sectors and firms, would be determined largely by the interplay of the activities of international firms, the state and, crucially, organized labour.

The process of slow integration should not be taken as suggesting that Poland would be integrated into the global economy simply as a national economy acquiring peripheral status in relation to the core economies of the EU. Whilst at a very general level this may be true, the process of combined and uneven development works in a more complicated fashion. Different regions and sectors, and thus different firms will be integrated to a varying degree and in a variety of ways. We explore this in detail when examining the experience of FDI in Poland at a national level, in Krakow, and in individual firms. Whilst in general we support Hudson (1995) when he suggests that the best hope for peripheral regions is one of limited branch plant investment, marginal small firm formation and some investment in the service sector, there will be particular industries and thus regions that develop relatively successful and advanced systems. Islands of relative success in a sea of peripherality will be the order of the day. As we examine the transformation of Poland in general and Krakow in particular, as well as the restructuring of particular firms, combined and uneven development emerges as a major theme. In the following chapter, we examine how these complex sets of forces and tendencies manifested themselves in the development of the Polish economy from 1948 to 1994.

SECTION II POLAND, 1948–1994

2 FROM AUTARCHY TO INTERNATIONAL PRODUCTION

The purpose of this chapter is to outline the development of the Polish economy from the 1948 through to 1994. This is necessary, firstly, in order that developments in the Krakow economy over the same period can be put into context. Secondly, and more importantly, because it is our contention that it is impossible to understand the patterns and processes of development between 1989 and 1994 without an understanding of the dynamics of development in the previous forty years.

The period 1948 to 1989 must be understood as one which demonstrated the process of development and subsequent disintegration of a particular politico-economic formation within a world economy that was simultaneously increasingly integrated and crisis ridden. We argue that the integration of Poland into the world economy contributed to the process that Morawski (nd) describes as regulation by crisis. We describe the same phenomenon as a dialectic of development, involving a continual, and ever deepening, cycle of crisis, revolt, reform and repression. However, this process became increasingly incapable of either reforming a failing system or deflecting popular opposition to that system.

Although development behind closed doors delivered rising standards of living for a large proportion of the Polish population up to the mid-1960s, economic conditions grew ever more problematic over the next twenty years. As the world economy faltered in the 1970s, the Polish economy opened up to the West seeking salvation for its own problems at precisely the time that help was least likely to arrive. A series of more and more desperate reform measures only served to exacerbate the problems that Poland was facing, with internal revolt growing ever stronger and better organized.

As we saw in Chapter 1, autarchic development did not take place in isolation from developments in the rest of the world economy. Development behind closed doors, depending heavily on the CMEA in general and the Russian economy in particular, could not have taken place if the world economy had not been experiencing the longest and most sustained boom in its entire history. However, increasing internationalization of the world economy meant that the conditions that allowed for relatively successful autarchic development were historically specific. The long boom of the 1950s and 1960s held within it the seeds of the destruction of this particular form of development. As the boom sucked larger and larger areas of the globe into the world capitalist order, increasing internationalization and integration meant that national development behind trade barriers became increasingly impossible. These same tendencies also demanded a radical reassessment of the limits and possibilities of macroeconomic management.

From 1948 to the Mid-1960s

Poland emerged from the destruction of World War II with most of the characteristics of a developing country. The population was rural and most of the workforce was employed in agriculture. Educational levels were low and birth rates, death rates and infant mortality rates were all high. Much of the fixed capital had been destroyed or damaged during the war (Schaffer 1992: 240). Forty-five years later, Poland was largely, but not entirely industrialized with all the peculiar characteristics of a command economy and with living standards, taking into account other social indicators, comparable with higher income economies, as Table 2.1 shows. An apologist for the system argued that Polish governments pursued radical egalitarian programmes up to the mid-1970s resulting in a diminution of what had been rigid class and income disparities in pre-war Poland (Szymanski 1984: 116)

According to Szymanski, during the first five year plan (1950–56) between 25 and 30 per cent of national income was reinvested, with 45 per cent of all investment in (mostly heavy) industry. Total industrial output increased threefold between 1948 and 1955, and fivefold between 1948 and 1960. The proportion of gross national income originating in industry grew from less than a third in the 1930s to almost

Table 2.1 *Social Indicators, 1950–1989*

	1950	1960	1970	1980	1989
Population					
At mid-year, millions	24.8	29.6	32.5	35.6	38.0
percentage urban	36.7	48.0	52.0	58.4	61.3
Per 1000 inhabitants					
Live births	30.7	22.6	16.6	19.5	14.8
Deaths	11.6	7.6	8.1	9.9	10.0
Rate of natural increase	19.1	15.0	8.5	9.6	4.8
Infant mortality rate					
(per 1000 live births)	111.2	54.8	33.4	21.3	15.9
Employment					
At end-year, millions	12.4	13.9	16.4	17.8	17.6
Participation rate	85.5	85.3	89.7	83.8	80.2
Men	98.0	95.7	93.9	88.4	84.3
Women	73.9	75.1	85.2	79.1	75.8
Share of women (%)					
In working population	44.7	44.3	46.8	46.3	45.7
In socialized sector employment	30.6	33.1	39.4	43.5	46.7
Education level of full-time					
socialized sector employees (%)					
Higher	3.8	5.3	8.1	9.9	
Secondary	11.2	19.2	27.2	31.2	
Basic vocational	8.2	17.0	24.2	28.7	

Source: Schaffer 1992: 241

two-thirds in 1979. The rate of growth in industrial production averaged 8.3 per cent per annum in the 1960–70 period. This was reflected in growth in personal consumption of 5 per cent per annum in the period 1960–70. Szymanski claims that these rates of growth considerably exceeded those of the USA and Western Europe at the same time, leaving Poland as the ninth strongest industrial power in the world in 1979 (Szymanski 1984: 117). Though one must take these figures with a massive pinch of salt, nevertheless for a while extensive accumulation achieved impressive results.

By the end of the 1960s the basic structure of the Polish economy was firmly established, being dominated by giant, highly integrated firms, principally in the heavy industrial sector, which in 1975, accounted for nearly two-thirds of industrial output. A third of the value of production of heavy industry was contributed by the fuel, energy and metallurgy subsectors. Agriculture, in contrast to other Soviet-bloc countries, remained in private hands. Services accounted for less than 15 per cent of GNP, an extremely low proportion by market economy standards.

This structure was formed at the end of the 1940s and the beginning of the 1950s, during the period of so-called 'accelerated industrialization'. The whole process was driven by military demands imposed by the Soviet Union (Haynes 1992a and b) and based on the Soviet experience. The necessity of building a militarized economy in competition with the West meant extreme centralization, complete state control of distribution and, structurally, the development of heavy industry, such as steel, mining, heavy machinery and chemicals at the expense of consumer goods. Tittenbrun (1993) suggests that these are features pertaining to a period of 'socialist primitive accumulation'. Growth was generated by increasing inputs of raw materials and labour, in particular involving the large-scale conversion of peasants into an urbanized industrial working class. This not only provided a readily available source of cheap labour, but the migration from the country to the towns introducing large numbers of peasants to membership of the industrial working class, allied to open access to higher education provided a mechanism for upward social mobility. Readily available supplies of cheap labour and a captive Soviet market dampened any drive to increase productivity or invest in new technologies. This form of growth was predicated on an extremely high participation rate (particularly for women) and low wages, which made workers particularly susceptible and sensitive to any increase in the price of food. The outcome was that, by the late 1970s, Poland had the highest female participation rate of any European country. Until 1981 Poland had a standard 46 hour working week (five full days and six hours on Saturday), longer than in the West and most other CMEA countries.

Although apparently producing growth rates that were reasonable by world standards and a steady, if uneven, rise in standards of living, rhetoric and reality were detached as evidenced by the uprising of 1956. The revolt, firstly in Poznan, closely followed by Warsaw and other cities, was triggered by demands against the effects of subordinating consumption to production. As Morawski (nd:7) demonstrates: 'The protesting workers put forward material postulates which led plans to allocate a larger amount of national income for individual consumption. This correction was followed for only a few years, however, and then once again over investment and recentralization threatened consumption.' The revolt had its roots in minor reforms initiated early in 1956 by the new Communist Party leader, Edward Ochab, motivated at least partly by the Khrushchev denunciation of Stalin. Political prisoners were released, industrial decentralization promoted and measures taken to improve living standards. But simmering grievances over wage levels erupted in June 1956, and after a series of demonstrations troops were sent into Poznan and, officially, fifty-three people were killed and three hundred wounded. Initially the Communist Party (PZPR) responded with an element of reform, promoting the development of workers' councils particularly in workplaces in and around Warsaw. However, the PZPR leadership was divided with an anti-reform group becoming increasingly concerned about the threat of Soviet intervention. Khrushchev arrived in Poland, and the PZPR leadership managed to assuage the fears of the Russian Communist Party, but the price was the replacement of Ochab by Gomulka. Gomulka left the spontaneous decollectivization of agriculture by peasants untouched, but central control over the Party was swiftly reasserted and press freedom limited. Furthermore, by 1958 the workers' councils set up in 1956 had been effectively neutralized. In so doing Gomulka removed the threat posed by conservative elements within the Party, agreeing that in Poland the Party was too weak to rule democratically (Lewis 1994: 173).

Here we have the first indication of a cyclical pattern that would re-emerge with increasing severity over the following decades; a slowdown in the ability of the economy to deliver rising standards of living, culminating in revolt triggered by rising prices, leading to reform based on decentralization and worker self-management to be followed rapidly by recentralization and repression. Writing in 1987, Pankow argued that Polish collective enterprises were a scene of permanent social conflict, sometimes hidden, sometimes open (Pankow 1993: 38). We can go further and, following Morawski (nd) argue that there existed within Poland a remarkable political economic cycle, with social outbursts performing the function of 'regulation through crisis'. This cyclical pattern is not accidental, and follows the increasingly obvious sclerotic tendencies inherent in the system (see Kyn *et al.* 1979, quoted in Barker and Weber 1982: 121):

> The economy goes through periods when everything is alright, plans are well balanced and can easily be over fulfilled, no shortages in the material supplies occur etc. These are the periods when the ratio of actual output to the capacity level is increasing. Then for some reason the economy begins to discoordinate. Plans cannot be fulfilled or even well balanced, scarcities and bottlenecks begin to grow, and the ratio of actual to capacity output begins to decline.

Growth was therefore uneven, and a cyclical pattern was evident even in periods of growth. We can see consistent factors in the economic crises that appeared with increasing severity in Poland from 1956 onwards. These factors are: a deterioration in the efficiency of investment, a fall in the average rate of utilization of productive capacity, a fall in the rate of growth of productivity of fixed capital, a decline in the rate of economic growth and growing inflation accompanied by stagnation or a fall in average real wages. Typically, the ruling class reacted by introducing more control in enterprises, a higher turnover of managerial and political cadres, intensified propaganda against ideological revisionism, suspension of certain investment projects in progress and the reallocation of investment favouring the consumption goods sector and services. However, by the end of the 1960s it was becoming clear that a policy of extensive growth could no longer deliver either positive growth rates or rising standards of living.

The 1970 Crisis and Gierek's Reforms

The slowdown in the economy was apparent from the mid-1960s, and in 1970 a political crisis was triggered by an increase in food prices. Polish wage levels, it is worth noting, were low even by Central European standards. The background was the increasingly obvious impossibility of co-ordinating production and consumption in an economy more and more prone to cycles of overproduction. By 1970, the Polish state was faced by revolt on two fronts: firstly, by the students and intelligentsia who had joined their colleagues in other Central European countries in the revolt of 1968; and secondly, by workers. In an attempt to boost the falling rates of growth of labour productivity, capital productivity and national product, the government led by Gomulka designed an incentive system to be implemented at the end of 1971. Although it was intended that this would bring about a closer relationship between the growth of labour productivity and the growth of wages, in practice this meant higher norms for workers.

On 13 December 1970, the government decreed an increase in commodity prices of up to 30 per cent. This met with violent opposition from workers in the Baltic coast towns. Although initially driven by food price rises, Gdansk workers also demanded open elections to trade unions and workers' councils as well as increased powers for the workers' councils themselves. Once again the response of the state was twofold. Troops were sent in and even official figures admitted that forty-five people were killed. However on 20 December 1970, Gomulka was replaced as head of the Polish Party by Gierek, who promised to be more responsive to the working class and raise standards of consumption. Under strong pressure from workers, the new leadership under Gierek was forced to rescind the announced price increases and the unpopular new 'incentive system'. However, the replacement of Gomulka by Gierek was symptomatic of a deeper *malaise*. Chronic economic crisis and the inability of successive leaderships to provide policy solutions led Poland to experience an unstable political situation with a large number of leaders and rapid policy change, particularly when compared with the situation under Kadar in Hungary and the leadership in East Germany.

Gierek promised tangible growth in the standard of living, modernization of obsolete machinery and the restructuring of production in order to be able to meet the envisaged rapid growth in consumption. From the economic point of view, however, Gierek faced the same basic dilemma as Gomulka had done, namely a choice between high economic growth with massive capital accumulation and modernization of productive structure, on the one hand, and a visibly higher standard of living, which was necessary to pacify rebellious workers and to stimulate growth in labour productivity, on the other. The adoption of an import-led growth strategy involved the large-scale importation of modern machinery and equipment, industrial inputs and grain from the West. These were largely financed by Western credits and, as we shall see, temporarily suspended the dilemma of choosing between the high growth of capital accumulation and consumption. Poland could, it appeared, have them both simultaneously. In fact the Western credits helped Gierek's policy of consumerism, by which he sought political support and legitimacy in exchange for a visible increase in the standard of living. Political stability and the quiescence of the working class was to be bought at a high cost, and initial high rates of growth rapidly tailed off (Lewis 1994: 183).

By 1976 it was clear that reforms had failed to placate the working class, as once again riots erupted in response to an increase in the price of basic foodstuffs. There was a steady decline in the growth of industrial production from an average of 10 per cent per annum between 1971 and 1975, to less than 2 per cent in 1979 (Nuti 1982: 19–21). The deteriorating economic position was echoed in other factors. The burden of debt service rose from 12 per cent of export earnings in 1971 to 75 per cent in 1979, with inflation, an unfamiliar phenomenon since the mid-1950s, reappearing. This was compounded by shortages of consumer goods, a familiar feature of central planning, which now became persistent and endemic. This led to the rapid growth of black or grey markets within which shortage goods were obtained at a high price or through connections, position or corruption, with most people busily fixing and exchanging each other's purchases. The population resented not only the shortages but also the resulting unequal distribution of access to goods and services.

Thus in the first half of the 1970s (after the slowdown and stagnation of the late 1960s) the Gierek reforms had started to deliver rising standards of living, but by the middle years of the decade were having disastrous consequences. In fact, the reform programme was abandoned after the 1976 uprising. Part of the explanation for this phenomenon is to be found in an examination of exogenous factors, those reasons which lie specifically in the increasing integration of Poland into the world economy. The traditional mechanism insulating a centrally planned economy from international trade had been dismantled. International inflation, which reached unprecedented levels in Western economies in the late 1970s, was imported and built into price formulae as the prices of imported consumer and capital goods increased. This in turn spilled over into wage demands. Prospects for Polish exports of manufactured goods, the income of which was intended to repay the debt, deteriorated in the face of the world recession.

In addition, monetarist policies, adopted in Western capitalist countries to deal with inflation, led to a trebling of interest rates. As Polish debt was mostly short and medium term, the increase was immediately reflected in the mounting burden of debt servicing. Recession in advanced capitalist countries encouraged Western companies to seek trade with Central and Eastern Europe and to offer attractive terms, but as a result Poland was induced to raise imports over what was strictly required by Gierek's import-led growth strategy. Therefore, some of the credits that were supposed to finance investment were diverted into consumption. Finally, the world recession adversely affected the viability of precisely those sectors in which Polish investment had concentrated, such as metallurgy and machine building – sectors particularly prone to a fall in demand during downturns in economic activity.

Whilst these factors are underplayed by those who wish to see the breakdown of Eastern European economies as rooted in the shortcomings of planned economies, this is not to deny that endogenous factors contributed to the culminating crisis. The fact that the level of investment exceeded the absorptive capacity of the national economy, particularly in construction, meant that projects had a long gestation period and contributed to inflation. Moreover, most investment was in greenfield projects, with modernization outlays playing a marginal role. Herein lies a contradiction in so far as, on the one hand, Poland was pushed by the logic of opening up to the world economy towards capital intensive production. On the other hand, it continued to be pulled by the soft markets of a captive CMEA and a declining, but still extant, supply of cheap labour, which militated in favour of old fashioned extensive investment. This was coupled with the fact that the reward system within the *nomenklatura* favoured large prestigious projects. Thus in capital accumulation inefficient and inappropriate structures meant that there was a failure to modernize existing plant, which eventually led to its dereliction. Not only did the investment programme perpetuate the traditional structure of heavy industry, it was also highly import-intensive. By the mid-1970s, imported machinery and appliances contributed over 50 per cent of total supply on the domestic market. Licences purchased from the West to facilitate technology transfer were barely used.

Thus Poland attempted to resolve the problem of slowdown and stagnation in its own economy by moves to integrate more closely with the global economy, whilst the world economy was experiencing its deepest crisis since the 1930s. The slowdown in all advanced economies was exacerbated by the oil crisis of the early 1970s (Maddison 1991). In response to stagnation, falling domestic demand and increased competition on global markets, the mid-1970s saw the resurgence in the West of free-market economics associated with Hayek and Friedman and the Chicago school, which in policy terms was reflected (*inter alia*) in deregulation, privatization and anti-trade-union legislation. Within organizations, the competitive pressures drove moves towards downsizing, decentralization and demands for what was euphemistically known as labour flexibility. Thus Western capitalist economies and units of capital responded to the crisis with a variety of policies and with varying degrees of success. Such remedies, although no guarantee of success in themselves, were not even on the agenda of the countries of Central and Eastern Europe. For example, bankruptcy and liquidation, used to discipline capital, simply did not exist. Combined with an ossified institutional and political structure and obsolete products and processes, room for man-oeuvre and the potential for restructuring to compete was severely inhibited. For Poland, then, the most significant outcome of its strategy of import-led growth was not that it managed to become more efficient but that the economy was increasingly stagnating and debt ridden.

The Crisis of 1980 and the Decade of the Unplanned, Planned Economy

The outward manifestation of these problems was, firstly, the riots of 1976 and then the crisis of 1980. On 17 September 1980 a co-ordination committee was formed in Gdansk which became the founding committee of the independent self-governing trade union known as Solidarity. Early the following year a network of enterprise-level organizations from Poland's leading enterprises, including the Lenin steel works, Gdansk and Szczecin shipyards and mines, was established. This is important for a number of reasons. The strike action that followed was initially triggered by a rise in food prices and a shortage of meat, but was symptomatic of a much deeper malaise, that being the increasing alienation of workers both politically and materially, especially as the system now revealed a chronic inability to deliver rising standards of living for the vast majority of the population. In other words, this was a reaction to the increasingly obvious fact that a particular form of organizing production had reached its limits of development. The second reason is that for the first time in a 'socialist' society, there appeared an independent working-class movement organized against the very state that was supposed to embody the power of the working class.

The leadership of the PZPR was divided over the appropriate response to the rise of Solidarity, and Gierek was forced to resign, deemed incapable of dealing with the crisis, to be replaced eventually by General Jaruzelski. Though initially espousing a conciliatory policy, under pressure from the conservative wing of the Party, Jaruzelski imposed martial law in December 1981. Solidarity's leadership and activists were arrested and trade unions suspended, and the PZPR purged of reformist elements. Martial law was used as a means of pushing through major price rises (Lewis 1994: 187). However, repression was accompanied by attempts at economic and social reform, which are commonly characterized as a move towards 'market socialism'. This represented a recognition by significant sections of the ruling class that the planned economy, as it had functioned up to 1980, could no longer deliver rising standards of living for the workers and indeed now threatened the material basis of the privileged position of the *nomenklatura* themselves. In an attempt to introduce market forces certain aspects of the planned economy were dismantled, particularly centralized control over enterprises, accelerating tendencies that had been under way from the mid-1970s.

A central feature of the reform was that enterprises should be independent, self-financing and self-managed (known as the '3S principle', after the Polish initials). Independence meant that enterprises had much more freedom about production decisions, without direct administrative guidance from the centre. Self-financing meant that the income of an enterprise and its employees were to be determined by the enterprise's financial performance. Kornai's hard budget constraint and financial discipline would be enforced by allowing ailing enterprises to go bankrupt. Self-management meant that powers were given to workers and Workers' Councils. In addition to moves towards decentralization, aimed at giving enterprises increased autonomy, re-strictions on small business formation were relaxed, and a more positive attitude to foreign investment encouraged.

The attempt at limited marketization produced a series of contra-dictory tendencies in the economy. Although formal central control of enterprises was not to be a feature of the new system, the centre did in fact retain substantial powers over enterprise activity. Informal guid-ance was commonplace, and could be reinforced through a wide variety of formal and informal measures. Control was also maintained through the manipulation of tax liabilities and subsidies by the centre and access to scarce industrial supplies. The central control of investment was of critical importance and had significant implications for the structure and performance of the economy. The bias towards heavy industry impeded rather than aided restructuring and contributed to a further deterioration in the stock of capital, efficiency and competitiveness.

After drastic and haphazard cuts in investment between 1978 and 1982, investment in fixed assets started to grow from 1983. Although by 1985 investment was still only just over 70 per cent of the pre-crisis level, it was in theory sufficiently high to implement restructuring. In prac-tice, however, this did not happen. The pattern of investment only served to reinforce the traditional structure of the economy. For example, a high proportion of investment outlays were expended on the continuation of unfinished projects from the Gierek era, with only a small proportion allocated to replacement of obsolete machinery and equipment. A combination of the low completion rates of investment projects and the small investment allocation for modernization and replacement of obsolete fixed assets led to rising disinvestment in the stock of physical capital. As a result, a growing proportion of capital stock machinery and transport became worn out, unreliable and caused frequent breakdowns. Furthermore, the planned growth in engineer-ing output concentrated on goods which were in excess supply in the world economy. Unsophisticated production techniques used to pro-duce these goods and a lack of innovation meant that they were uncompetitive on world markets. Insufficient investment in renovation and modernization of the chemicals, light industry and food processing industries imposed additional strain on the domestic consumer market, which was already fully stretched. This had a marked effect not only on the ability to compete but also on people's material conditions of existence.

Increasingly contradictory tendencies manifested themselves. Progressively more scarce investment resources led to an increase in centralized decision-making, whilst at the same time the reforms loosened the control of the central authorities over individual enterprises. Not only had the economy ceased to be a classical centrally planned economy, but decision-making and ownership had descended into chaos and uncertainty. The decade of the 'unplanned' planned economy had arrived.

Lurching Towards Crisis

As we have already seen, Poland was increasingly driven by a dialectic of development encompassing a cyclical response involving crisis, revolt, reform and then repression. The emergence of workers' councils as part of the reform package is a recurring feature of reforms attempting to pacify or buy off working-class revolt throughout Poland's history after 1945. However, their resurgence, decline and re-emergence in the 1980s was to be of central importance to the dynamics and pattern of the 1989 reforms, and in particular the debate about privatization, as we shall see in the next chapter.

In addition, there were important changes taking place within the ruling class. By the end of the 1980s, many managers followed the call of the leadership and engaged in private enterprise. Typically, what happened was the so-called *nomenklatura* privatization, a state-owned enterprise would sell its non-core operations, such as a computer centre, repair facilities, or the sales centre to a group of insiders that included managers and party activists. The purchasers were typically offered favourable terms in sales, leases or licences, thus stripping state owned enterprises (SOEs) of their most profitable operations. As enterprises were restricted from raising prices, the private purchaser could buy cheaply and make a handsome profit by selling on the unrestricted black market. The *nomenklatura* privatizations further weakened the management of the state-owned enterprises. Decentralization allowed them the option of shifting their power base, either by acting as owners of small businesses or as a result of *nomenklatura* privatizations, or more commonly as increasingly powerful managers in quasi-governmental, decentralized enterprises. Zubek (1993: 811) describes the so-called Rakowski privatizations as the last profound attempt at systemic reform, with the aim being to unleash Poland's petty entrepreneurs and independent peasantry whilst simultaneously attracting investment from Polish *émigrés* via joint ventures. These three basic groups – petty entrepreneurs, peasants and *nomenklatura* capitalists – would now have to operate in market conditions. The importance of this was that the *nomenklatura* now found themselves pulled in different directions. On the one hand, maintaining contact with the Party was vital but, on the other, their position and experience told them that the old order was unsustainable, that reform was inevitable and, further, that they were well placed to take advantage of, if not lead, those reforms.

Most accounts treat the *nomenklatura* ruling class as an homogeneous group with similar interests. In fact, for a significant section it became clear that, whilst it was still important to maintain Party membership, their interest lay in increasingly close involvement with foreign capital. What emerged was a series of ambivalent and ambiguous positions. Members of the *nomenklatura* had a foot in both camps, either setting up the 'agents' system' whereby *nomenklatura* operated an outlet of a state-owned corporation, usually a retail or service outlet, on a franchise basis, whilst retaining management positions in the SOE, or by taking advantage of blockages and distortions in the formal economy through operating in the informal sector. Cieochinska (1992: 215) concludes that:

> As a result, towards the close of the 1970s there were more ambitious solutions which allowed the political elite to transform itself into management staff and entrepreneurs. The communist doctrine was dead, and there was only the apparatus which, in the name of reforms, could see to the interests of the nomenklatura in getting rich. This philosophy engendered demands for foreign capital and the establishment of the first joint venture companies ... Therefore there were grounds for the thesis that the elite was distributing the benefits of the development of the market economy outside agriculture in the final stage of the command economy, which in Poland occurred in the 1980s.

The outward manifestations of this process were twofold: firstly, the number of foreign small scale enterprises in Poland (joint ventures) increased from 100 in 1981 to 841 in 1989; secondly, the number of firms in the private non-agricultural sector increased from 351 000 in 1981 to 572 400 in 1988, with employment in these firms doubling during the same period. The rate of growth of employment in the private sector was faster than that in either the state or co-operative firms. It is also worth noting at this point that some of the most high profile cases of foreign direct investment in Poland (for example Fiat and Asea Brown Boveri (ABB)) had a significant presence before 1989. Non-agricultural private sector employment grew from 611 700 in 1980 to 1 521 500 in 1989. By December 1989 there were 291 250 private enterprises in industry. These were, however, mostly very small and often depended on larger state enterprises.

It must be stressed that though political leaders throughout Central Europe, including Poland, were aware of the need for reform and made many attempts to initiate such processes, the consequence of partial reforms and deepening economic crisis was increasing political instability. The rapid deterioration of the system and its increased inability to deliver economic, social or political benefits meant people experienced a marked deterioration in their quality of life in a number of ways. In the workplace, managerial ineffectiveness and the inefficient organization of production coupled with job security and low wages served to reduce workers' morale even further. Inadequate conditions in the workplace and falling standards of living were reflected in the physical health of workers. Morbidity and disability rates among the workforce increased rapidly, and many employees retired prematurely because of ill health (Kondratowicz and Okolski 1993: 14). Between 1981 and 1988 there was a significant exodus from Poland's working population with about 640 000 people in the 18 to 64 age bracket leaving the country.

Shortages became a common phenomenon of daily life. In the early 1980s the average time devoted to shopping rose to more than two hours per household per day. Speculation and blackmarket activities became ubiquitous (see Kondratowicz and Okolski 1993: 15):

> Over time the consumer market became disorganised; large scale bribery, queuing, waiting list systems, speculation, direct exchange of goods between enterprises and various privileges in access to scarce commodities were typical symptoms of this process. A flourishing underground economy with its invisible hand mechanism (i.e. the black market) played a particular destructive role.

Households adapted to the conditions that prevailed in consumer markets in two ways. The majority simply reduced the quantity and quality of their purchased goods, giving up the consumption of certain goods and services and resorting to do-it-yourself practices. Other individuals, and particularly although not exclusively those within the bureaucracy, sought to generate additional income by setting up small businesses, or joining the underground economy. The shift towards the black or second economy became particularly strong as controls on foreign contacts weakened. Between 1980 and 1986, it is estimated that up to 25 per cent of personal incomes were from secondary activities, with foreign trade transactions providing up to 10 per cent (Grzegorczyk 1989, quoted in Myant 1993: 68).

This was to make a nonsense out of any pretence that the authorities could influence the pattern of income distribution. A study of high income earners (the top 10 per cent) suggested that hardly any of this group were dependent primarily on salaries from the state sector, with a large number having made gains from dealings involving international trade or hard currency. Society became ever more sharply differentiated, with many households declining to the brink of poverty, whilst others accumulated, at least by Polish standards, substantial fortunes. The class nature of society, always both obvious and resented, became even more stark.

Societal degradation extended to environmental decay (see Kondratowicz and Okolski 1993: 16): 'All the while the environment deteriorated. Rampant expansion of the coal-based energy sector contributed to unprecedented air and water pollution. This and other factors ... transformed Poland from an almost environmentally clean country into a conglomerate of lands plagued by biological disasters.' This included dramatic air pollution, an acute deficit of clean water, soil contamination and intensified acid rain. The environmental degradation led to a deterioration in health, particularly among men of working age, reflected in an alarming increase in the rate of retirement due to ill health. Between the mid-1960s and late 1980s, the mortality rate amongst men aged between 30 and 60 increased by between 30 and 60 per cent, particularly in the rise in deaths caused by cancer and cardiovascular diseases. The most dramatic rise in mortality in the 1970s and 1980s occurred in those regions where environmental pollution was highest. Finally, this impairment of the quality of life manifested itself through mental stress which could be observed in aggression, depression and neurosis. This phenomenon, it is claimed, also led to the appearance of a fundamentalist orientation, an outburst of interest in religion, and desire to return to 'traditional' family life (Kondratowicz and Okolski 1993).

By the end of the 1980s, the systemic implosion triggered by the weight of all these factors, combined with the actions of the re-emergent Solidarity crystallized out as an agreement between the leadership of Solidarity and a significant section of the ruling class that 'socialism' could not be reformed and wholesale change was inevitable. Agreement was aided by the purge of conservative elements within the PZPR, carried out immediately before the Roundtable talks. The reforms had been a failure at almost every level. As we have seen, crisis was endemic in Poland almost from the inception of the Soviet-style system. One effect of this was that though Solidarity appeared to be a spent force in the mid-1980s, the failure of the Jaruzelski reforms to initiate anything other than a holding operation in the face of growing political and economic troubles, provided a platform for the re-emergence of the movement.

It is important to note that these developments coincided with the rise of the Gorbachev doctrine. Faced with acute systemic crisis throughout the whole of Central and Eastern Europe, after 1986 Gorbachev adopted an increasingly *laissez faire* attitude to satellite states such as Poland. The new found freedom and the bankruptcy of the Jaruzelski programmes were reflected in the 1987 referendum on proposed reform measures. The referendum sought support not only for economic and political reforms but also for an austerity package. The referendum required support from two-thirds of the electorate, but a third did not bother to vote. Therefore, although two-thirds of those voting supported the reform package, the required majority failed to transpire. The outcome was that Jaruzelski pushed forward with price rises in 1988 regardless, provoking the largest strike wave Poland had ever witnessed.

As we shall see in the next chapter, Solidarity had been transformed over the course of the 1980s. Beginning as an organization committed to some form of democratic socialism, by the end of the decade the dominant ideology had become neoliberalism. This had partly come about because the organization had been destroyed as a mass movement by martial law and repression. Solidarity came to be represented by a small group of individuals, such as Walesa, and intellectuals, such as Balcerowicz, who were firm adherents of the free-market philosophy. In January 1990, Poland introduced a series of measures, known as the

Balcerowicz Programme, which came to be characterized as 'shock therapy'. This programme comprised a massive dose of IMF type stabilization, intended to bring pain in the short run, but a speedy adjustment to the benefits of a market economy. The programme was made easier because neoliberals occupied the most important economic portfolios in the first non-communist government, led by Mazowiecki (Adam 1994: 607). It is worth emphasizing the degree of support that Solidarity had in 1989 for the reform package. The union had only been reregistered in 1989, but in the semi-free elections in that year Solidarity took all bar one of the 35 per cent of seats it was allowed to contest in the lower house (Sejm) and 92 of the 100 places in the less powerful upper house (Senate). The extent of changes that had been made is witnessed by the fact that the PZPR dissolved itself in 1990, to re-emerge later as the SdRP (Social Democracy of the Polish Republic).

The Leap to the International Economy: Trade and Foreign Investment

If the 1970s and 1980s were seen as a partial and increasingly uncontrolled attempt to integrate into the world economy, the Balcerowicz Programme could be regarded as a leap to international markets. Neoclassical ideas and a belief in the powers of the market, at least initially, underpinned Poland's trade policy and integration into the world economy. The dramatic liberalization of Poland's foreign trade sector in 1990 had two main components: firstly, all restrictions on foreign trade were completely eliminated, including quantitative restrictions on imports, with customs' duties lowered, eliminated or suspended for a large number of goods. Furthermore, immediate convertibility of the currency was urged by those supporting the 'big bang' approach. This policy was seen as an integral part of the seamless web of reforms suggested by Lipton and Sachs (1990), who argued that it was necessary to allow Poland to integrate into the world economy by reaping the benefits of trade liberalization. The rationale here was that importing competitive pressures from abroad would facilitate the economic pricing of imports and exports, thus providing the necessary competitive stimulus to jump start the market economy.

The effects of immediate trade liberalization are perhaps most clearly illustrated with respect to East Germany, where large sections of manufacturing industry were simply wiped out when exposed to the chill winds of international competition. The effect in Poland was not quite as dramatic, but the economy was poorly equipped to compete on the world market. As we have seen, the legacy of the 1980s was that large sections of productive capacity were either completely obsolete or at best lagging significantly behind their new competitors. In addition, whilst changes in trade patterns in general, and within the CMEA in particular, were not unexpected, nobody had anticipated the speed and scale of the collapse of the Soviet Union and the disbanding of the CMEA in January 1991. In 1989, the CMEA accounted for a third of Poland's external trade, the Soviet Union being Poland's most important trading partner. The collapse of trade within the CMEA had two immediate effects: firstly, the cushion of subsidized prices of raw materials and energy was removed in one fell swoop; and secondly, Poland faced a collapse in the main market for its relatively advanced technology goods. Poland's exports to the Soviet Union consisted mainly of manufactured goods, with machinery and equipment playing a leading role. Thus the cutback of Soviet purchases severely affected key sectors of Polish industry, and factories that had specialized in producing equipment for the CMEA countries, such as rolling stock and large-scale machinery could not find customers outside of the bloc. The dissolution of the CMEA imperilled the existence of around sixty large Polish enterprises, many of which were major employers in small urban centres.

Thus the collapse of the CMEA and trade liberalization produced a profound shift in the geographical structure of trade, reflected in a huge increase in trade with the European Union. In 1989 the European Union accounted for 32 per cent of Polish exports and 34 per cent of imports, with these figures rising to 63 per cent and 57 per cent respectively by 1993. At a general level, not only has there been an increasing trade deficit, widening from US$ 2725 million in 1992 to US$ 4691 million in 1993, but the deficit with the EU accounts for an increasing share of this total, rising from 31 per cent in 1992 to 39 per cent in 1993.

The changing composition of trade can be illustrated by looking at trade with Poland's main partner, Germany, which accounted for a third of exports and a quarter of imports. Although the structure of exports to Germany included an increasing share of manufactured goods, Polish imports from Germany comprised machinery and equipment, consumer electronics and cars. Exports to Germany from Poland mainly comprised raw materials and semi-processed goods; coal, timber, cement, copper and clothing. This apparent comparative advantage in semi-processed or raw materials was also reflected within industries. For example Poland had tended to specialize in bulk chemicals, whilst increasing imports at the sophisticated end of the product range such as pharmaceuticals. Some individual products had simply been unable to compete. This was reflected in a 14 per cent fall in the production of colour television sets in the first nine months of 1994 and a corresponding fall of 34 per cent for tape recorders. The manufacture of integrated circuits had all but disappeared, falling by 94.5 per cent between January and September 1994, the result being that much electrical equipment and all circuitry is now imported (EIU 1994).

It would appear then, that the European Union rather than Poland has been the main beneficiary of trade liberalization and increased integration. Furthermore, it would appear that the integration of Poland, at least into the European economy, would be as an exporter of raw materials and semi-processed goods rather than the relatively high technology goods associated with innovation. The technology gap, however, had already widened between the East and West in the previous two decades with a sharp decline and decreasing share of exports in fine chemicals, electronics and telecommunications. These trends, should not, therefore, be taken as signalling a change in direction, simply a consolidation and acceleration of trends that were already firmly in place. Moreover, the exclusion of Poland from the EU simply served to reinforce the tendency toward peripherality.

However, this paints a rather simplistic picture of the integration of the Polish economy into the global scene as it takes no account of the role of transnational corporations (TNCs) or foreign direct investment (FDI). We return to a central theme of Chapter 1, the way that FDI rather than trade is increasingly the major factor locking economies, regions and sectors into the pattern of international production. We explore this in detail in Chapter 4, but a brief overview of trends in FDI suggests a complex and uneven picture. A common prediction was that there would be increasing flows of FDI to Central and Eastern Europe on the basis of low costs. The picture that emerged, however, showed a small number of very large investments by TNCs, who invested not only on the basis of low cost but also had been motivated by questions of market access and domination. Foreign investment was largely confined to certain sectors within which oligopolistic competition predominated, such as food processing and tobacco. The effect of these developments was to slightly modify the picture of peripherality painted previously. For the time being it appears that Poland will remain on the margins of major flows of investment, though the process of uneven development characterized by the role of TNCs in FDI will mean that particular organizations in certain sectors will stand out as islands of relative development in a sea of peripherality.

Growth of the Private Sector: Mirage or Miracle?

We have argued that the image of a planned economy told us little of the reality. In the 1970s and 1980s complex organizations formed from partnerships between the state, *nomenklatura* management, foreign direct investors and Western finance capital emerged. The 1970s and 1980s also bequeathed an important, if often formal, role for workers' organizations, particularly in the form of the workers' council. The 1990s witnessed a reconfiguration of these formulations, depending firstly on whether particular sectors are attractive to FDI. Secondly, the role of the state is changing from dominant owner to attractor of FDI. The outcome is that though the balance amongst the various partners in complex organizations may be changing, the emergent formulations do not correspond to the textbook types supposed to typify planned or market economies. Thus, though the rhetoric of transformation in the early 1990s was that of eighteenth-century *laissez faire*, the state had an important though changing role to play in promoting development. In particular, of increasing importance was the role of promoting the institutional and infrastructural supports thought to be necessary to promote both FDI and privatization. One irony was that in the light of the ambiguous nature of property relations that had developed in the 1980s, the state had first to restate its claim to property in order that it might be redistributed via privatization.

Both by default and by design the state remained a crucial actor in the process of economic development. This was due, at least in part, to the fact that the privatization process was described, two years in, as a damp squib. This was not only due to reliance on a level of FDI that never transpired, but also to two further crucial reasons: firstly, attempts to copy British style privatization proved to be spectacularly unsuccessful with only 120 companies being privatized by this method by late 1994. Initial prescriptions for privatization emphasized speed, immediacy and comprehensiveness; however, the proposal for the mass privatization programme was only finalized in April 1993, and by early 1995 was still waiting to be implemented. It also remained the case that there were a large number of companies that were excluded from any part of the privatization programme. Firms remained outside the programme for a number of reasons, including strategic considerations, failure to fulfil financial criteria and resistance of trade unions and workers' councils. This has meant that the state has actively discouraged FDI in some sectors, whilst negotiating directly with major transnational corporations and giving sweeteners in others. We examine the Polish experience of privatization in greater detail in Chapter 4.

The idea that the state is somehow being marginalized in the process of transformation might appear to be supported by the apparently spontaneous re-emergence of a vibrant private sector. However, a closer examination of the picture revealed in Table 2.2 raises some interesting points. Firstly, it is important to note that in 1989 over 30 per cent of total employment and more than 70 per cent in the trade sector was already in the private sector, accounting for nearly 30 per cent of GDP. Therefore, any evaluation of the 're-emergence' of the private sector must start from an understanding of the fact that this process was already well developed before 1989. The second point is that, though the figures appear to show a dramatic increase in the importance of the private sector after 1989, as Blanchard (1994: 1173), amongst others, has pointed out, these figures need to be treated with some caution. Firstly, part of the shift represents little more than a reclassification of co-operatives. The 1.5 million people who were employed in co-operatives at the beginning of the period were rapidly reclassified as working in the private sector. Furthermore, an initial increase in the private sector reflected rapid small privatization undertaken at the local or regional level. However, this often involved local authorities simply leasing shops and stores previously under their direct control. It is also the case that the re-emergence of the private sector, and in particular the growth in the service sector may be partly a product of the re-structuring of large state-owned enterprises. As we discuss in some detail later on, many large firms have spun off peripheral or unwanted parts of their operations. These may include catering, transport, design and marketing functions as well as establishments that provided social and welfare functions. Such a restructuring will appear in statistics as a decline in the size of SOEs (and may be taken to be a sign of successful restructuring) and an accompanying growth in the service sector and, in some cases, small and medium-sized firms (SMEs). This is illusory, as we demonstrate in an investigation into the relationship between restructuring of SOEs and the re-emergence of SMEs in the former Lenin steelworks in Chapter 8.

Small firms are often taken as representing the shock troops of economic transformation, being apparently dynamic, innovative and carriers of the entrepreneurial revolution. This treats small firms as an undifferentiable, homogeneous mass, and belies the fact that, though

Table 2.2 *Private Sector Share (Percentage), 1989–1993*

	1989	1990	1991	1992	1993
Total employment*	31.2	33.6	40.3	42.2	46.2
Employment in industry	29.1	31.2	35.8	40.5	46.9
Employment in trade	72.7	82.2	88.3	90.7	92.5
GDP†	28.6	30.9	42.1	>45	n.a.
Industrial production sold†	16.2	18.3	24.6	30.8	37.4
Trade†	59.5	63.7	82.8	86.5	87.8
Exports†	0.0	4.9	21.9	38.4	42.0
Imports†	0.0	14.4	49.9	54.5	58.0

* Without private agriculture

† Current prices

Source: Adam 1994: 612

there may be some dynamic organizations, the vast majority of Polish SMEs are members of the flea market rather than the free market. Most SMEs are in sectors with low barriers to entry, but equally high rates of exit. Few will ever provide any significant employment growth, and most SMEs in Poland, according to Blanchard (1994: 1173), reported a profit rate of approximately zero in 1993. Despite all the problems associated with small firms, SMEs have remained at the centre of both national and regional economic development policies.

Accounts of the re-emergence of the small firm sector must be treated with some caution on a number of counts. Firstly, the growth in the private sector did not start in 1989. The economic problems of stagnation and spiralling debt that Poland faced in the late 1970s and early 1980s, referred to in earlier chapters, led to the introduction of the 'market socialism', in a desperate attempt to bring some flexibility into a sclerotic economy, and as a means of pacifying a suffering and rebellious population. This programme attempted to attract FDI, decentralized a degree of control to management in SOEs, and also encouraged the growth of SMEs. The growth of SMEs was partly the result of the exodus of workers from large state firms, with half a million workers leaving to join the private sector. Nearly one in five engineers and technicians employed by state-owned firms left to form their own firms. By the end of the 1980s the private sector accounted for more than 80 per cent of land cultivated by agriculture, nearly 50 per cent of the output of household services and close to 20 per cent of construction (Bloch 1989: 98).

At the beginning of the 1980s there were approximately 5000 private manufacturing firms nationally, employing around 12 500 people. Ten years later the number had risen to around 40 000. The number of firms in the non-agricultural private sector increased from 351 000 in 1981 to 572 000 in 1988. Employment in these firms rose from 654 000 to 1 287 000 (i.e. almost doubled) in the same period. Wisniewski (nd: 2) argues that by the last year of the old political system, Polish industry was dominated by small firms, thanks to the private sector. However, this must give pause for thought. Most SMEs formed in the 1980s survived in niches left by incompetent state enterprises, which may disappear, thus depriving some of the SMEs of their *raison d'être*. Alternatively, new competent large firms may appear, better able to pay decent wages, leaving SMEs no longer an attractive option to disaffected technicians and engineers.

Finally, the SME figures include not only the small privatizations and newly formed firms, but also firms coming out of the informal sector. According to Wisniewski (nd: 8), the shadow economy accounted for between 10 and 20 per cent of production in the 1980s. Unlike the informal economy in the West, the shadow economy complemented rather than substituted for the formal sector. Three forms of shadow economy could be differentiated: firstly, rendering services or small scale manufacturing without formal permission (this was previously connected with regulations requiring craftsmen to have qualifications); secondly, illegal trade in goods, particularly those in short supply; and finally, typical criminal offences or economic fraud. Under new conditions the first two forms ceased to be criminal and thus formal recognition would appear as formation of a 'new' SME.

In essence we draw three conclusions about small firms: firstly, they are not homogeneous – some will fit the image of the dynamic and innovative organization creating jobs, but the vast majority will not; secondly, small firms are not the shock troops of the enterprise culture – whether an individual small firm develops or not will largely be determined by the activities of large firms and the state; finally, the fact that most small firms will have a marginal existence has important implications for the lives of the people who work within them. This raises the question of poverty, unemployment and transformation.

More Shock than Therapy

The people of Poland were led to believe that three months of pain was the necessary sacrifice before the market economy could start to deliver the rising standards of living supposed to exist in the West. Six years on the reality of increased pauperization, unemployment and job insecurity is undermining illusions about the panacea of the market. The social wage has been slashed with access to basic services such as health, childcare, leisure and education curtailed. The inequality, poverty and unemployment endemic, to one degree or another, in all European market economies was not the image of capitalism sold to the people in the economies undergoing transformation. There is nothing unusual or surprising about this, the experience of so-called IMF stabilization policies is that invariably working people pay the price in terms of plunging living standards, with little evidence that this short-term pain results in long-term gain.

Mainstream economists are sharply divided on the success of the Balcerowicz 'shock therapy'. Views range from those such as Berg and Sachs (1992) who regarded the programme as so successful that Sachs has gone on to espouse the same treatment for Russia. Many, including those who initially supported the programme, are much less sanguine (Rosati 1990, Winieckie 1992). In conventional economic terms certain aspects could be considered a success, including the marked slowdown in inflation, the elimination of shortages, the stabilization of foreign currency with internal convertibility and the initiation of many institutional changes. Table 2.3 shows that the cost of these achievements turned out to be high in terms of output and employment, as Poland plunged into a recession. The sharp initial contraction in output and investment led to a fall in GDP of 11.6 per cent in 1990. In the same year, unemployment rose from negligible levels to 6.3 per cent of the workforce with industrial output falling by 24 per cent. Table 2.3 shows that although by 1993 production and investment were beginning to recover, they were still significantly below 1989 levels. In particular, it should be noted that wages and salaries were still only 70.8 per cent and pensions only 90.2 per cent of their 1989 rates.

The focus on a range of macroeconomic variables and dry statistics, however, gives us an inadequate picture of the material effects on the majority of the population. Apologists such as Sachs suggest that despite falls in output, which are in their view exaggerated, other evidence can be put forward to support the view that living standards and welfare actually increased. Reduction in queues (people had previously spent on average two hours a day queuing), the elimination of shortages and better quality and variety of goods are cited as 'welfare improving' aspects. However, whilst shortages are given as the main obstacle to purchasing goods in the period before the reforms, the liberalization of prices meant that in reality most working people could not afford the goods now appearing in the shops (Myant 1993). Freeing up prices meant an end to shortages and queuing, but this meant that not only were some goods not affordable, but more importantly there were significant increases in the prices of basic goods such as food and energy as subsidies were withdrawn. This has been estimated as representing a 15 per cent fall in real consumption (Myant 1993: 94, Rosati

1993: 218). Food took up an increasing proportion of household income, rising from 44 per cent to 52 per cent of household income in

Table 2.3 *Performance Indicators, 1990–1993*

	1990	1991	1992	1993	1993(1989 = 100)
GDP*	88.4	92.4	101.5	104.0	86.3
Industrial production sold*	75.8	88.1	103.9	106.2	74.0
Gross agricultural output*	97.8	98.4	87.2	102.2	85.6
Gross investment*	89.9	95.9	100.7	100.0	86.5
Real wages and salaries*	75.6	99.7	97.3	98.2	70.8
Real retirement pay & pensions*	84.9	114.5	93.5	97.3	90.2
Inflation rate*	685.8	170.3	143.0	135.3	
Average profit of enterprises†	106.0	−13.0	−15.0	4.0	
Unemployment rate‡	6.3	11.8	13.6	15.7	
Budget deficit in % of GDP§	−0.4	3.8	6.0	approx. 2.8	
Foreign debt in $ bn¶	48.5	48.4	47.0	46.8**	

* Previous year = 100; the first four indicators are based on constant prices.

† Net profit zl. 1000 of receipts; the figure for 1993 is for October.

‡ End of the year.

§ The minus sign indicates a surplus.

¶ In 1989 the foreign debt was $40.8 bn.

** This figure refers to the end of November.

Source: Adam 1994: 608

employed households and reaching levels of over 60 per cent in pensioner households.

The fact that there was increased consumption of certain consumer durables such as cars and videos, rather than being a sign of success as some suggest, simply reflected the uneven distribution of the benefits of transition (Zielinski 1993). This was reflected in the appearance of the *nouveaux riches*, who were to be seen in the new luxury shops and restaurants. To suggest that the possibility of increased consumption by a small minority can be interpreted as an increase in welfare for the majority is disingenuous. For many this polarization of consumption simply served to underline the unevenness and unfairness of the reforms.

The losers and winners of transformation are clearly illustrated by the household surveys of the Polish Statistical Office, outlined in Table 2.4. Table 2.4 provides startling evidence of a large-scale redistribution of incomes away from workers and farmers and in favour of entrepreneurs. We do not share Gomulka's rosy view that pensioners have been protected and therefore poverty avoided. Instead, we suggest that this represents a high degree of hidden unemployment, as former wage earners are given early retirement in preference to appearing as part of the unemployment statistics. However, we are not trying to suggest that Polish society now consists solely of the *nomenklatura* and *nouveaux riches* as the sole beneficiaries of transformation, with the working class being driven into poverty *en masse*. As we have argued, the implications of the unwinding of the process of combined and uneven development means that workers in some sectors and some firms will experience rising standards of living. Equally some SMEs will thrive and grow. However, the general picture to emerge is an increasingly elongated spectrum with the rich getting richer, and a growing proportion of the working class getting poorer, but with certain groups of workers occupying segments of varying degrees of relative affluence along the spectrum.

By 1991, reaction to shock therapy was reflected in the ballot box. In the elections of that year, the five political parties associated with Solidarity regained a comfortable majority in the Sejm. However, signs of equivocation were appearing: firstly, the turnout at the election was low; and secondly, the post-Solidarity parties only managed to gain just over 40 per cent of the votes cast (Lewis 1995: 783).

Table 2.4 *The Level and Composition of Personal Real Incomes in Poland, 1985–1991*

Source of income	Level (1985 = 100)			Composition (%)		
	1988	1990	1991	1988	1990	1991
All income	113.6	102.7	108.8	100.0	100.0	100.0
Wages	111.5	75.5	73.4	46.3	38.2	35.1
Private agriculture	124.4	70.7	57.5	12.7	6.6	5.1
Other private activity	118.8	157.4	170.0	25.6	37.9	38.6
Welfare payments	111.5	95.6	124.0	15.4	17.3	21.2

Source: Gomulka 1993

Unemployment

Despite the fact that employment in the private sector grew throughout the whole period, overall employment levels declined and unemployment continued to grow. The number of registered unemployed grew from 2 155 600 in 1991, to 2 951 300 in the first quarter of 1994. Official figures, however, have to be treated with caution in that the falling rate of unemployment growth in 1992 resulted from changes in the regulations which altered the definition of unemployed and limited the number of people who were entitled to claim benefits. According to research carried out by the Government Statistics Office (GUS) in May 1992 between 30 and 35 per cent of unemployed people were not registered at unemployment benefit offices. This would include those who are working illegally or those whose savings enabled them to survive the worst period (Hausner *et al.* 1995: 226).

Two further groups of people were giving cause for concern. The number of unemployed in the countryside, in the early 1990s, was estimated at 600 000, but only 200 000 were registered as unemployed. Peasants who had previously worked both on the land and in industry, found themselves ineligible for benefits when they were made unemployed, and they had little chance of finding alternative employment. Changes in the regulations relating to unemployment benefit have undoubtedly contributed massively to the growth of poverty in Poland. In 1991, 93 per cent of families affected by unemployment had incomes below the poverty level. Despite this a lowering of benefit levels and a tightening of conditions for receipt of benefits were justified on the basis that they were acting as a disincentive to work. The Employment Act of December 1991 restricted entitlement to benefit with the immediate effect that nearly half of all the registered unemployed no longer received any benefits, and at the end of 1992 a further 400 000 unemployed people ran out of benefit entitlement (ILO 1995: 124). With the rapid growth of long-term unemployment, a declining proportion of the unemployed are likely to receive benefits. This situation is especially dramatic because people in this group have lost their right not only to unemployment benefit but to family allowances and free medical services in addition. So large groups have been deprived of the most elementary social security, and will be forced to seek help from charitable institutions as their last line of defence against absolute poverty (see Hausner *et al.* 1995: 228):

> Thus, in many unemployed families the syndrome of poverty has begun to appear in a drastic form. It does not only consist of professional degradation (the loss of work); it also means the loss of free medical care, few possibilities to find a flat (or to maintain one that is already owned), consumption limited to the most basic foodstuffs and increasing debt.

However, not all sections of society were suffering equally. Unemployment in the years immediately after 1989 was rising faster in rural areas than in conurbations. This may have been due to reluctance to bankrupt large politically sensitive workplaces based in urban areas, for example Huta Sendzimira. However, small and medium-sized enterprises in rural areas could be allowed to disappear without the risk of a backlash. The regional pattern of unemployment in 1994 continued to show Warsaw, Krakow and Poznan least affected, with unemployment rates in the 8–9 per cent range. Areas with the highest unemployment remained the peripheral regions clustered around each other in the north-east, as well as provinces to the west of Gdansk. These regions had unemployment rates in the 28 to 30 per cent range, as did some areas in lower Silesia (EIU 1994: 18). This situation generated numerous conflicts including a strike wave at the end of 1992 and the beginning of 1993. During this time there was an escalation of demands to confer the status of high unemployment areas upon various districts and regions, because unemployment benefit could be claimed for six months longer in such areas than elsewhere.

Poverty

After the initial shock of the Balcerowicz Programme, the pain continued and for increasing numbers of people therapy failed to materialize. Ksiezopolski (1991: 179) argues that Polish society had undergone a gradual process of pauperization starting in the early 1980s, a process which accelerated after 1989. Between 1980 and 1989 the proportion of workers' households falling below the poverty line grew from 7.6 per cent to 13.7 per cent, but within a year that figure had risen to 40 per cent. By 1992 50 per cent of all households had incomes below the poverty level (ILO 1995: 113). By 1991 between 25 per cent and 40 per cent of the population were having to rely on social security for their income at a time when the philosophy behind social security was going through a fundamental change (Hausner 1993: 304).

Despite the fact that shock therapy was causing extreme poverty, the government saw the social costs as a necessary sacrifice. Social policy was driven by two considerations: the first was subsidiarity, meaning that the state would only provide a service where voluntary or private sector organizations could not be encouraged to step in; secondly, the policy was aimed at providing a minimal safety net, not at stopping people falling into that safety net (Ksiezopolski 1992: 231–2). Under the previous regime, basic goods such as housing, heating and lighting were subsidized and social and welfare benefits provided, usually, by major employers, though it is important to note that the *nomenklatura* had disproportionate access to these 'benefits'. The provision of these basic services came under attack in two ways: firstly, major employers began to withdraw from the provision of non-core facilities such as childcare and leisure; and secondly, though legislation now imposed on the gmina (local government) responsibility for the provision of these services, as we shall see in Chapter 6, the gmina did not have the financial resources to provide the same level of support. Therefore, access to childcare, housing and health care rapidly moved out of the reach of an increasing number of people, both through decreasing provision and the introduction of charges (Ksiezopolski: 1992: 235). The impact of this was that large sections of the population became increasingly dependent on voluntary welfare benefits with charity and the voluntary sector filling the gap. In the absence of affordable services such as childcare, women workers increasingly found themselves having to rely on family networks and juggling shift patterns to cope with the formidable demands of work and family responsibilities.

The right to free medical care provided by state-run medical institutions supposedly guaranteed by the constitution came under threat. Actual expenditure on health care fell systematically and the government was constantly searching for new short-term measures to prevent its complete breakdown. These measures consisted either of the introduction of partial or higher charges for certain kinds of welfare services or giving health departments the power to levy charges (Supinska 1995).

Furthermore, postcommunist Poland inherited a disastrous housing situation. In 1989 there were 14 per cent more households than housing units with the result that 60 per cent of young families (below the age of 30) shared accommodation with parents. Commercial rates on housing loans, introduced in 1990, made such loans prohibitively expensive, affecting not only the demand for new property but also those people who had contracted cheap credit many years earlier. As a result, housing associations were increasingly unable to find people to take over newly built flats, even though people had waited for them for more than ten years. Negative equity is alive and kicking in Poland with people who thought that they could afford the new prices quickly finding themselves not only in debt, but also with the level of debt exceeding the market price of the property. The result was that new investment in house construction, in both the co-operative and private sectors, began to fall away. While the number of dwellings built in 1978 (the post-war record year) amounted to 284 000, in 1988 this figure fell to 190 000 and 127 000 in 1992. The trend continued downwards with only 93 000 new flats expected in 1993. Yet rents are occupying a growing share of family expenditure, with the inability to pay evidenced by the fact that 20 per cent of families in communal and co-operative buildings fail to pay their rent (Supinska 1995).

We have already seen that working-class people both in work and out have borne the brunt of the costs of restructuring. However, women have shouldered a disproportionately large share of both the economic and social costs of transformation. Poland had comparatively high female participation rates before 1989, reaching levels of 58.7 per cent in 1978. For women between the ages of 25 and 49, participation rates ranged from 75 per cent to 83 per cent. This should not be taken as any proxy measure of equality. We have already seen that Polish economic development was based on extensive accumulation (i.e. low wages and full employment). This required maximum employment, entailing turning the peasantry into an industrial working class and as many women as possible working full time (part-time work was unheard of). As far as families were concerned this meant that as many members of the household as possible had to be in employment. In the old regime, women were formally and administratively equal, but gender relations remained male dominated. Evidence for this comes firstly from pay levels. In 1990 women's average earnings varied between 73 per cent and 82 per cent of men's, depending on sector. Women predominated in poorly paid professions such as education and the health service. The outcome was that managing the extreme contradictions between the necessity of full-time employment on the one hand, and domestic labour on the other (particularly with inadequate welfare support) produced an almost unbearable burden for Polish working-class women (Watson 1993: 476). The transformation process not only did nothing to address questions of discriminatory pay rates, but Polish women found themselves over-represented in the ranks of the un-employed. Female unemployment stood at 17 per cent early in 1994, compared to a male rate of 15 per cent, with a greater proportion of women than men joining the ranks of the long-term unemployed.

Women were also confronted with an emergent ideology that cast female domesticity as a virtue. This process had gone largely un-challenged and unnoticed. For example, stereotyping is so entrenched that the Polish feminist association challenged a Warsaw primary school for its practice of giving boys computer lessons and girls cookery classes (*Warsaw Voice*, 45, 1994). This is partly because, before 1989, work was not considered defining by any section of the population. Home was were the informal survival networks were based. The result was that 'traditional' gender relations were set in aspic and then idealized. The former regime was seen to be preventing men and women from fulfilling 'normal' functions. The burden of full-time work was seen as preventing women from being 'proper' wives and mothers and poverty wage levels were seen as preventing men from earning a 'family wage' (Watson 1993: 484). However, the rhetoric of a return to traditional family values clashes with women's wish to work and the necessity of working at a time when prices of basic goods are rising rapidly and many social and welfare functions are either disappearing completely or being priced beyond the pockets of most working women. The deep division between the public and private spheres of life, far from suppressing or transforming gender relations had simply served to reinforce a highly reactionary notion of the role and the function of the family (Watson 1993). As we shall see in Chapter 9, women workers were becoming increasingly disenchanted with the process of transformation. Increasing poverty and personal commitment to employment meant that many demanded the right to work, but at the same time women were being driven out of work, and out of the labour market. Furthermore, a resurgent reactionary ideology of the family bolstered the marginalization of women's position within the labour market.

Conclusion

By 1989, reaction to deepening and ever more frequent crises had resulted in important structural changes within the Polish economy. The decade of the unplanned, planned economy resulted in growing private sector employment, particularly in small firms, *nomenklatura* privatizations, and joint ventures with foreign capital, none of which proved capable of providing solutions. In 1989 a decisive attempt to jettison the last vestiges of a planned economy and leap towards integration into international production was made. However, the shift from plan to market has not developed as expected. Privatization, far from being rapid and comprehensive, has been slow, tortuous and contentious. FDI has not arrived in anything like the volumes expected or indeed necessary. We investigate these factors in more detail in Chapters 4 and 5.

In general, by the mid 1990s, for most members of the Polish working class, transformation was causing as many problems as it had solved. Standards of living were falling for many both in work and out, and unemployment was a major problem. Disenchantment was reflected in strike figures with the number of disputes rising from 305 in 1991 to 6362 in 1992. Disillusionment was reflected in changing voting patterns between the 1991 and 1993 elections. In 1991 parties associated with Solidarity, despite shock therapy, got over 40 per cent of the vote. Two years later, a coalition led by the SdRP (the former Communist Party) returned to power though it still only received slightly more than a third of the votes cast.

We have argued that the role of organized labour is crucial to an understanding of the process and pattern of change within Poland. In the next chapter we examine the development of Solidarity from its emergence in 1980 through to 1994. In so doing we look at the way in which growing disenchantment with the process of transformation has altered the structure and action of the union itself. Furthermore, we argue that the change in the attitude of workers to the process of transformation has both altered and been altered by the experience both of privatization and foreign direct investment.

3 DESPERATELY SEEKING CAPITALISM: TRADE UNIONS AND RESTRUCTURING

The previous chapter emphasized the dialectical process of development that Poland underwent in the period from 1948 to 1989. We pointed to a deepening cycle of crisis, revolt, reform and repression, culminating in the political and economic crisis of 1989. Within this formulation the role of the working class in general, and Solidarity in particular, is central, but Solidarity itself underwent a profound transformation during this period.

In four months in 1980 Solidarity's membership grew from almost nothing to over 10 million. Illegality and repression under martial law in the 1980s drove the movement underground, so a return to legality later in the decade left the union with a lot of ground to recover. By 1994, the union's membership had reached around 1.5 million, though it was still significantly lower than that of OPZZ, the old Stalinist trade-union federation. However, surveys in 1991 suggested that less than one in ten of the population were members of Solidarity, and even in industry only around one in four workers were members of the union. More worrying still for the union, two-thirds of all workers believed that membership of a trade union brought no tangible benefits (Morawski nd: 29–30). This does not mean, however, that transformation has brought about industrial peace. A report on Poland (WERI, 1994b: 74) concluded that:

> Because of the role played by the unions, especially Solidarity, in the social, political and economic transformations and the great expectations of employees, the process of change in the relations of production is giving rise in many workplaces to considerable tensions and conflicts. The situation is

complicated by the lack of any clear cut vision of a new system of industrial relations and the existence of an extensive grey area in the economy.

Most orthodox analyses of transformation of Central and Eastern Europe only consider labour in so far as it constitutes a factor of production or as an indicator of unemployment or poverty statistics. Although we stress the centrality of and interlinked nature of foreign direct investment (FDI), privatization and small and medium-sized enterprises (SMEs), we argue that the pattern and process of these factors are inextricably bound up with workers and their organizations. Thirkell *et al.* (1994: 85) argue that, for Central and Eastern Europe as a whole, analyses of patterns of transformation have tended to ignore the importance of labour relations. The same authors stress the significance of trade unions as agents in strategy formulation at both enterprise and national level, as well as their key role in interest representation, with some commentators advocating an incorporationist role.

Therefore, rather than treating workers either as a group having things done to them, or as the residual in an economic equation, we prioritize the role of the Polish working class. We combine an analysis of the change in Solidarity's organization and ideology with the continuing importance of the notion of self-management. In so doing we suggest that part of the unions' problems can be laid at the door of an enthusiastic and uncritical embracing of free market ideology along with tensions emerging from the organizations multifaceted role as union, social movement and quasi political party. We begin, however, with an analysis of Soviet-style trade unions in general, and the pattern of trade-union development in Poland after 1948.

Soviet-style Trade Unions

The role of trade unions in Central and East European countries represented a Stalinist distortion of the Leninist view that unions should be a transmission belt from the Party to the masses in particular and schools of communism in general. Officially, trade unions had a dual function: firstly, to represent the interests of workers; and secondly, to represent the policies of the Party – state. In practice, the latter

dominated the former, with there being little in the way of representation or bargaining taking place at factory level. As Clarke *et al.* (1993)
point out, the interests of the working class were identified, at least
rhetorically, with those of the Party and the state. Therefore the role of
trade unions at the workplace would be to ensure the implementation
of these policies, nominally representing the interests of the workers in
opposition to managerial neglect, incompetence and corruption. As
Clarke *et al.* (1993: 93) comment: 'From this point of view the "dual
functions" of the trade union were their functions for the enterprise
administration, on the one hand, and their functions for the party –
state, on the other, and the tension was between these two roles'.

In Poland, a law of 1949 identified one of the chief tasks of the trade
unions as being the stimulation of the working class to carry out the
production plans, increase productivity and intensify competition and
to work for the constant improvement of the national economy. The
Trade Union statute was even more unequivocal, stipulating that trade
unions follow the lines of the Communist Party and recognize the
leading role of the Party as the vanguard of the working class (Dzwonczyk and Sobczyk 1993: 15).

The outcome was that the trade union operated, to some extent, as
the personnel department of enterprises, maintaining the discipline
and motivation of the labour force. Through the patronage link the
union was integrated into, and worked alongside management, providing a route into the *nomenklatura.* In order that we might understand
how the union maintained membership, never mind control, in these
circumstances, we need to examine the way that welfare structures were
attached to the enterprise and administered by the union.

Trade unions had very high membership levels, with 97 per cent of
employees in state-owned enterprises in Poland being members of
official unions. Unions were not just concerned with wages, but also
with childcare, housing, education, holidays, sport and culture. Unions
represented the interests of old, young, unemployed, producers and
consumers in both welfare and social function terms. In Poland, state
owned enterprises (SOEs), at plant level, provided more than 500
'houses of culture', just under 3000 clubs, 340 cinemas, 4378 trade-
union libraries and more than 7000 amateur artistic groups. Unions
were also concerned with the distribution of food in winter, small loans
and children's camps (Morawski nd: 9), with the result that access to a
whole range of essential social and welfare amenities were not only in

the hands of the union, but depended on membership of the union. Membership was, therefore, essential, and acquiescence helped to gain access to necessary benefits in an economy where wages were low.

Trade Unions in Poland

A simple reading of the post-war trade union history of Poland would suggest that the period can be divided into three sections: the first is from 1945 to 1980; the second starts with the rise of Solidarity and runs through to 1989; and the third traces developments after 1989 (Dzwonczyk and Sobczyk 1993). The first period is taken as being a close approximation to the Stalinist Soviet model outlined above, when the system of labour representation was highly centralized, with labour organizations functioning through a system of 23 branches, united in one umbrella organization – the central council of the trade unions (CRZZ). They were organized, in theory, following the principles of democratic centralism, which is supposed to allow for the influence and experience of individual members, whilst subordinating lower level structures and members to higher level bodies. The actual practice was centralist rather than democratic.

Unions were organized in branch structures with three distinct levels – national, regional and enterprise. According to statutory regulations, the enterprise level organizations were obliged to respect the resolutions and recommendations of higher level organizations. The centralized character of the system was reinforced by the fact that all unions were obliged to be members of CRZZ, and it was the council rather than enterprise-level unions that was seen as the partner with the state. The actual participation of branch-level unions in decision-making was negligible (Dzwonczyk and Sobczyk 1993: 11). The role of the union in the workplace was further marginalized, these authors argue, by the influence of party organizations and workers' councils within the enterprise, effectively reducing the role of the union to welfare work. Unlike local party organizations, unions had little influence on decisions taken by company directors. Even their influence over welfare work was limited by party initiatives which were used to try to gain favour with employees.

However, the situation was not quite so clear cut. Morawski (nd) argues that the imposition of the Stalinist system met, initially, with great resistance from a Polish working class which had a strong and rich trade-union tradition, based heavily on socialist but not communist doctrine. Yet it cannot be argued that for the first few years after the formation of CRZZ in 1948 the new trade unions fulfilled anything other than the standard Soviet-style function (see Dzwonczyk and Sobcyzk 1993: 6):

> The period described was characterised by the dependence of the trade unions on the political system, but it was not a uniform period. We can distinguish two sub periods in it. In 1948–56 the trades unions had no chance to perform any other role but that of a special kind of welfare department, a department that could have been organised just as well by the administrations of enterprises. The function of the defender of workers' interests was then performed by the trades unions in a ritual manner. All of the most important decisions were made by the party organisation or by the management of the enterprise. If a trade union activist was also a party activist (which was often the case), one could get the false impression that the trades unions were participating in the decision-making process.

However, Morawski argues that, after 1956, the situation began to change, and herein lies the first intimation of our class-struggle driven dialectic of development. In June 1956 spontaneous workers' protests broke out in Poznan, followed by similar protests in Warsaw and other cities in October of the same year. Apart from the material demands which resulted in a temporary shift in national income from production to consumption, workers raised the demand for democratic socialism through the slogan 'Socialism – yes, deformations – no'. Crucially, central to this idea was the concept of workers' councils. In workers' eyes, unions were no longer credible organizations.

Workers Self-management

Many accounts of centrally planned economies present a picture of static, hopelessly inefficient, and repressive bureaucracies. Morawski, by contrast, has suggested that there existed within Poland a remarkable political economic cycle, with social outbursts performing the function of regulation through crisis (Morawski nd). We go further, as we saw in Chapter 2, and argue that a dialectic of development existed within Poland consisting of a cycle of crisis, revolt, reform and repression. Successive attempts to deal with economic crises by savage increases in the price of basic foodstuffs in a desperate attempt to subordinate consumption to the needs of production, triggered revolt in 1956, 1970, 1976 and again in 1980. Furthermore, as successive crises were growing deeper, the revolt that they engendered increasingly threatened the existence of the whole political structure. This was exacerbated by the disastrous attempts to turn to the West in the 1970s and 1980s, which simply resulted in accumulating debt problems and the political crises of 1980 and 1989. We can get a more concrete idea of the implications of this dynamic for the post-1989 patterning of Poland's development by examining how workers' self-management fitted into this process.

Pankow (1993: 57) argues that Polish SOEs in the post-war period were scenes of permanent social conflict, sometimes hidden, sometimes open:

> They [workers] try, with varying consistency, to rebuild a true worker representation: with one of the main 'shields' guaranteeing the functioning of normal enterprise. Sometimes this representation takes the form of workers' councils, at other times the form of independent trades unions. Communist employers, disposers of collective enterprises, try to counteract these efforts, but it seems they are doing so with decreasing success.

Workers' self-management is strongly rooted in Polish radical trade-union tradition. The spontaneous seizure of factories by militants in 1945 resulted in the formation of Factory Councils, and in 1956 workers turned to self-management in the form of workers' councils. By 1970 the movement took on the form of workers' commissions (Kolankiewicz 1982: 7). However, self-management is not an unproblematic concept, and three variants on the theme can be recognized that will recur throughout the whole of our period. The three variants are syndicalist, technocratic and co-administration forms of self-management.

The syndicalist conception sprang out of the workers' councils formed in the 1956 uprising. Here all control was to be ceded to the workers' council both by the ministries and by the management of SOEs. The role of central planning would now be limited to co-ordinating the plans emerging from various enterprises. This is the most inspiring, the most democratic model, reaching its finest moment in the wave of factory occupations in 1980–81.

The technocratic model has similarities with the syndicalist variant only in so far as its adherents advocated a decentralization of economic control to individual enterprises. Here the similarity ends, as the technocratic model envisages self-management as comprising 'experts' at enterprise level, working in conjunction with the central planning authorities. It can thus be seen as an attempt to retain bureaucratic centralized control in the hands of the *nomenklatura* whilst simultaneously accessing some of the perceived advantages of decentralization (one can see similar patterns of restructuring in major corporations in the West in the 1980s and 1990s).

Finally, the co-administration model assumed a greatly reduced, though still extant, role for central planning, allied to decentralization and a form of democratization. Factory management would remain intact, but a factory council with representation of all workers would exist. However, the role of the factory council would be almost entirely cosmetic, functioning as little more than a consultation exercise whereby management explained and outlined plans to worker representatives who would have no statutory powers to alter or amend management decisions. The model is best understood as a form of participation designed to inculcate incorporation (Morawski 1987: 80–3).

The three models rise and fall in importance in the years after 1956. Whichever is in the ascendancy is largely determined by the level and strength of working-class opposition to the regime at any particular time. The various forms recur at different points in the cycle of crisis, revolt, reform and repression. On this interpretation then, self-management cannot be taken as a monochromatic concept, rather it takes on different hues, reflecting the ebbs and flows of the class struggle. It can be a reflection of the highest point of workers self-organization at the very heart of opposition movements. Yet it can be manipulated by the factory management and politicians, and thereby used as a means whereby revolt is contained.

By the time that Solidarity burst onto the scene in 1980, disillusionment with the practice, if not the theory of self-management, meant that, initially at least, the idea of self-management did not figure high on workers' lists of demands. On the contrary, the demand was for the legal right to form independent trade unions (Morawski 1987: 83). By the time the Gdansk agreements were signed one year later, self-management was back on the agenda, but must be placed in the context of the events of that year. On 19 March 1981, Solidarity activists were brutally beaten up by security police in Bydgoszcz. Solidarity immediately mobilized a four-hour protest strike and called a full general strike for a few days later. In the intervening period, and under pressure from the Catholic Church and close advisers, Lech Walesa called off the strike. If the four-hour strike represented the high point of Solidarity's ability to mobilize the population, then the internal crisis that followed the cancellation of the strike brought a shift in direction.

It is crucial to an understanding of what follows to recognize that Solidarity must not be treated simply as a trade union. It was, and remains, simultaneously a trade union, a quasi political party and a social movement. The tensions and clashes between the various elements of the organization's activities have important repercussions throughout the whole period under examination. It is also important here to understand the concept, central to Solidarity's strategy, of the self-limiting revolution. Solidarity continued to recognize, formally at least, the leading role of the Party, but had three aims: firstly, the self-organization of society, the aim being the reconstruction of civil society; secondly, the immediate defence of workers, but with a longer term strategy of removing the Party's influence from within the workplace; thirdly, the expression of the national aspirations of society (Morawski 1987: 11). Within this context it is easier to understand the speed with which Solidarity's national leadership moved to call off the general strike. Even before the cancellation of the general strike, managers were once again attempting to defuse the situation by promoting the co-determination model. However, after Bydgoszcz, militants from seventeen of the major factories which had been selected for strike headquarters came together to form the Network (Siec). This 'horizontal' organization had two key aims: firstly, a high degree of decentralization of decision-making; and secondly, democratization of enterprises. The aim was to allow Solidarity to play a role in 'renewal' without accepting responsibility for macroeconomic decisions. In effect, the aim of 'renewal' was to clear workplaces of the influence of the Party and the state machine. In this case, self-management was to give workers the power to elect the enterprise director. We have then the re-emergence of the syndicalist model. Solidarity was calling for self-managing, self-financing and independent enterprises, whilst the government was stressing, yet again, the co-determination model (Barker, 1986: 96–7, Kolankiewicz, 1982: 140).

In the event, the 1981 law on self-management represented a compromise giving workers' councils some form of control over key long-term conditions, but limited if enterprises were in the defence sectors, in a monopoly position, or in key public service areas. Paradoxically, this relatively liberal law was being passed just as martial law was being declared and thousands of Solidarity activists lost jobs, were arrested or went underground. Prior to martial law being declared, self-management in some form or another existed in half of all enterprises but there was insufficient time to consolidate before it was suspended (Morawski 1987: 107). Writing in 1982, Kolankiewicz argued that 'the Sejm in what may prove to have been an historic declaration of legislative independence, passed a law that, whilst not acceptable to the Solidarity radicals, will be a solid cornerstone to future economic reform' (144–5). As we shall see, later in the decade the re-emergence of self-management on the back of the 1981 law was to have a vital role to play in conditioning the pace and pattern of reform, but not in quite the way that Kolankiewicz envisaged.

The 1980s: The Primacy of the Market

If, as Touraine has argued, in 1981 concentration on self-management represented a retreat from the height of Solidarity's struggle, driven by the image of a self-limiting revolution (Barker 1986: 104), then the rest of the decade was to witness this retreat turn into a full-scale rout of any element of socialism within Solidarity's analysis. Ost (1993: 13) argues that the support for the notion of participation declined within the country as a whole, allied to the emergence of simple notions of the operation of the market, incorporating a belief that, if markets were allowed to operate unhindered, a 'good' worker would always be rewarded. Both the revolt of 1980 and that of 1989 were at least partly driven by responses to the economic crisis of the late 1970s and the continuing descent into economic chaos during the 1980s. During the

1980s, the decade of the unplanned planned economy, attempts were made to introduce market forces in the form of increasingly decentralized control over enterprises, as well as encouragement of small business development and foreign direct investment. The outcome was chaos and uncertainty, a rapid growth in the black market, and a drastic decline in standards of living for most members of the working class.

There were however a number of other material factors driving this transformation. The first was that as Solidarity was driven underground, what public face it had was that of individuals such as Walesa, who by 1981 was already in favour of marketisation. Ost argues that, paradoxically, as far as Walesa was concerned, it was fortunate that the Solidarity revolution did not succeed in 1980–81, as he would not have been able to deliver the Polish working class in terms of accepting market-based reforms. At this time, the mass of activists were loosely grouped around notions of decentralized democratic socialism but by 1989 all this had changed. This can be partly explained by the fact that, during the early to mid-1980s many of the reforms that the Communist Party introduced into the economy were almost carbon copies of those advocated by the Solidarity leadership in 1980–81. These were largely to do with moves to decentralization of financial and managerial responsibility, which gave firms increased autonomy. The reforms only served to exacerbate chronic economic crisis and in so doing contributed to the discrediting of the ideas that had dominated Solidarity's activities and policies at the beginning of the decade (Weinstein 1994: 2). By 1984, the rout of democratic socialist ideas had reached the level whereby the view that Solidarity had failed because it was too left-wing was commonplace. At the same time, Solidarity's struggle to create a civil society came to mean precisely what it had meant to Marx, that is the struggle to create a bourgeois society (Ost 1989: 78). During the 1980s, liberal discussion groups came to be dominated by the works of Hayek and Friedman, and key individuals such as Balcerowicz, a proponent of self-management in 1981, became a major architect of 'big bang', the shock therapy of the post-1989 government. This emphasized the immediacy and comprehensiveness of the reform package, compared to the piecemeal nature of earlier failed attempts to escape the economic stagnation of the 1970s and 1980s. What emerged was a jump to the market, accompanied by draconian macroeconomic policies, embodied in the Balcerowicz Programme instigated in January 1990.

By 1987, the policies of major sections of the ruling class, and the leadership of Solidarity were united around the question of the necessity for market-based reforms. The only differences centred on questions of speed and sequencing. However, even these differences had disappeared by 1989 with Walesa arguing that the Mazowiecki government was being far too cautious in its pace of reform, and further, that although shock therapy would provide three months of pain, things would rapidly improve thereafter (Weinstein 1994: 28, Ost 1993: 15). This unconditional surrender to the myth of the market by Solidarity's leadership was to have important consequences for the union in the years after 1989.

Lewis (1994: 788) argues that Solidarity re-emerged as a political giant and a trade-union dwarf. In the first partially free election in 1989 only 35 per cent of the seats in the Sejm (parliament) were open for free election, although all seats in the upper house (senate) were to be contested. Solidarity took 160 of the 161 non-reserved seats in the Sejm and 92 of 100 seats in the senate. However, the tentative nature of the process of change was reflected in the first and second Solidarity governments which accepted General Jaruzelski as president and gave the defence and interior ministries to the former Communist Party.

However, Kloc (1993) argues that the experience of the ensuing years forced Solidarity to change from being a social movement with political ambitions to becoming a trade union which supported market reform. The period after 1989 would not only bring about tensions between Solidarity's various roles, but would also witness a growing distance between the government and the union, as well as a growing tension between the union's national organization and its workplace and regional organization. To understand how these tensions developed, we must look briefly at Solidarity's organizational structure, as it emerged in the early 1990s.

Solidarity appeared to be a far more democratic and accountable organization than most British union structures. The union had a territorial and branch structure, although locals (workplace organizations) related directly to regional boards and only about half were members of the relevant sector group. The union was organized in thirty-eight regions and ten branch secretariats, with the largest region being that around Katowice with 237 000 members in 1350 locales, and the smallest in Chelm which has 7248 members in 150 locals. Solidarity is not a federation, as is OPZZ (the official Federation), rather it has claimed to be an homogeneous organization based on the territorial-branch system. The basic unit of organization was the enterprise, and then there rose above that a representative system based on the enterprise. All positions (until the mid-1990s) were elected, and all delegates had to be, at least nominally, employed at a place of work. Furthermore, delegates could only hold a major position for three years before having to return to their workplace and start to climb the representational ladder again. There was evidence, however, that pressures were emerging at the national level for the professionalization and bureaucratization of structures. Enterprise commissions (workplace locales) elect delegates to regional congresses, which in turn elect delegates to the national congress. Members of the national congress then elect members to the national commission, the national audit commission and the president of the union, all of whom hold office for three years. Membership of regional branch sections is voluntary, and each regional branch section contributes to forming a national branch section. The chairpersons of the national branch secretariats are also members of the national commission. Solidarity also has a national section of women, a national youth section and a national section for the disabled.

Trade Unions and Restructuring after 1989

We have seen that restructuring is driven by three core elements: privatization, foreign direct investment and the re-emergence of small firms. Though the first two had failed to live up to expectations, and emergent small firms were more reminiscent of a flea market than an enterprise culture, all three presented Solidarity with problems. The rapid growth in the number of SMEs found the union incapable of responding and trade-union presence is minimal in these establishments, with surveys indicating that only 20 per cent of workers in such firms believed trade-union membership would be beneficial. Furthermore, in organizations privatized through liquidation, primarily SMEs, trade-union presence fell from a figure of nearly 90 per cent in pre-privatization organizations, to just over 40 per cent after privatization. Overall, surveys indicated that Solidarity claimed only 28 per cent of employees in businesses privatized through liquidation (see Chapter 5), whilst OPZZ represented 22 per cent of the total workforce in these organizations. These are primarily smaller organizations and the picture is not so bleak in privatization of larger organizations wherein Solidarity's presence remained virtually intact, the union being present in just under 90 per cent of collectivized firms and businesses privatized through the capital track. However, OPZZ presence fell from a figure of 75 per cent in collectivized firms to less than 25 per cent in privatized firms (Pankow 1993: 158–60).

There are a number of factors contributing to declining union membership. The first is that much foreign direct investment and many small and medium-sized enterprises are hostile to unions and Solidarity has had trouble recruiting in both these sectors. SME owner-managers exhibit similar characteristics across national boundaries, including active anti-unionism (Rainnie 1989). National officials argued that SMEs dictated conditions, with employers arguing that because the firm has a human resource department, then not only is a union superfluous but it would also impose extra costs on the firm which would preclude the firm from offering the best terms and conditions available. Unfortunately, initially, workers tended to accept management's arguments.

Even the concept of recruitment is problematic. Solidarity has been at pains to distance itself from the forms and functions of OPZZ, and its national policy statement concludes: 'NSZZ Solidarnosc does not co-operate with any national trade union centre. Contacts with other national centres (OPZZ, Solidarnosc 80, etc.) take place only within the activities of tripartite bodies at the national level, as mandated by national law.' As we shall see later, this rule does not always hold at local level, but the principle of establishing difference and distance is important, and this has meant a policy of not actively recruiting people at workplace level. The justification, according to national officials, for this apparently suicidal policy is that under the old regime union membership was *de facto*, if not *de jure*, compulsory. People were, in effect, forced to join a union if they did not want to cut themselves off from social and welfare benefits. Workers, it is believed, are reluctant to join a union if they feel that they are being forced, being afraid of associations with old-style unions. Therefore, the union made no attempt to actively recruit people, preferring to wait for workers to express an active interest in joining themselves. This policy was changing by the mid-1990s, with the first moves towards national and local recruitment drives beginning to develop.

Solidarity was also suffering attacks on a number of fronts. By 1993, sections of the press as well as a supposedly Solidarity-dominated government had come to perceive the union as a problem. Mass circulation papers such as *Gazeta Wyborcza* regularly carried articles arguing that Solidarity had moved in the space of two years from 'the only right positions' to the 'decidedly wrong and backward positions'. The articles were reminiscent of those in the press during the Gomulka era (Pankow 1993: 156).

Disillusionment was reflected in changing voting patterns between the 1991 and 1993 elections. In 1991, the five political parties associated with Solidarity got over 40 per cent of the vote. Two years later, only one of these five parties (the Democratic Union) managed to gain any parliamentary representation at all, although post-Solidarity parties gained over 30 per cent of the vote. By contrast, the SdRP now formed a coalition (the Democratic Left Alliance, SLD), which raised its share of the vote from just over 20 per cent in 1991 to nearly 36 per cent in 1993 (Lewis 1995: 785).

So far we have concentrated on the experience of Solidarity, but there were also significant changes taking place in other labour movement structures. The All Polish Trade Union Alliance (OPZZ) had been formed in 1984 as an attempt to reform CRZZ into a quasi-official alternative to Solidarity. Attempts to act as a third party during the Roundtable talks were limited in their effectiveness by the continued association of the federation with the Communist Party. OPZZ had been restructured in 1990, and attempted to differentiate itself from Solidarity and act as a real trade union by stressing problems of housing, youth unemployment, regular payment of wages, full indexation for public sector workers and indexation of old age pensions. Early in 1991 OPZZ staged its first major public demonstration in opposition to the 'excess' wages tax (Popiwek), which established a wage norm for a given firm or sector and then taxed all wage increases above that up to one hundred per cent. In January 1992 OPZZ organized a nationwide protest against the increase in energy prices, culminating in a demonstration in front of the parliament building. In 1993 OPZZ claimed to have over four million members, although this figure is generally taken to be inflated by the inclusion of large numbers of retired members.

Solidarity 80 was founded in 1990 by Solidarity activists connected with the work group of the national committee who did not accept the Round Table talks. As early as 1981, the group had expressed opposition both to communists *qua* capitalists, and trade unionists *qua* reformists. Solidarity 80 emphasizes its union character and blames NSZZ Solidarity for betrayal of union ideals and for becoming a political party (see Morawski nd: 24):

> It accuses Solidarity for betrayal of the ideals of the movement since 1980–81, especially for not respecting democratic principles in the internal operation of the confederation, for a deep involvement in politics, for supporting the neoliberal strategy of shock therapy, for selling out the national property to foreign capital, for far reaching privatization program etc. Its positive programme has the following elements: employee ownership ideas (it proposes the sale of 51 per cent of shares to the employees of the enterprise at preferential prices), a housing program on a massive scale, a policy of various safety nets (social minimum), etc.

Membership of Solidarity 80, in 1994, was put at anything between 160 000 and 280 000. It is claimed that is the only trade union whose membership is growing. The union has a history of direct action, organizing hunger strikes in HTS (the steelworks) in Krakow in 1991, and in 1992 organizing an occupation of the State Coal Mining Agency. There have also been cases where Solidarity 80 has participated in strike committees with other unions, but has refused to accept a negotiated agreement and then continued the action. In addition, the union withdrew from negotiations with the government over the Pact on State Owned Enterprises.

There is evidence of another phenomenon threatening Solidarity and OPZZ, that being the increasingly pluralized nature of the trade-union movement. Completely new organizations such as the Union of Air Traffic Controllers are emerging and workplace organizations have been splitting off from both Solidarity and the OPZZ federation. A survey in 1991 indicated that Solidarity was losing membership in 45 per cent of firms and OPZZ in 36 per cent. The Mineworkers Union federation split from OPZZ in disillusionment with what was taken as the excessive willingness of OPZZ to compromise in the face of drastic restructuring of the coal industry. The

Polish Teachers Association left OPZZ to put distance between itself and a federation that was still associated with the old regime.

Solidarity, the Protective Umbrella and the National Government

To understand how we have arrived at this confused and confusing picture, we must start by examining the role that Solidarity played in the months after the election of the first non-communist government. As Weinstein (1994: 13) has pointed out, in the months leading up to the creation of the first post-war, non-communist government the National Executive Committee of Solidarity publicly stated its support for market reforms, and within a week following the nomination of Mazowiecki as prime minister, Solidarity mobilized to support the introduction of the marketization programme. Walesa went so far as to call for a six-month strike moratorium, and asked that workers seeking wage rises should not resort to the strike weapon. This was the first sign that Solidarity, at least at a national level, saw its role as providing a protective umbrella for the new government. The shield would be necessary from the potential backlash of the effects of shock therapy, seen by Walesa as three months of pain followed by recovery. In the longer term the protective umbrella would be necessary to allow for the introduction of an unfettered market economy. In effect, as Pankow (1993: 155) argues, it is ironic that the protective umbrella held up by Solidarity over the reforms differed only slightly from the Leninist concept of trade unions as a transmission belt from the authorities to the working class, at least in its distorted Stalinist variety.

In the early days workers tended to heed the call of the union leadership, with railway workers immediately suspending a two-week strike in response to Walesa demands, and even the OPZZ affiliated Federation of Metallurgical Trade Unions echoed Walesa's appeal. However, after a brief honeymoon period, and as the full horror of the effects of shock therapy sank in (falling living standards and rising unemployment), then underlying tensions between Solidarity's role as a social and political movement, on the one hand, and its role in defending workers interests in the workplace, on the other, started to reveal themselves.

Within the first year of the new Solidarity government, it became clear that the role as protective umbrella would take primacy over the normal trade-union function with Solidarity's national leadership stating that it was prepared to accept 80 per cent wage indexation and later even lower levels, as a price deemed worth paying for macroeconomic stabilization. However, as Kloc (1993: 128) concludes, 'the social consequences of the economic changes, leading in the first place to a decline in real incomes and to growing unemployment, have widened the gap between the union's policies and its members expectations.'

The national leadership of Solidarity was shielded to some extent from major revolt at grassroots level, by the operation of the excess wage tax, Popiwek. Blame for lack of wage increases could be foisted on the government rather than the union itself (though the differences between the government and Solidarity's national leadership were difficult to detect). Popiwek was introduced initially to cover all enterprises, but then restricted simply to SOEs as a means of persuading workers to accept rapid privatization of enterprises. Restriction of Popiwek to state owned enterprises was designed to give the impression that a rising standard of living could only be gained in privatized enterprises. Crucially though, privatization also abolished workers' councils by law and we return once again to the importance of the concept of self-management.

Self-government after 1989

It is important to remember that the comparatively liberal laws on self-management, dating from the period of martial law, remained on the statute book, and were further strengthened by the Employee Self-government Law of September 1989. Whilst it appeared that the codetermination model of self-management was being reincarnated in its traditional role, the reality was very different. The self-management law posed problems for Solidarity, at least at a national level, given that the union's policy was now far removed from support for employee control. However, the self-government legislation did give workplace trade-union organization an important, if contradictory, role to play in determining the process and pattern of privatization and restructuring at workplace level.

Under the terms of the self-management legislation, the general meeting of employees elects members of the workers' council, and the director and all high- and medium-level managerial staff are excluded from running for the council. The council has broad powers which include, among other things, drawing up the annual plan, auditing the annual balance sheet, making resolutions concerning investment to be made, approving co-operation or partnership arrangements with other economic entities, and approving the acquisition of fixed assets (Dzwonczyk and Sobczyk 1993: 8). Furthermore, the workers' council, together with the ministry responsible for the enterprise, has the power to appoint and dismiss the director, and decisions of the council are binding on the director. The workers' councils powers are then, at least in theory, extremely wide-ranging. However, gains that would have been welcomed by Solidarity in 1981 began to cause problems. At a time when the introduction of market reform was the only item on the agenda, employee self-government was now perceived as an obstruction to restructuring of enterprises and rationalizing employment. On the one hand, workers and management were taking advantage of the powers invested in them under self-management and, in a few cases, privatizing their own companies, and echoes of self-management could also be found in a form of privatization known as the management/ employee buyout, an option under the liquidation route. However, in these cases employee ownership is usually transitory and often illusory, as we shall see in Chapter 9. On the other hand, Solidarity's own analysis of the nature of the crisis of state socialism meant that it would be difficult to argue for self-management or even significant representation on the government of the new enterprises (see Weinstein 1994: 15):

> The purpose of the macroeconomic reform program and the privatisation of the economy was to create 'real' owners who would have a material interest realising a profit from their assets. For Solidarity trade union leaders, promotion of employee control of privatised firms would undermine the basis of the economic transformation strategy. There would be little point in creating the legal and economic conditions for the establishment of private owners if the workers could effectively preempt managerial prerogative on strategic issues that impact firm level restructuring. Although there was widespread sentiment among shop floor Solidarity activists that managers who owed their position to the nomenklatura system of advancement should

be removed, there was an equally strong sentiment that newly appointed managers in state-owned firms should be permitted a relatively free hand in directing firm-level restructuring to hasten the enterprises eventual privatisation.

In the view of the Solidarity leadership, the major problem facing the economy was state ownership of the means of production, and this problem could only be overcome by creating a proper private sector, with a proper private sector (i.e. non-*nomenklatura*) management. This scenario did not include worker self-management. Therefore there was little resistance, at a national level, to sections of the privatization legislation that abolished employee councils at the point of privatization. There was a further carrot, in so far as self-management could not be abandoned completely, but had to be turned into the legal right of workers to buy a guaranteed (20 per cent) proportion of their companies' shares at the point of privatization. It is becoming clear, however, that most ordinary workers could not actually afford to take up their options (Tittenbrun 1995).

The education programme for its own representatives, run by Solidarity after 1989, gives some clue to their thinking on questions of ownership and control. The union produced, in conjunction with the YS (Norwegian trade-union confederation), a workbook called *Understanding the Market Economy*. The idea behind these courses, according to the head of Solidarity's national education department, was an attempt to change the way that their members thought, so that they might understand the market economy better. It was essential, the officer said, to get ordinary members away from the idea that, under a market economy, everything would be available for everybody. He concluded that people had got to learn that they couldn't claim a wage increase if the enterprise was unprofitable. Evidence from workplaces in and around Krakow suggests that Solidarity is pushing at an open door. For example, in a cigarette factory, the union had brought in outside experts and introduced a performance-related pay system, negotiated successfully with the incumbent management. The general view encountered from Solidarity workplace representatives was that effort and reward would be inevitably and irrevocably linked as long as the old *nomenklatura* management could be replaced by Western-style managers with new management practices. Here we have echoes of the contradictory role of Solidarity at workplace level. The policy of the union is to campaign for the replacement of *nomenklatura* management in favour of 'proper' capitalism, and until the point of privatization workplace union leadership can act as a proponent of change rather than an orthodox trade union, under the umbrella of rights granted by self-management legislation. In the early days of transformation this apparently contradictory role – union as agent of change and worker representative – could be reconciled under the banner of a demand for 'proper' management structures and reward systems. The two roles would, however, increasingly come into conflict with each other.

In general, in the early days of the post-1989 governments there was a widespread acceptance that the old approach (including self-management) had been tried and failed, and that drastic economic change was needed. Furthermore, Pankow (1993: 115) argues that the influence of activists and experts on self-management in 1989 and 1990 had a considerable role in influencing the privatization law adopted by the Sejm in July 1990. Concessions were, however, made to both workers and the concept of self-management. Evidence for this is taken to be employees being given the right to buy 20 per cent of stock at 50 per cent of the nominal price, as well as the privatization through liquidation track giving workers the possibility, in theory, of buying out the whole enterprise. However, the influence of self-management legislation has certainly not been that envisaged by the legislators, in so far as it has given workplace trade-union representatives the ability to force the pace and pattern of change in a direction that mostly involves relatively unfettered management, coupled with a nod in the direction of limited employee share ownership.

Disenchantment and Dissent

A further stabilizing factor in this early period was the mediating role played by regional structures of Solidarity and local activists. It was inevitable that disputes would occur given the strictures of shock therapy, allied to the effects of Popiwek at plant level. Weinstein (1994: 18) argues that being wedged between managers and workers in state firms, Solidarity activists utilized their open door access to managers, who often owed their positions to workers' councils dominated by Solidarity, to negotiate worker grievances and diffuse potential conflict.

When more serious disputes emerged between Solidarity factory committees and management or government ministries, then regional or national Solidarity leaders, wedged between firms and the government, performed a similar mediating role. This process of mediation and accommodation at a regional and national level was facilitated by the easy flow of Solidarity personnel and ideas from union to ministry and back. This reflected another important factor in Solidarity's position – the multifaceted nature of its activities. Solidarity operates in a quasi management function at workplace level as well as in a trade union function, as a union organization but also as a quasi political party attempting to construct a local microcorporatism at the regional level, and as a political organization and social movement as well as a union at national level (Kloc 1992).

A picture of the relative quiescence of labour organization at a time when shock therapy was being administered can be gained from an examination of strike statistics. The number of strikes in Poland fell from 900 in 1989 to the figure of 250 recorded in 1990. The state railway PKP accounted for over half the strikes in 1990, mostly to do with the effects of the Popiwek. However, the ability of Solidarity's national leadership to continue to keep a lid on simmering discontent would be threatened by two factors; the first being that shock therapy was providing a lot of the first element and little of the second, and also was lasting far longer than Walesa's promised three months. The second factor was the organizational legacy of the years of repression and underground activity in the 1980s. When Solidarity re-emerged in the strike wave of 1988, many of the new workplace leadership were unknown to the Union. Its workplace organization had withered in the 1980s. However, the national leadership was able to put itself at the head of the new movement, but this could not disguise the distance between and the weakness of the links between Solidarity at a national level and workplace organization. As Kloc (1993: 127) comments:

> Employee disappointment was first noticed by Solidarity organisations in the workplaces. That led them to adopt a more radical attitude which was then picked up by sector-level union structures. This occurred especially in the areas worst affected by the recession which were experiencing the most rapid rises in the levels of unemployment. Factory, regional and sectoral level Solidarity structures began pressing more and more for a removal of

the 'protective umbrella' held by the unions Home Commission over the economic policies of successive governments.

Kloc (1992) has argued that worker attitudes to the process of transformation went through three stages. The first was based on a general belief that the new market model would quickly and unproblematically bring benefits to all, and, therefore, there was a willingness to make sacrifices in the short term. The next stage was disenchantment and social disintegration, followed by the third stage which was characterized by the rise of groups representing sectional interests. As the strike figures for 1992 demonstrated, there was a growing willingness to take industrial action. The number of strikes rose from 305 in 1991 to 6362, with teachers leading the fight against falling real wages.

The transfer from Kloc's first stage to the second stage of disenchantment and social disintegration can be gleaned from the strike statistics and the threat to Solidarity posed by the restructured OPZZ and the breakaways such as Solidarity 80. Danger signs could be seen in the 1990 PKP strike where rank and file strike leaders were arguing that Solidarity leadership had lost touch with grass-roots feeling. Furthermore the strike committee was led by OPZZ and Solidarity 80, whilst Solidarity's leadership were instructing strikers to return to work. The outcome was a break between regional structures of Solidarity and its rank and file, and a strong indication that workers, though members of Solidarity, would turn to OPZZ or Solidarity 80 if Solidarity itself failed to provide leadership.

The distance between Solidarity rank and file and the leadership was demonstrated by Walesa's presidential campaign in 1990. At a time when the upsurge in disputes showed growing discontent with the appalling effects of shock therapy, Walesa argued that the major problem was that the government was proceeding too cautiously, that the pace of reform should be increased and that 'self-interested strikes' would only cause further delays. However, the immediate aftermath of the presidential election was an outbreak of industrial unrest in the mines, railways and municipal transport authorities, mostly driven by wage and state subsidy concerns. There was also a less publicized wave of industrial unrest in SMEs driven by wage demands and calls for the abolition of the Popiwek. At the same time polls showed only 6 per cent of the population believing that workers benefited from privatization

(Weinstein 1994: 33). There is also evidence that a more complex attitude towards FDI is beginning to emerge. Within the Krakow region there have been cases where workforces have opted for worker/management buyout rather than FDI. In another case, the union had managed to call into question the financial status of a company wishing to take over a regional power plant, thus precipitating a re-tendering process. In general, it appears that a nationalistic theme is emerging precipitated by adverse reaction to foreign consultants 'mishandling' the disposal of Polish enterprises. What was needed, it was suggested, was Polish investors and Polish management with Western management methods for Polish firms, in other words capitalism with a Polish accent.

By 1991 delegates at the National Congress were more or less equally divided between those who supported the continuation of Popiwek and wage restraint and those who opposed it. However, the national leadership was finding it ever more difficult to continue to play a mediating role between the government and an increasingly discontented rank and file. Equally, at regional level, officials who had played a mediating role were being replaced by more radical candidates in a wave of elections.

At a conference called by Solidarity's national commission in May 1991, Andrzej Slowik, leader of the Lodz region argued that 'Solidarity supported the government and had been betrayed. The government is not paying any attention to its partner. Discussions with the government lead nowhere.' (Kloc 1992: 36). Through the rest of 1991 and into 1992 a pattern developed of Solidarity responding at a national level to unilateral action taken by a Solidarity-supported government. Talks were usually unsuccessful from a union point of view. What emerged was a growing discontent, witnessed by rising strike statistics, and increasing calls for the union to call national protest actions against government policy. The Solidarity leadership found themselves torn between the need to put some critical distance between the union and the government, and yet not wishing open conflict with a government still associated with the pre-1989 opposition, and still in broad agreement with the restructuring aims of the national union leadership.

In mid-1992 an increasingly embattled government, facing a wave of strikes, presented its proposals to conclude a whole series of social pacts, the most important of which would be the Pact on State Owned

Enterprises, covering their status, method of restructuring and clearance of debts. It was to be accompanied by a series of smaller pacts, covering amongst other things a social minimum, housing and the problems of agriculture. The government's main intention was to grant effective guarantees of a minimum level of security as a condition for the continuation of reforms (Hausner and Morawski 1994: 9). In September 1992 the government invited fifteen trade unions for negotiations, however Solidarity 80 rapidly withdrew. The Pact on State Enterprises in Transformation was signed separately by NSZZ Solidarity, OPZZ and seven other federations in February 1993.

The pact covered three areas: firstly, the instruments and processes of privatization; secondly, financing of state enterprises; and thirdly, social issues. The first provides for employees to have some choice of the method of privatization to be adopted; employees to have rights to purchase shares in the privatized company; participation of employees in the management of the company will be guaranteed; employee partnerships will be able to lease their enterprises on more favourable terms. Here we see the legacy of self-management transformed into limited employee share ownership and the (limited) possibility of worker/management buyouts. The second element allows for state-owned banks as well as state-owned enterprises to undergo financial reorganization so as to accelerate and simplify conversion of debt; the tax on net profits (*dywidenda*) was to be replaced. The third element allowed for agreed principles covering collective agreements at plant level; a guaranteed employee wage fund to secure benefits in case of bankruptcy; to extend the labour code to cover International Labour Organization (ILO) standards of health and safety; to establish social insurance funds in all places of work.

By the time that negotiations on the pact had been concluded, pay disputes in the public sector had exploded into major industrial conflict which led to a vote of no confidence in the Suchocka government in 1993. It has been argued that the strike wave was led by militants who were not members of any union and alienated from unions. However, the situation may be more complicated than this. There is evidence to suggest that there is far more co-operation at workplace level between supposedly antagonistic unions than national posturing would suggest. Both Solidarity and OPZZ have rules regarding non-co-operation with each other at workplace level, but it has been suggested (Kloc 1993) that a way round these strictures is for union activists to combine to set up an apparently non-union strike committee, which in reality is dominated by union activists seeking to conceal their co-operation from their respective leaderships. In the September 1993 parliamentary election that followed the vote of no confidence, the parties emerging from the pre-1989 opposition were resoundingly defeated and the Solidarity trade-union ticket did not even reach the 5 per cent threshold needed to gain seats in the new parliament. Paradoxically, the new government led by the reformed communist party provided Solidarity with a possible means of release from some of the problems and contradictions of the previous three years. National officers of the union argued that people were disillusioned with the changes that had taken place and blamed Solidarity for the disasters, because they were associated with the pre-1993 governments. But now, according to Solidarity national officers, the old regime had become the new government, and OPZZ was now inside the new government. In the national union officers' view, the new government's election promises had been unrealistic, and the ex-communist *nomenklatura* were now just business people with an economic policy which was little more than a continuation of market-based reforms.

The roles of OPZZ and Solidarity were to some extent reversed. When the new government prevaricated in signing the Pact on State Owned Enterprises, demanding significant changes, Solidarity called a national demonstration in Warsaw in February of 1994, claiming a turnout of around 40 000. This did not interrupt production as Solidarity members took holiday entitlement to attend. However, a demonstration called later in the year to protest at attacks on standards of living, and the continuing dominance of the 'red bourgeoisie' attracted less than half that number. As a direct result of the effects of campaigning during the 1993 election, and in the face of falling membership, the union in 1994 abandoned its non-recruitment policy and was moving to adopt a more proactive policy. However, interviewed in 1994, Kaziemiericz Kloc, sociologist at the Warsaw Academy of Economics and arbitrator for the ministry of labour, argued that Solidarity was still not a typical union at factory level. Their target was not defence of workers *per se*, but rather taking responsibility for restructuring of the enterprise. Therefore, anything that was not good for restructuring was not good for workers, Solidarity or the firm. In reality, Solidarity are usually seeking a change in management and therefore will precipitate strikes over wages as a means of discrediting the old *nomenklatura* management. In the Krakow tobacco factory, the Solidarity workplace representatives had been impressed by the calibre of the Phillip Morris executives with whom they had had a long-standing licensing arrangement. They wanted to replace their old management with a younger, more dynamic group, essentially new style Polish management with a Western business philosophy.

However, there is evidence that belief in the wonders of the market and the beauty of unfettered 'real' management may be starting to wear a little thin. Regional officials of the union now espoused a belief in a mixed economy, rather than a need to privatize everything. Already there is evidence of disputes in the privatized companies and in companies that are subject of major foreign direct investment. Disputes are usually driven by disappointed expectations, as increased standards of living fail to materialize. There is evidence of major private sector enterprises attempting to use voluntary redundancy as a means of sidestepping the job-protection elements of privatization legislation. Furthermore, employers are simply disregarding labour law and cutting wages to avoid social security tax, avoiding written contracts and resorting to hiring and firing at will (Dzwonczyk and Sobczyk 1993: 36).

Conclusion

The particular history of Solidarity may be unique in Central Europe but demonstrates, perhaps *in extremis*, that the process and patterns of transformation of these economies cannot be understood without reference to class and class conflict. However, it is also clear that the role of Solidarity has been complex.

Firstly, the historical and political importance of the union allows Solidarity a presence at national, regional and local level that far outweighs its actual membership. The union's moral power, though waning, still far surpasses its numerical strength. At a national level, Solidarity acted in the early days after 1989 effectively as a political party shielding the government from any backlash over the effects of shock therapy. There was little to separate the policies of either government or national union leadership. However, despair and disillusion brought on by the terrible impact of shock therapy brought about an increasingly obvious gap between workplace and regional trade-union organization and the attitude and activity of the national leadership. This forced the national leadership to create some distance between themselves and the national government, culminating in the collapse of the 1993 government. However, there is no simple and straightforward dichotomy between leadership and the rank and file.

The influence of Solidarity and the traditions of self management became embodied in legislation that crucially affected the patterns and processes of transformation, particularly privatization. The self-management legislation gives workplace Solidarity leadership an important role to play in the introduction of changes that have little to do with self-management. Paradoxically perhaps, acting as an agent of change rather than a trade union, Solidarity has used the form of workplace trade-union organization and self-management legislation in an attempt to introduce 'proper' capitalism. It was held that if 'real' investment and 'proper' management could be secured then efficiency and effectiveness would increase, leading inevitably to increases in levels of employment and individual reward. Thus, in the early days at least, the apparently contradictory roles of workplace trade-union leadership and agent of restructuring could be reconciled. It would appear though that this is now being called into question. There is some evidence to suggest that, at workplace level, the increasing problems of poverty and the threat of unemployment are driving workplace-based trade-union organizations to act in a more representational role, defending the terms and conditions of employment of their members, as we shall see in Chapter 9. The balance of organizational activity is shifting slowly in the direction of a more critical examination of the process and outcomes of restructuring.

The attitude toward FDI is more ambiguous, as we saw in the far from isolated cases where workplace Solidarity organizations have organized effective campaigns against the takeover of their plants by foreign capital. There appears to be a growing belief in Polish capital and Polish management providing solutions for Polish plants. Desperately seeking Polish capitalism in a world where FDI will be central to the process of transformation is a tactic fraught with problems. The problems are multiplied by the complexities and contradictions between Solidarity's functions as union, political organization and social movement as well as between its workplace, regional, sectoral and national structures. This will become clear as we examine the process of FDI and privatization in the next two chapters.

4 'CLOSER TO THE WORLD': FOREIGN DIRECT INVESTMENT AND TRANSNATIONAL CORPORATIONS

A Solidarity bulletin in 1994 described the Wedel confectionery factory in which Pepsico had bought a 40 per cent share as being 'closer to the world'. This was contrasted with the Wawel chocolate plant, which had taken the worker/management buyout route to privatization that was said to be 'closer to the people'. This captures succinctly the way in which foreign direct investment (FDI) by transnational corporations (TNCs) brings closer integration with the global economy with important implications for individual firms and their workers. The main thrust of this chapter is to locate the restructuring of Central and East European economies in general, and the Polish economy in particular, in the context of changes in the global economy, particularly emphasizing the internationalization of production through FDI, with transnational corporations as the main driving force behind that process. The TNC is a powerful primary force in shaping and reshaping the geography of the contemporary global economy, with FDI increasingly replacing trade as a way of linking individual nation-states through complex strategies and intricate network structures. We begin by discussing the motives for foreign investment in Central and Eastern Europe and its wider implications for the economy, taking this as a starting point from which to draw out the implications for sectors and firms and the workers within them.

The central question is how the economies of Central and Eastern Europe will fit into the emerging international division of labour, given the trend whereby trade and FDI are heavily concentrated within and between major market economies to the virtual exclusion of large sections of the globe and the marginalization of other parts. This is particularly relevant given the paradox of disintegration and integration. The expansion of the European Union (EU) and consolidation of the North American Free Trade Association (NAFTA) increases the integration of major economies, whilst the years since 1989 have seen the political and economic fragmentation and disintegration of former Committee for Mutual Economic Assistance (CMEA) economies.

The internationalization of finance, trade and production has been reflected in a tendency to talk about the system as if states were being increasingly marginalized, proclaiming the age of the stateless corporation (Ohmae 1990). The corollary of this argument is taken to be a diminished role for the state, as described by McMichael and Myhre (1991: 99):

> The nation state is yielding its primacy of place in the regime of accumulation – its role as political mediator. In its stead the institutions and mechanisms of the global regime are setting the terms of political debate and economic policy. As a result there is a growing tendency for the state to act more as a facilitator between global capital than as a mediator between global capital and national bourgeoisie and the working class.'

This view of a global village with footloose and extremely mobile giant corporations divorced from competition, distorting the effects of national policy, is misleading. There are very few firms that can claim to be truly transnational (that is, not reliant on a particular home state). Governments, both host and home, continue to play a crucial and, perhaps paradoxically, even greater role in providing the framework which determines or influences the location of transnational firms. As a consequence it follows that one of the motives firms have in seeking mergers or joint ventures is not that of just gaining access to new markets, but of searching for access to previously closed nexuses of power, foreign communities and foreign governments. Thus the state–business relationship does not disappear, but rather multiplies the number of states and national capitalist networks to which TNCs are linked. We are not suggesting that this process is straightforward, but rather that contradictory tendencies between the internationalization of production, the nation–state and labour must lie at the centre of any analysis which seeks to explain the changing form of capitalist development in Poland.

Internationalization of Production

In order to understand the changing form of integration in the world economy we begin by presenting a thumbnail sketch of recent developments already outlined in Chapter 1. Traditionally, patterns of international economic integration were determined by patterns of trade. The 1950s and 1960s saw a huge increase in world trade, and economies were locked in via this shallow integration. In addition, integrated international production by TNCs grew in importance, with its structure shaped by the pattern of FDI. More recently an explosion of investment can be observed. Whilst world trade volumes grew at a compound annual rate of 5 per cent between 1983 and 1988, FDI grew at 20 per cent annually in real terms.

The number of TNCs and their foreign affiliates has expanded enormously, and they come from an expanding range of home countries (UN 1993). Transnational corporations are a powerful force binding national economies together through complex corporate strategies and intricate network structures, engaging in international production characterized by a sophisticated inter and intra firm division of labour. As a result one-third of the world's private sector productive assets are under the common governance of TNCs. Even these figures understate the sphere of influence of TNCs, not only because of difficulties in measuring flows, but also because firms carry out their transnational activities by exerting control over foreign productive assets through a variety of non-equity arrangements (subcontracting, franchising and licensing) as well as through the formation of strategic alliances. The TNC universe is highly concentrated in terms of the share of foreign assets controlled by the largest firms, with roughly 1 per cent of parent TNCs owning half of the global FDI stock. The largest one hundred TNCs accounted for roughly $280 billion of the world stock of outward investment in 1990 (UN 1993).

In examining transnational and foreign investment there are two other important observations that need to be made. Firstly, the rapid increase in FDI throughout the world has been accompanied by a pronounced change in its sectoral composition, away from the primary sector and resource based manufacturing towards services and technology-intensive manufacturing. Stopford and Strange (1991) suggest a simplified typology which shows foreign investment taking place in a series of waves. In the 1960s, a concentration in labour-intensive industries such as textiles, shoes or simple assembly shifted in the 1970s to capital-intensive goods such as automobiles, machinery and chemicals. Moves towards consumer electronics and telecommunications in the 1980s were replaced by a shift in emphasis to information and financial services in the 1990s. This suggests a decline in importance of resource intensive, low cost and low skill activities as primary attractors of TNCs. We explore the implications of this in more detail shortly.

Central and East European economies were far from excluded from these developments. Although capital/equity investment appeared to be low, this masked a wide range of franchising and licensing agreements that proliferated in the 1970s as large firms extended their operations and influence into these economies. Thus Central and East European economies, to a greater or lesser extent, were increasingly integrated into the international division of labour. In the case of Poland, the effect of this process was accelerated by the government's adoption of a strategy of import-led growth in the 1970s which involved attempting to break out of economic stagnation by, amongst other things, buying imported technology from the West and taking a more liberal attitude towards foreign investment.

It has been suggested that moves from 'simple' to 'complex' integration by TNCs in national economies have important ramifications for states (UN 1993). Under simple integration, stand alone affiliates engaged in international production serve a single host country or region. They are responsible for most of the activities that comprise their value chain and may act as self-contained entities. More recently, many TNCs have gone beyond these simple integration strategies. They are now regarding all activities across the entire value chain as potentially being performed by one or more affiliates. It is not suggested that this is the inevitable path of development for all TNCs, and it is recognized that strategies will vary between and within sectors. Nevertheless, this new approach of 'complex integration' made possible by huge improvements in communication or information technologies, allows transnationals to co-ordinate a number of activities in a widening array of locations. This poses problems for governments in devising appropriate strategies, where the nature of new technologies both redefines and blurs traditional lines between sectors. The implication of this is that policies aimed at sectoral transformation may have decreasing relevance.

Transnational corporations should not however, be treated as mono-lithic entities with a single strategic direction and intent. Using the example of production led by high technology, research and development to examine integration developing at an international level, Hirst and Thompson (1995) observe the existence of quite different forms of collaborative agreement between firms and national subsidiaries. The form of FDI and the strategy of individual firms will be influenced by the unique institutional arrangements of particular countries. Certain innovations, such as new technology, can more easily be detached from their original setting and transferred to other settings than organiza-tional processes. Thus Japanese firms will install different factory re-gimes in their Malaysian and in their German subsidiaries (Elger and Smith 1994). In other words, the international division of labour and internationalization of production through transnational capital means an unequal installation of personnel practices, manufacturing techniques and training programmes. Therefore, whilst we can point to new possibilities and directions in the strategies of TNCs, their form will depend not only on the sector and the country of origin of the TNC, but also the conditions within the recipient country.

The State and FDI

Thus far a framework has been outlined in which the processes and outcomes of restructuring are set in wider tendencies in the global economy. Further, following Stopford and Strange (1991), it is argued that the nation-state is not simply a passive conduit for the policies and actions of TNCs, but that the state both influences and is influenced by FDI and large companies in an elaborate bargaining process. Central to the analysis is both a rejection of the simple state/market dichotomy underpinning the neoclassical paradigm, and at the other extreme, a rejection of the argument which suggests that the role of the state is now reduced to that of a mere facilitator of global capital.

States are not independent of firms and their policies are, at least in part, influenced by the necessity of attracting foreign investment. This is not only true at the wider level of putting in place institutions and legal frameworks, but a bargaining process is also evident at the level of individual transactions. Examples would include the assiduous courting of General Motors by the Polish government, where negotiations took

place directly. Further, the entry of three telecommunications operators (AT & T, Alcatel and Siemens) was on condition that 50 per cent of
the value of communications equipment was supplied by producers
who were privatized Polish firms (*British News From Poland* 15 October
1993).

Pragmatism and bargaining are further complicated by different
attitudes to different sectors. FDI by TNCs in confectionery has largely
been non-contested and the bargains struck were the outcome of
competition between different TNCs for individual firms. Tobacco, by
contrast, has been something of a political football. This is illustrated by
the way in which the state moved from a position where the tobacco
industry was initially excluded from the privatization programme for
monopoly reasons, to a situation where the state was in the process of
attempting to negotiate the privatization of a tobacco company which
produces 40 per cent of Poland's cigarettes (*British News From Poland* 26
July 1993). The participation of a central player, Philip Morris, was
initially opposed by Solidarity. We explore the twists and turns of this
story in more detail in Chapter 9.

In the steel sector, the policies of those holding the 'aid purse
strings', such as the IMF and World Bank, coupled with the constraints
of debt, have severely limited the ability of the Polish government to
modernize on anything like the necessary scale. Ironically, integration
with the global economy means that that they are now operating in a
sector which, at a European level, far from being a free market, is
intensely sensitive to political influence with a high level of state
intervention evident in (nearly) all economies. The overall picture, at a
European level at least, is one of national restructuring and consolidation bolstered by varying degrees of protection and with only limited
and small forays across national boundaries.

Radice (1994b) suggests three ideal-types of transformation paths in
which attitudes to FDI can be understood. Firstly, the neoliberal path,
where internationally traded goods and services are determined according to their marginal productivities at international prices, and this
will be achieved through the unfettered working of the market mechanism, with market prices serving to allocate resources according to
comparative advantage (see Dornbusch 1992, Rodrik 1992). Two policy
prescriptions flow from this analysis: firstly, the removal of any domestic
market distortions, whether due to government or institutional factors,
thus allowing markets to operate freely; and secondly, the liberalization

of international trade, by removing any trade or exchange controls. In this scenario there is no distinction between transnational processes and domestic ones. The second ideal type is the protectionist path, where the construction of a viable national economy secures the well being of all groups. The state and institutions are essentially interventionist, with foreign interests viewed with suspicion and as a result are closely monitored. Thirdly, the state developmental path, in which a highly conscious strategy for gaining comparative advantage and success on world markets is deployed. Such an approach is exemplified by Korea (Chang 1993, Jenkins 1991, Wade 1991), where markets are managed and manipulated to this end, with foreign ownership directly controlled.

The neoliberal approach conforms to the rhetoric of transformation. However, despite the apparent willingness of the states of Central and Eastern Europe, and particularly Poland, to embrace the Adam Smith model of eighteenth-century liberalism, we question the degree to which it has been translated into practice. A rhetorical commitment may have been trumpeted by many in the early days of transformation, but harsh realities quickly led to what has been described as a more pragmatic approach. The approach of the state to foreign capital appears to have been one that reflects the tensions between the competing demands of powerful interests, both domestic and international, tempered by concessions to workers. The necessity of foreign investment for modernization is undeniable, and this is reflected in legislation favourable to FDI, which not only removes any constraints, but in some circumstances gives tax holidays. In addition, large investors such as General Motors in Poland and Volkswagen in the Czech Republic demanded protection via tariffs and quotas against competition from imports as a precondition for investing. The car industry in Poland, an area dominated by foreign capital, has enjoyed the highest degree of tariff protection. Ironically, the same powerful TNCs which have successfully claimed tariff protection in order to ensure themselves privileged operating conditions have been known to default on their investment commitments, although they have derived profit from their protected markets in Poland. This protection was reinforced in 1994 by the government's refusal to sanction the proposal by the antimonopoly commission to drop tariffs from 35 per cent to 10 per cent in a situation where Fiat currently has 88 per cent of the domestic car market.

The degree of integration and scale and type of foreign investment cannot simply be seen as a bargaining process between large firms, on the one hand, and nation-states attempting to balance competing national and international interests, on the other. The position of Poland (as well as the other Visegrad countries) with respect to important trading blocs, in this case the European Union, is of crucial importance. The disingenuous attitude of the EU is exemplified by the Association Agreement (1992), which has been given a high profile in terms of claims to liberalize trade between the PIT (Partners in Transition) countries and the EU. In reality, its impact in terms of encouraging trade is severely limited by the fact that those goods in which Poland has a short-term comparative advantage (steel, agriculture, textiles, chemicals, which provide 35 per cent of exports, are still subject to protectionism (Messerlin 1992). In addition, it includes contingent protection such as anti-dumping and safeguard clauses which may stymie the export potential of new industries. Even more insidious is a clause relating to rules of origin, which potentially may have a significant effect on foreign investment in Poland, in that it places barriers to exporting goods to the EU whose content is less than 60 per cent Polish. This may have the effect of discouraging firms wanting to take advantage of relatively cheap labour costs from investing in assembly production. The (not so hidden) agenda is to ensure that other trading blocs do not gain a backdoor entry to EU markets. Therefore, formal integration (or lack of it) is likely to significantly affect real integration via foreign investment. Thus Poland is potentially limited in its ability to be locked into other sections of capital from, for example, the US or Japan, whilst being unable to reap the benefits of being fully integrated into the EU.

Poland and FDI: Behind the Figures

Optimism regarding the level of FDI in Central and Eastern Europe, particularly in the financial press and investment journals, appears on first sight to be justified. The number of registered joint ventures increased from 1685 in 1990 to 6187 by early 1993 (WERI 1993). In addition, by January 1994 foreign investment in Poland amounted to US$2.2 billion. The arrival of international firms such as ABB, Alcatel, AT & T, Coca Cola, Gerber, IKEA, Siemens, Thomson and Unilever was taken to be a further sign of the attractiveness of Poland as a location for foreign investors. On closer scrutiny the picture is far from one of unqualified success. Not only have flows of foreign investment to Central and Eastern Europe been much less than anticipated at a general level but, relative to other countries, Poland's record is disappointing. Poland has attracted only 16 per cent of the total FDI in the region and in terms of foreign capital per head, the position of Poland looks even more dismal (see Table 4.1).

Table 4.1 *Foreign Capital in Central and Eastern Europe and Russia*

	Total foreign capital (US$bn)	Percentage of total	Foreign capital per head (US$)
Hungary	5.2	37	505
Russia	3.0	21	20
Poland	2.2	16	57
Czech Republic	1.9	14	184
Bulgaria	0.7	5	78
Romania	0.7	5	30
Slovak Republic	0.3	2	55

Source. Adapted from figures issued by the Polish State Agency for Foreign Investment (PAIZ) (January 1994).

Figures on joint ventures need to be treated with caution on a number of counts. Firstly, foreign direct investment figures prior to 1989 may underestimate the level of foreign participation. Long-standing co-operation agreements, both for local marketing and for sourcing where there was no equity investment to be measured, had already existed in Poland for about two decades (Levcik and Stankovsky

1979, Paliwoda 1981). Focusing specifically on Poland, it should be noted that, in some cases FDI may represent simply an acceleration of trends that had already been established in the 1970s, rather than new investment. For example, firms such as ABB and Philip Morris have been producing in Poland since the 1970s, and Fiat's presence can be traced back to the 1950s (Maxcy 1981). In addition, registration may simply signal intention or a process of testing the water and many early 'testers' have failed to develop. Similarly, a survey of investment intentions of major companies, undertaken by the Commission of European Communities (1993), revealed that, although companies were taking an interest in Eastern European economies, it was largely on a wait and see basis.

An examination of the relative weight of individual projects reveals a picture of a small number of large investments by transnational corporations, surrounded by a large number of much smaller investments, often contributing insignificant sums. For example, of the 197 major foreign investors, recorded by the Polish state agency for foreign investment (PAIZ) in 1994, 107 investors (54 per cent) contributed US $5 million or less. In 1994, according to official government statistics, ten major foreign investor countries account for 90 per cent of realized foreign capital commitments. Over a short period of time the nature of investment projects has changed. At the beginning of 1992, the highest number of investment projects were registered in industry, followed by wholesale and retailing. Later figures (see Table 4.2) show a marked change in the balance of FDI, with electronics (this includes investment by Fiat) ranking highest followed by food processing, finance, building, chemicals, paper, telecommunications and trade. Finally, it should be noted that large sections of the economy had received little or no foreign investment, in particular heavy industry. For example, although five firms are shown to be investing in steel, the bulk of the realized investment is accounted for by one project – the Lucchini Group investment in Huta Warszawa steelworks.

Low Costs or Market Domination

There is an extensive literature which attempts to explain and theorize about the strategies and motives of TNCs (see Pitelis and Sugden 1991).

We focus on low labour costs and market growth, the two most commonly proffered explanations of foreign direct investment by TNCs in Central and Eastern Europe. The first motive is rooted in the

Table 4.2 *Foreign Investment in the Polish Economy by Sector*

Sector	Investment realized (US$m.)	%	Investment committed (US$m.)	%	Number of firms	%
Electrical	566	18.6	2 007	43.8	25	12.7
Food	450	14.8	418	9.1	37	18.8
Finance	435	14.3	288	6.3	16	8.1
Construction	351	11.6	172	3.7	15	7.6
Chemicals	230	7.6	40	0.9	14	7.1
Paper	225	7.4	297	6.5	10	5.1
Telecommunications	217	7.1	413	9.0	10	5.1
Trade	155	5.1	104	2.3	31	15.7
Minerals	117	3.8	196	4.3	7	3.6
Energy	109	3.6	301	6.6	9	4.6
Light industry	103	3.4	199	4.3	8	4.1
Metallurgy	40	1.3	150	3.3	5	2.1
Transport	15	0.5	0	0.0	5	2.5
Miscellaneous	14	0.5	3	0.1	3	1.5
Agriculture	8	0.3	0	0.0	2	1.0
Insurance	4	0.1	0	0.0	1	0.5

Source: Adapted from statistics issued by the Polish state agency for foreign investment (PAIZ) (January 1994)

traditional theory of comparative advantage, which asserts that given differential labour costs between countries, firms will take the opportunity of producing wherever is cheapest. Another version of this argument is to be found in the new international division of labour (NIDL) literature (Froebel *et al.* 1981, Jenkins 1984), which draws similar conclusions but whose starting point is that of Marxist analysis. This theory asserts that the desire of capital to maximize profits will lead to a restructuring and relocation of industry to cheap labour countries on the periphery. The result is a new international division of labour where products are conceived and designed in advanced countries and assembled in low cost locations such as developing countries, or in this case Central and Eastern Europe, and returned to developing countries for distribution, sales and marketing. With average wages at just over $200 per month, and a highly educated workforce, Poland is, on this reading, an attractive investment proposition. Table 4.3 provides examples of firms, which may have been attracted by low labour costs and have opened up production or relocated facilities from elsewhere in Europe to Poland. Such firms would include ABB, Curtis, Thomson and Philips.

Both the neoclassical and NIDL theories, with the motive of cost minimization at their core, have been subject to extensive criticism. The assumption that 'All simple production is going East' (*Business Week*, September 1992) cannot be taken for granted. It is not axiomatic that low wages means low costs. The important measurement for firms is that of unit costs (costs divided by productivity). Productivity is determined by a complex set of factors, ranging from the quality of capital through to less tangible but equally important variables such as the quality of human capital, which depends in turn on education, training and motivation. In addition, given that most firms operate to some degree in international markets, the concept of relative unit labour costs, incorporating the exchange rate, is significant. For example, Tungsram's 30 per cent wage cost advantage over West European competition was lost when the Hungarian forint was not devalued in line with inflation, and costs rose faster than export prices. The assumption is also static, in that it neglects the possibility of any potential for restructuring production sites in developed market economies to reduce unit labour costs. Marginson (1994) quotes two separate studies of UK based multinational textiles companies (Elson (1986) and Walsh (1989)) which showed how British based operations significantly

Table 4.3 *Major Foreign Investors in Poland*

Number	Investor	Equity and loans (granted by an investor) (US $ m)	Commitment (US $ m)	Country of origin	Branch
1	Fiat	260	1,750	Italy	Manufacture of passenger cars
2	Coca-Cola	180	50	USA	Soft drinks
3	Polish American Ent. Fund	164	63	USA	Capital participation in private sector
4	Thomson Consumer Electronics	147	37	France	TV tubes and sets
5	IPC	140	175	USA	Paper products
6	EBRD	138	0	International	Banking, capital participation in enterprises
7	International Finance Corporation	123	0	International	Investment in private sector projects across all sectors of industry
8	ABB	100	20	International	Power supply systems, turbines, electric engines
9	Curtis	100	0	USA	Electronics, construction
10	Unilever	96	0	International	Washing powder, food processing
11	Epstein	90	110	USA	Construction development, meat processing
12	Proctor & Gamble	60	130	USA	Personal hygiene products
13	Philips	60	26.5	The Netherlands	Electric appliances
14	ING Bank	56	0	The Netherlands	Banking
15	PepsiCo	55	50	USA	Sweets, soft drinks, potato snacks

Source. Polish state agency for foreign investment (PAIZ) (February 1994)

reduced costs through the application of new technology and production rationalization. In addition, pronounced changes in the sectoral composition of FDI (UN 1993), away from primary and resource based manufacturing towards services and technology-intensive manufacturing, suggests a decline in competitive advantage based on resource-intensive, low cost and low skill activities.

Marginson (1994) examines the pursuit of a low wage, low skill strategy in attracting FDI in Britain. Whilst examples of social dumping can be found, notably the relocation of Hoover from France to Scotland, his research suggests that the primary concern of multinational companies is the quality and productivity of labour. Thus, in the case of Britain, the attractiveness of labour resting on a cheap, unprotected and semi-skilled workforce, gives only a limited and specific advantage in the emerging European and global division of labour. The greatest shortcoming of the NIDL literature is, however, its failure to account for the dominant pattern of investment flows that remain primarily amongst advanced countries rather than between advanced and developing countries.

Furthermore, the possibility of actually realizing the comparative advantage of low labour costs through increased exports may be constrained by the political economy of international trade. As we have argued, the Association Agreements with the European Union, which purport to liberalize trade, may have the effect of inhibiting both trade and foreign investment (Messerlin 1992, Hindley 1992). Thus, whilst the rest of the world is moving towards the consolidation of three powerful trading blocs, the disintegration of the Soviet bloc and the peripheral status of Eastern European countries with regard to the European Union has implications for Poland's ability to attract foreign firms on the basis of low costs. The surge of foreign investment into Spain after its accession to the European Union underlines the attractiveness of investment in a large internal market, and highlights the problem of exclusion from membership of the European Union for Poland and the other countries of Central and Eastern Europe.

The possibility of coupling low cost production with domestic market penetration is also questionable. In Poland, a population of 40 million and a low level of ownership of consumer durables offers the possibility of market growth. However, this has to be set against the fact of rapidly growing inequality with many people facing falling real wages and rising unemployment. Further, there may not be location specific advantages (Dunning 1993) which justify opening up new production facilities, because markets may be more easily served by other methods. Sony, for example, has put money into consolidating its existing distribution network (Collins 1993), whilst textiles, clothing and footwear, which constitute the bulk of cheap labour exports to the West, are characterized by contractual arrangements. Therefore, for some Western firms, firm specific advantages lie in market access rather than in direct ownership or joint ventures.

The expected advantages of securing low cost production have to be offset against the risks and uncertainties of producing in a new country, particularly one where structures that underpin market economies, such as financial institutions are still embryonic. According to the ministry of industry and trade in June 1994 (*Privatisation News* November 1994: 4), there are a number of problems at a state level, including an unresolved reprivatisation issue, delays in banking and insurance reform and high loan servicing costs. This is reflected in *The Economist*'s Investment Risk of New Markets, in which Nigeria heads the world list as the most risky country for investors, with Poland high on the list behind Venezuela and Brazil and ahead of Argentina. *The International Competitiveness Report*, prepared by the International Institute for Management Development in Lausanne, placed Poland in 41st and last place. Poland was criticized mainly for inexperienced bureaucracy, taxation policy, rising protectionist tendencies, a low share in international trade and complicated investment procedures (*Privatization News* November 1994).

At a very basic level there are resource implications for negotiating entry, and reports of the speed and ease with which negotiations are successfully concluded are mixed. The experience of individual investors gives a flavour of the investment environment in Poland. Esso, the European subsidiary of Exxon, supports (in *Privatization News* November 1994) complaints about bureaucratic impediments voiced by almost half of all foreign investors:

> Last year Esso applied for a permit to build two more gas stations. For several months the application crawled through different commissions: urban planning, ecological impact, municipal services, surveyors – even the

town's cultural patrimony commission. Finally when the matter was almost resolved and Esso had assembled all the building materials, it turned out that the magistrates court has some objections. Esso had to threaten to move all its business to the Czech Republic before the application was approved.

Despite the bureaucratic hurdles, some FDI has taken root and the primary motive for Western investors has been the acquisition of local market share and the establishment of access to regional markets, rather than low cost sourcing or tapping into Western markets. However, it is not simply a case of establishing and extending markets, but in particular establishing and maintaining market power and product domination as part of global competition. In Poland the top thirty foreign investments are dominated by food processing, detergent manufacturers and telecommunications. The strategies employed by these companies, particularly in the confectionery and food processing sectors, exhibit classic oligopolistic characteristics of collusion and rivalry (Sugden and Cowling 1987).

An example of collusion is provided by the Polish tea industry. After 1989 when the state owned monopoly lost its right to exclusive national distribution, a large number of independent suppliers set up direct contracts with Indian tea producers. This situation closely corresponds to the kind of market economy envisaged by Lipton and Sachs (1990), with many suppliers, no one of whom could influence the price. However, this neoclassical notion of markets was quickly shattered by the entry of Unilever and Tetleys, which reduced competition to a two horse race. Backed by heavy advertising, relatively cheap by Western standards, but expensive for a Polish company with little capital, these two firms segmented the market, with Lipton's (Unilever) tea regarded as an aspirational brand and Tetleys aimed at the mass market. Thus transnational corporations producing non-durable consumer goods need to be firmly located in the national market in order to realize their firm specific advantages in consumer branding, backed by advertising and marketing. Rivalry has been seen in the degree of competition in acquiring companies, particularly evident for example in the confectionery sector, as we shall see in Chapter 9.

The distinction between low cost sourcing and market access is, however, often blurred. In the case of Philip Morris and other tobacco companies, their increased interest in the whole of Central and Eastern Europe and China is driven by the search for lower costs and new markets as smoking declines in domestic markets. In addition, the huge planned investment by Fiat is driven by both low costs and the existence of a large market in which uncertainty is reduced by decades of experience in the Polish economy.

Investment in telecommunications could be viewed as directly linked to the transformation process. This is understandable given that domestic investment has been insufficient to update obsolete equipment and the programme is facilitated by a loan from the World Bank. However, this is only part of the picture and investment should be put in the context of changes in the telecommunications market, which grew globally by 13 per cent in 1992 alone. Already a large number of telecommunications privatizations have taken place in the world economy with more planned for the remainder of the 1990s. The scale of operations is deemed to be so huge that it is estimated that telecommunications could be a larger equity sector than the banks by the end of the 1990s (*Financial Times Survey* 18 October 1993), with the result being serious international competition between rival alliances of telecommunications companies. Thus technology and global competition have driven privatization which in turn has spurred further competition, and triggered a massive restructuring in the forms of alliances and mergers in the industry on a global scale. A similar argument could be applied to services, particularly in the financial sector, where there is also a lack of basic institutions. However, FDI in financial services reflects a worldwide increase in this sector (UN 1993). FDI is progressively substituting for trade because it is not possible to trade services internationally as they are locationally specific, so TNCs must invest abroad to provide services. In these sectors then, whilst the starting point in terms of the existing technology and development between Western economies and those of Central and Eastern Europe may be different, the pattern of FDI and restructuring is part of a wider trend of deregulation and privatization, not a simple function of transformation.

Thus far we can draw several conclusions. It appears that Poland will be drawn into the international division of labour in a very limited way, with large sections of industry untouched by the necessary FDI, and the remainder dominated by large TNCs as part of their global strategies.

However, the influence of TNCs extends far beyond simply the numbers that inhabit a particular economy.

Cathedrals in the Desert?

The optimistic view of FDI is that, at a micro level, it will introduce expertise at both the level of technology and management in economies where productive processes and capital equipment are outdated and obsolete (Donges 1992). According to this view, it follows that the diffusion of technology and know how will stimulate competition and increased integration into the global economy. This view of foreign direct investment can be questioned on two counts. Firstly, in terms of its economic impact, particularly on technological transfer, employment and exports, and secondly, the impact on competition and market structure.

The claim that foreign direct investment means updating products and processes through the transfer of technological know how needs further examination. We have already pointed to the pattern of a small number of large TNCs surrounded by a large number of small investments contributing little capital. This picture is substantiated by a survey of 515 joint ventures by the Polish state agency for foreign investment (PAIZ 1993), which shows that the capital invested by foreign investors has been relatively low, with the initial capital contributed by 74 per cent of firms not exceeding US\$270 000. Further, the survey suggests that the role of investment in terms of updating technology is limited, revealing that 50 per cent of joint ventures were using equipment that was five years old or less, and 15 per cent of companies were using equipment that was up to ten years old.

In many cases, those firms that have invested for low cost motives have transferred simple assembly line production, whilst retaining the high technology parts of the process in the country of origin. As Radice (1994a) suggests, the key question is whether these companies have been integrated into the TNC parents at the lowest point of the value added hierarchy, producing low level products with relatively unskilled labour. This may, however, simply be reinforcing structural change induced by changing trade patterns. Before 1989 Poland largely exported primary products and semi-processed goods to the West and continues to do so, whilst the CMEA market for 'high technology' finished products has collapsed.

However, it would be simplistic to suggest that there has been no upgrading and technology transfer and the corollary of this, that Poland will only fit into the international division of labour producing low grade goods with unskilled labour. In the case of telecommunications, a kind of leapfrogging has taken place whereby several stages of technological development have been skipped with the installation of equipment that is more sophisticated than that found in some Western market economies.

Linked to the large FDIs is the possibility of a multiplier effect on local industry opening up the possibility of local suppliers providing inputs and services. Grabher (1992), however, suggests that high profile TNCs may remain as 'cathedrals in the desert', producing little in the way of a multiplier effect. This depends, however, on the extent to which components or raw materials are imported or purchased locally, and the extent to which sales to the domestic economy generate a demand for intermediate services.

In November 1994 General Motors (GM) opened their first assembly facilities, rolling Opel Astras out of the state-owned FSO auto plant in Warsaw. The impact of this joint venture will have beneficial spin offs, with some technology transfer as part of an agreement to assist in the updating of the Polonez, one of FSO's own cars. However, although the initial investment is worth US$20 million, in 1995 only 130 jobs had been created on the line. Initially, the investment is in simple assembly with components being imported from Western Europe with the engine already on the chassis. Integration is thus at a low point on the chain of value added. The possibility of multiplier effects in the future are unclear as GM parts subsidiaries are currently working with Polish companies to produce compatible parts consistent with GM standards. The advantages to GM are clear in that they not only gain a foothold in the market, but at the same time avoid paying costly import duties. The joint venture status of the investment means that they can take advantage of existing facilities and have access to a trained workforce without having to commit the scale of resources that would be necessary on a greenfield operation.

Other experiences of foreign investment are mixed. The purchase by Gerber of a controlling share (60 per cent) of the Alima plant in February 1992 for US$11 million was hailed as a 'clear success story of foreign investment in Poland' (*Privatization News* May 1994). This is evidenced by an increase in wages from 20 per cent below the national average to significantly higher. The US$31.1 million spent on upgrading production is reflected in the improved quality of goods receiving a licence to export to Europe. In addition, a multiplier effect is evident as key suppliers bought Huta Jaroslaw Glassworks to supply the new plant with baby food jars. The downside is the announcement of 250 voluntary redundancies, constituting 23 per cent of the workforce, a significant number in a small town where other industries may not absorb the unemployed. According to the company, the 'modernization and computerization programme at Rzeszow works has reduced the need for personnel' (*Privatization News* May 1994). As we see in Chapter 9 modernization will have significant effects on firms in the course of restructuring and therefore for workers FDI will be a mixed blessing.

There is little evidence to suggest that even in cases of large TNC driven FDI that strong local linkages are emerging in terms of the development of local supplier networks. This seems to be a reflection of a general tendency where the importance of proximity in primary supplier relationships is diminishing, although some local small and medium-sized enterprises (SMEs) will be locked into supplier networks in secondary, peripheral and often dependent relationships. In effect, incoming FDI provides development in a region, but not necessarily development of a region. The issue at hand extends beyond a few TNCs, standing like cathedrals in the desert; their presence has important implications for existing firms, privatized or otherwise.

Competition and Market Structure

The issue of competition is important given that the legacy of the planned economy was one where most large plants were in effect monopoly producers both within these economies and the bloc as a whole. Where Western economies are characterized as being pyramidically structured with a large number of small firms at the base and a few large ones at the top, centrally planned economies were usually characterized as precisely the opposite. It should be stressed that the size of firms did not simply reflect the scale of their core operation, but also the degree of provision of other functions ranging from catering and transport through to social and welfare functions such as hospitals and nurseries. These distortions, however, go further than this in that, ironically, substantial numbers of firms and plants are actually too small to compete in global terms. In terms of their core operation they were unable to derive sufficient economies of scale to compete on world markets and in particular against leading world oligopolies (Amsden *et al.* 1994, Haynes 1992b).

We have been working so far on the assumption that, in comparison with Western economies, processes and products are obsolete or at best lagging behind and that this gap widened in Poland in the 1980s. The reality is not quite so simple and this assumption requires closer examination. Amsden *et al.* (1994) note that in planned economies technology was often focused on the process of production rather than the product with the result that processes were not always backward. For example, in the early 1990s, the Polish textile industry had more modern equipment than many other countries and therefore did not face the costly burden of introducing new technologies or buying completely new systems of machinery. The major problems were non-cost related, in particular too narrow a product line and poor quality goods. The importance of quality is crucial not simply in terms of competition, but also in terms of access to important markets such as the European Union. For example, whilst not a legal requirement, ISO 9000 standards are increasingly recognized and demanded by Western firms as a quality control standard. The acquisition of a certificate requires know how and resources, both of which may be difficult for many indigenous Polish firms to access. It would probably require either co-operation with a foreign partner or the costly fees of a management consultant. Although many firms are in the process of applying, in 1994 there were only twenty firms holding ISO 9000 certificates in the whole of Poland.

We can develop this point of 'soft' versus 'hard' skills further in relation to the presence of large TNCs. It is not simply that, generally, some potential entrants are kept out of production by economies of scale or the benefits of research and development, but more im-portantly – in sectors dominated by oligopolies – market experience and large advertising budgets are crucial where product differentiation is the key to competition. The exercise of power in overseas product markets is related to the ability to differentiate products and services and mould them to local tastes. Demand within and between sectors is a complex mixture of a desire for Western products and brand loyalty to local products. In the case of the latter, overseas companies may be seen as foreign in the eyes of local customers and therefore disadvantaged compared with local producers and products. Localness becomes one dimension of product differentiation and since there are advantages accruing to being a local producer, rival multinationals are expected to follow each other in local markets. In Chapter 9 we examine two sectors, tobacco and confectionery, in which TNCs have pursued a twin strategy of taking over well-established local brand names, at the same time as introducing and establishing western brands. The importance of Pepsico retaining the brand name of Wedel, a renowned quality Polish chocolate firm, led to a protracted legal battle to maintain ownership of the brand name. This, as we shall see, leaves domestic capital at a grave disadvantage. Wedel now has both name and reputation, but also the backing of a multinational corporation's expertise in areas such as marketing, as well as budgets for such activities.

Work, Workers and FDI

In themselves, however, the relationship between the state and TNCs is insufficient to explain the process and outcomes of restructuring because they fail to build in an adequate analysis of the role and influence of labour. In many accounts, collectivism, particularly when it manifests itself in workers' participation is seen as a blemish on the workings of the free market. Other economists take a far more sympathetic view emphasizing the impact of FDI on the power, wages and working conditions of labour. Nevertheless, labour is treated as the object of externally determined policies, a passive group on the receiving end of the policies of states and firms. A crucial point of departure is to posit that labour is also the subject of change, where the resistance of groups (formally organized or otherwise) will in turn impact on the actions and policies of states and firms.

In Poland, as we saw in the previous chapter the legacy of the last twenty-five years, and in particular the long tradition of workers' councils, which have exercised varying degrees of influence over the period since World War II, impact upon individual firms and sectors. From 1989 onwards Solidarity has attempted to function not only as a trade union in the work place, but also as a principal agent of restructuring. A particular privatization cannot go ahead without the approval of the workers' council. Union recognition in most cases of FDI was usually negotiated prior to investment taking place as part of a social package which includes guarantees of employment levels for up to two years. Thus, in cases of competition between firms, winning the support of the workforce may be decisive.

There are examples of FDI where the unions have remained strong and satisfied, but in general FDI simply adapts to local conditions rather than bringing in superior terms of employment. It is difficult to generalize about the attitudes of workers to FDI as they are varied and often contradictory, in later chapters, for example, we report attitudes ranging from apprehension to outright hostility. These were motivated by two concerns: firstly, the direct impact of FDI on employment levels; and secondly, a strong nationalistic streak wishing to see strategically important industries remain under Polish control. The few cases of outright rejection of foreign investment have been underreported, as this behaviour is obviously not conductive to encouraging the interest and entry of other firms. In the case of Wawel, one of four major confectionery plants in Poland, the union backed a management/workers buyout in the face of attempts by Suchard to take a controlling interest. However, a realization that raising capital for modernization would be difficult but necessary in a market dominated by TNCs has led to a softening of attitudes, with an acknowledgement that there may be advantages in having a strategic investor. A similar change of attitude was in evidence in ZPT, the Krakow tobacco factory, where in the face of pressure from the government Solidarity resisted an attempt by Philip Morris (already producing Marlboro in the factory, under licence) to take a majority shareholding. From initial rejection, Solidarity's position has shifted to one of attempting to influence the speed and conditions under which privatization takes place. The effect of this resistance has led to a kind of rolling privatization involving FDI where Philip Morris will be allowed to own an increasing share of the stock, conditional upon the level of promised investment materializing.

Although some workplaces have successfully blocked FDI, more commonly some sort of negotiated and progressive takeover by foreign firms has been the order of the day. In other firms an initial welcome for FDI has turned sour as the reality of competition in practice becomes clear. A Solidarity news bulletin (*Tygodnik Solidarnosc* 47 1994) compares two firms in the confectionery sector that have taken different routes to privatization; the first, Wedel, where Pepsico bought a 40 per cent share in 1991, and the second, Wawel, which refused the overtures of foreign investors and took the route of worker/ management buyout. In the case of Wedel, workers clearly receive benefits from working for a firm with new facilities such as a canteen, and a social fund which provided mortgage loans, other benefits however, such as holiday homes, nurseries, kindergartens and flats, are now off the menu. The company clearly regarded the sphere of social responsibility as being outside of its scope. Workers complained about a feeling of insecurity, with poor communications exacerbated by the winding up of the broadcasting centre to which Solidarity had access, being replaced by a company newsheet. Increased hierarchy reinforced by wage differentials led to poor relations between employees and supervisors. So whilst restructuring clearly guaranteed the future of the firm, at least in the short term, workers felt more insecure about their jobs. There are other reports of conflicts, not only around wages, conditions and social packages, but often over the style of management given the long tradition of some kind representation, consultation and communication (*Rzeczpospolita* 219: 2 1994).

There is evidence that foreign investors, aware of the labour conditions attached to Polish investments are experimenting with ways to avoid or overcome restrictions. Interviewed early in 1994, Solidarity officials in Gdansk pointed to the example of a foreign takeover of a telecommunications plant in Wroclaw. The contract allowed for the conversion of the plant, and the inward investor wanted to raze the buildings to the ground. The problem of the incumbent labour force was overcome by offering severance pay far higher than that permitted by law, and most workers took the offer. Similarly, a ministry-sponsored mediator in industrial disputes, interviewed in 1994, pointed to the example of Alcatel, who wanted to reduce employment in the plant by 20 per cent but had signed an agreement guaranteeing employment for eighteen months. The company offered severance pay amounting to 21 months salary and 30 per cent of the company's employees applied to leave.

This ambiguous experience of FDI is raising suspicion, particularly at workplace level, regarding the wisdom of allowing foreign investors to take over Polish enterprises. Initial expectations that wages would rise and terms and conditions improve have generally been confounded. It should be pointed out that this is not a universal phenomenon. In one example, where foreign investment came to a cellulose company, not only were the union in favour of the venture, but the union organization in the workplace demanded that the city council grant the former minister of privatization honorary citizenship. As Solidarity national officers dryly pointed out, this contrasted with the attitude of the rest of the union to the former minister, in so far as everyone else wanted to hang him!

Conclusion

There is nothing unusual or surprising about the pattern of FDI in Poland, indeed to a greater or lesser extent it can be observed across other countries in Central and Eastern Europe. The picture is one of a small number of significant examples of FDI by TNCs surrounded by a large number of small FDIs, which often amount to no more than testing the water. The sectors that have dominated FDI are those in which companies are usually seeking access to markets that cannot be served or supplied from outside of Poland, either because of the nature of the service (e.g. telecommunications) or because of prohibitive import duties. In addition, although we have argued at length against simply equating investment with a search for low labour costs, there are examples of sectors that have experienced FDI driven by such a motive.

However, we want to stress that market access or low labour costs as locational determinants are simply subsets of the central force driving FDI, which is a search for market domination, the result of oligopolistic competition. It follows then that we reject simplistic formulations regarding the impact of FDI, be they either the pessimistic 'screwdriver' hypothesis, wherein FDI is taken simply to result in low wage, low value added operations, or more optimistic accounts suggesting automatic benefits such as the transfer of know how and technology. Although it is largely negative, states nevertheless retain a degree of bargaining power. However, we suggest that the limited ability of nation states to exert a positive influence leaves the pattern of FDI as largely determined by sectoral trajectories of development, with decisions ultimately taken in boardrooms rather than parliaments.

Transnationals will have an important impact on sectors within the Polish economy whether TNCs appear as significant carriers of FDI or not. If TNCs do appear, then to a greater or lesser extent (probably the latter), there will be examples of technology transfer, but what is certain is that the nature of the market within which they operate will be radically and irrevocably altered. Surviving Polish firms will then be inevitably locked into the global market either as competitors of the TNCs, or in junior or dependent positions as suppliers, if they survive at all. The failure of any FDI to transpire, combined with the collapse of the CMEA market, has accelerated the demise of some so-called high tech sectors. The positive effects of FDI are further limited by the 'cathedral in the desert' status of a large proportion of such investments. They may well bring development into a region, but development of the region is a more difficult question.

In the early days there was a polarization of attitude towards FDI, ranging from outright opposition to gung-ho optimism. There has, however, been a retreat from both of these positions, with, in general, a grudging acceptance of the necessity of FDI allied to a growing concern with its impact on jobs and working conditions. For workers, FDI would appear to guarantee the continued existence of their firm, at least in the short term, but the price of working 'closer to the world', that is being locked into global competition, has been increased intensity of working practices, coupled with redundancy, or at best increased insecurity.

On one level, far from being a panacea, FDI appears to be reinforcing Poland's position as a junior and unequal partner of the EU. The bulk of exports will continue to be in primary and semi-processed goods, with so-called high technology goods and consumer durables being imported. However, this picture of peripherality is too simplistic and does not capture the uneven impact of FDI. FDI will undoubtedly bring some modernization and updating locking some firms and sectors more firmly into the global economy. Those areas or cities with higher levels overall may experience a virtuous circle, with other FDIs simply standing as cathedrals in the desert. This tendency will be exacerbated by the inextricable link between FDI and privatization, which will be explored in the next chapter.

5 BEYOND THE NUTS AND BOLTS: PRIVATIZATION AND RESTRUCTURING

Although the trend towards privatization can be seen across advanced market economies and developing economies alike, it has been the very centrepiece of the transformation of postcommunist economies. We begin by describing the process and outcomes of privatization in Poland, emphasizing the theme of continuity, that is the way in which privatization has been conditioned by the tendencies set in motion in the pre-1989 period. In the second part of the chapter we go beyond the mechanics and develop three particular themes which, when combined, constitute a significant departure from conventional or standard approaches to the privatization debate.

Firstly, the rationale for privatization that flows from the neoclassical analysis is well rehearsed. In brief, it is argued that a system of private property is a fundamental precondition for a market economy (Hayek 1944). This case rests on a huge body of literature on the affinity of private property with the efficient operation of the market mechanism (Kornai 1990a, Lipton and Sachs 1990, Blanchard *et al.* 1991). From this point of view, any form of collective ownership distorts economic incentives and consequently managers, acting as owners, cannot adapt to an environment of hard budget constraints and market competition. The starting point of our analysis of privatization is that the assumption of perfect competition, deviations from which can be explained by market failure, can be turned on its head. Following Cowling and Sugden (1987) and drawing on arguments developed in Chapters 1 and 4, we take as our benchmark the existence of global oligopolistic market structures dominated by large transnational corporations. This allows us to develop an analysis wherein domination of certain sectors of the economy moves from the sphere of state ownership to that of large transnational corporations (TNCs): As Martin (1993: 162) puts it: 'Arguably the most significant change in power relations resulting from privatisation has not been from public to private, nor from the state to the market but from national and local political agencies to global centres of economic power.'

Secondly, the task of transforming Central and East European economies in the conventional literature is seen as a leap from one distinct economic system to another, that is from 'socialism' to 'capitalism'. It follows that the debate is framed by a set of polar opposites; the past was about state property and central planning and the future about private property and the free market. In the transformation of these economies, privatization is viewed as being of critical importance in undermining the power of the state (Lipton and Sachs 1990, Frydman and Rapaczynski 1994). The state, furthermore, is seen as being incapable of rectifying market failure, let alone initiating and implementing a nuanced industrial policy. Therefore, one of the main aims of privatization is to wrest power and control away from insiders, be they workers or the *nomenklatura*. Thus, within the mainstream debate, the only real question is whether it is better for the state to sell or give away its property via some kind of mass privatization.

This simple dichotomy of the state and the market lying at the core of neoclassical analysis, however, is something of a straw target. A cursory glance at real economies reveals a much more complex relationship between the state and the market (Polanyi 1944, Amsden *et al.* 1994). This is borne out by the vast array of privatization methods used by countries, be they advanced market or developing economies, showing that states are not ideologically wedded to a particular path to privatization. The routes taken by different countries and sectors will be contingent on both the historical legacy and institutional framework of those economies.

A third crucial element in the dynamic of change has been the role of organized labour. Conventional accounts by and large ignore the long tradition of workers' struggle in Poland from 1948 onwards. At worst, these accounts view workers as a stage army to be wheeled out to precipitate the downfall of communism, but now consign them to the role of utility maximizing and essentially atomized individuals. We explored the role and impact of labour in the process and outcomes of privatisation and restructuring in Chapter 3 suggesting that the union response has been complex and varied.

The challenge of transferring large sections of the public sector to private ownership has sent many economists scurrying to their drawing boards and spawned a huge literature and diverse set of solutions and prescriptions. We reject the approach to privatization that sees it as a mechanical task, peculiar only to economies undergoing transformation. Rather, we discuss privatization within a wider debate about restructuring, firmly located in trends in the world economy to which the Polish economy has been rudely and increasingly exposed since 1989. The logic of trends in the global economy towards the internationalization of production and increasing competition make restructuring an imperative. However, the particular path of privatization and restructuring will not be the result of some disengaged blueprint produced by economists or the product of some kind of crude economic determinism. Neither will it be the outcome solely of the unique circumstances to be found in Central and Eastern Europe or individual economies that comprise it. Emerging from these factors, we point to the development in Poland (in addition to other Central and East European economies) of 'hybrid' firms, where ownership and control is vested in a mixture of state, international and domestic capital, which is then manifested in a complex set of institutional arrangements. Furthermore, in order to understand the complexity of ownership and control in emerging firms, we must incorporate an analysis of the role of organized labour in conditioning outcomes.

The Legacy of the Past

Central and East European economies began the process of restructuring and privatization sharing similar basic characteristics. Firstly, they had all been bequeathed an industrial legacy dominated by large, monopoly firms with a high degree of vertical integration and often utilizing equipment that was largely obsolete and depreciated. This combination of inefficiencies, which intensified in the 1980s, was predicated on the existence of soft markets of the CMEA. In addition, market structures such as financial intermediaries and an appropriate legal framework were at worst non-existent, or at best embryonic.

Whilst to a greater or lesser degree, Poland shared these characteristics with other Central and East European economies, there are peculiar features which pertain to the particular outcome of restructuring in Poland. These are the result of the specific response to the economic crises at the end of the 1960s and 1970s and the legacy of the reforms which attempted to deal with them. In the 1970s, the strategy of import-led growth, designed to bring an end to stagnation and falling living standards, failed miserably, culminating in the economic crisis of 1979 to 1982. In a desperate attempt to extricate themselves from this latest crisis the state introduced 'market socialism' which brought limited marketization, one aspect of which was to devolve decision-making to individual firms. This increased autonomy, however, led to a large degree of uncertainty and the opportunity for *nomenklatura* privatization. Specifically the State Enterprise Law (1986) allowed state-owned enterprises to enter into association with private partners and contribute a part of the physical assets as a share. Physical assets were deliberately undervalued to create high profits for private partners who were most often the management of enterprises or local officials (Kierzkowski *et al.* 1993: 174). Its significance also lay in giving rise to feelings of anger and resentment amongst the majority of the population as they saw factory managers and party bosses using their position to transform themselves into fledgling capitalists.

In the end, the privatization legislation passed by the Sejm in July 1990 was a curious document, ambiguous both in terms of decision-making and its lack of a specific programme. Control was in the form of a two-tier decision-making system. The state was given the right to define annually the direction of privatization and to determine its revenues, whilst wide powers were granted to enterprises with respect to the decision as to whether privatization should take place or not. Decision-making within the firms was dispersed among the managing director, workers' councils and a general meeting of the workforce who had the right to veto privatization. The legislation recognized free mass stock distribution as a possible instrument in the privatization process, but did not specify how it was to be used. Almost as an afterthought, a paragraph was added that made it possible for the workers' councils, after the approval of the ministry to legally dissolve their firms, and rent, sell or lease the assets to a new corporation. Significantly this new corporation could be solely or partially owned by its employees, thus in essence this clause provided a loophole that allowed, at least in theory, employee ownership of firms.

The Long and Winding Road(s) to Privatization

The privatization programme in Poland was strongly influenced by the many international practitioners, academics and consultants who flooded in to take part in the great transformation. In practice, Poland adopted a blueprint which drew on what were taken to be successful models from the West, and in particular the experience of the United Kingdom. In January 1990, the Balcerowicz Programme announced an ambitious programme of privatization emphasizing speed and comprehensiveness, that would run alongside a stabilization package.

Commercialization

Following the UK method, in the initial stages of the privatization programme firms were to be commercialized, which meant the elimination of workers' councils and the transformation of firms into state-owned joint stock companies. Once commercialized, firms were to be sold on the open market creating a cycle of investor confidence and making it possible to sell off state assets rapidly. Paradoxically, commercialization reasserted the ownership claim of the state and was, in effect, renationalization by another name.

The reformers' faith in rapidly privatizing the state sector through public offerings expressed a naive belief in neoclassical orthodoxy in assuming that the market would determine an optimal distribution of ownership rights. This view seemed to almost wilfully overlook both the problems experienced by the UK, the country furthest down this path, as well as existing conditions in Poland. It is worth pursuing this comparison a little further. Firstly, the scale of the task facing the Polish government was simply not comparable with the UK. Whilst it has taken the UK government fifteen years to privatize approximately forty companies, the agenda set by the Polish government was to transfer 8500 companies into private ownership in the shortest possible time. Secondly, privatization in the UK context took place within the framework of well-developed legal, financial and regulatory institutions which had evolved over a very long period of time, whilst Poland lacked many of these institutions, such as an established legal infrastructure, a stock market and financial institutions. Thirdly, whilst the UK privatization depended essentially on the existence of institutional investors and mobilizing the savings of small investors, these sources were, initially at least, virtually non-existent in Poland, where recent statistics show not only that two out of three families have no savings, but in addition in 1994 50 per cent of Polish families were surviving at or below the poverty level.

Table 5.1 *Privatization Outcomes, 1990–1994*

	1990	1991	1992	1993	1994	Total
Number of companies sold in their entirety	6	22	22	48	28	126
Number of SOEs corporatized (joint-stock companies, owned by the treasury)	38	222	220	47	169	696
Privatization of small and medium-size enterprises (SMEs) under Article 37 of the Law on Privatization of SOEs	31	418	270	195	110	1024*
Liquidation (sale of assets belonging to a bankrupt state enterprise, according to Article 19 of the State Enterprise Act)	18	522	317	260	109	1226

* Number of privatizations of Small and Medium-Size Enterprises (SMEs) under Article 37: sales, 173; joint-ventures, 41; leasing (to employees or management of the enterprises), 743; a mix of the above, 67; total, 1024.

Source: Privatization Update February 1995.

The volatile economic situation and difficulties in establishing the worth of firms' coupled with the problems discussed above, meant that in the initial stages privatization was spectacularly unsuccessful. Table 5.1 shows that despite considerable effort and expense, only six firms were privatized through public offerings in 1990 and twenty-two in 1991. By the beginning of 1995, this figure has risen to 126 completed privatisations out of 696 companies which had been transformed into joint stock companies through commercialization, the result therefore was far removed from the anticipated scale and speed of privatization.

Liquidation

The second major procedure provided for by the legislation was liquidation, aimed at privatizing medium or smaller companies. Liquidated firms were either sold, included in the holdings of another company for sale or leased out. One of the most popular and widespread methods has been through leasing, which requires the creation of a new commercial company with the participation of a substantial portion of employees of the old enterprise. The new company leases assets from the state enterprise, which is then liquidated. The rent on the lease is calculated so that payments are an instalment on purchases of assets over a period of five to ten years, which then becomes the property of the lessees at the end of the term. Table 5.1 reveals that this has been by far the most prevalent form of privatization.

Mass Privatization Programme

Whilst public offerings attempted to avoid problems of redefining property rights by relying on the market, free stock distribution sought to redefine and establish property rights as quickly as possible. The debate over so-called mass privatization, however, was protracted and not finally resolved until April 1993. The title of mass privatization is something of a misnomer, in that it refers to the distributional element rather than the number of companies involved. Fifteen National Investment Funds (NIFs) have been established to act as holding companies for the 300 or so firms to be distributed between them. It is intended that the NIFs will play a leading role in restructuring the enterprises to which they are designated. Each enterprise has been designated a lead NIF which has 33 per cent of the shares of the enterprise privatized, with 27 per cent of the shares equally distributed as minority holdings to other NIFs. The remainder will continue to be held by the state (25 per cent) or distributed free of charge to enterprise employees (15 per cent). The contracts for the management of these NIFs have been given to consortia comprising a mixture of international and Polish firms. Each adult would be given the option of buying a certificate (*swiatdectwo*), for around 10 per cent of the average monthly wage (zl. 5.5 million or $246 in June 1994) which would give the shareholder one share in each NIF.

The argument for giving foreign firms such a high profile in the Mass Privatization Programme is that it is assumed that they bring expertise in Western management that may not exist in Poland, and furthermore they will bring with them credibility and contacts which will create a virtuous circle by encouraging further foreign investment. The legislation was highly contentious and several amendments had to be made before it was eventually passed. Firstly, the number of participating firms has been reduced from the original 600 to around 300, because of difficulties in finding firms which satisfied the dual criteria of wanting to be in the programme and fulfilling the necessary financial conditions. Secondly, concessions were made resulting in a proportion of share certificates being distributed free of charge to pensioners and state employers. In effect, these people have borne the brunt of the transformation, facing falling real wages as nominal wages were deliberately held back from keeping pace with inflation. Finally, in response to widespread criticism about the high level of involvement of foreign firms, supervisory boards were set up to monitor NIFs in a regulatory capacity. The composition of these supervisory boards, which were in themselves contentious, was intended to offset concerns that foreign influenced NIFs will have a free rein over the destinies of a sizeable tranche of the best Polish firms. By mid-1995 contracts had been awarded for the NIFs, with the 300 participating companies shared out by some sort of quasi lottery arrangement.

The Sectoral Approach

This approach is unique to Poland and has been described as an instrument of 'soft' but applied industrial policy. Whilst it is not a privatization path in itself (like public offerings, leveraged buyouts or the transfer of funds), it can lead to any of these paths and is intended to co-ordinate action in a sector as a whole.

The underlying intention was to offset concerns raised by the Anti-Monopoly Commission regarding the emergence of private monopolies as a result of early entry by foreign firms. It was argued that considerations of the development of monopolies demanded a more systematic approach which looked beyond the individual transactions of the firm and addressed the needs of the sector as a whole. Thus sectoral privatization was driven, at least in part, by a desire to stop the process of cherry picking, with Western firms shopping around for the most advanced and profitable units in each sector. This strategy emanated not from hostility to foreign investment, but in an attempt to focus and channel activities after the chaos of the early days. This pro-gramme, however, covered only twenty sectors of the economy, leaving the remaining eighty excluded from this approach.

Despite the production of lengthy and detailed, not to mention costly, surveys by management consultants, the results have been dis-appointing with large disparities in terms of the sale of firms both between and within sectors. In the final analysis, the government sold whatever they could to whoever was prepared to buy. Generally this meant that the most promising and profitable firms were sold, leaving the state with the residue of those in the poorest condition, in effect, an unprivatizable lump. A partial explanation can be found in the way in which the selection of companies has been determined by the activitives and strategies of TNCs. Thus there has been a high (and often highly competitive) interest in sectors such as confectionery and food process-ing, tobacco and telecommunications. In contrast, other sectors have received little or no interest. This raises questions as to the potency of formulating and implementing even a soft industrial policy in the light of the existence of powerful actors pursuing their own agendas and strategies.

Mass Commercialization

This initiative was introduced in the autumn of 1994 as part of the government's 'Strategy for Poland'. The aim was to clarify the owner-ship issue and to strengthen the hand of management in state firms. This ambitious policy initiative is a plan to commercialize around 1000 large state firms from early 1995. These firms will remain state property until fully privatized through sale or disposal of the majority of the assets. A central aspect of this development is the creation of a single authority, the state treasury, as the nominal shareholder for commer-cialized companies. The treasury will bring together firms currently managed by a variety of central state ministries, it will then agree contracts with managers who will, within the terms of the contract, have a largely free hand in managing the firms. The central thrust of this initiative is to tip the balance of authority in state firms away from workers' councils and in favour of management (EIU 1995). The new legislation will permit commercialization to take place irrespective of the views of the workers' council.

Small Privatization

Two important forms of privatization, especially in the early stages of the process, have been municipal privatization and the transformation of co-operatives. Both involved small scale business and were therefore called small privatizations. Most municipal privatizations concern the retail trade, and by the end of 1991, 33 786 premises owned by local councils moved from public to private sector users, but only 1074 (3.2 per cent) of them were actually sold. It has led to a form of privatization from below, based on leasing arrangements. This type of privatization, although generally regarded as the most successful, is not unproblematic, as we shall see later in the chapter.

An outline of the various paths and routes to privatization is crucial in that it provides an important reference point as well as the necessary framework in which to understand the discussion that follows. The complete fixation in the conventional literature with the nuts and bolts of privatisation, coupled with conventional assumptions has, however, obscured a number of crucial arguments.

Privatization: Competition or Concentration?

The discussion of the many and varied paths to privatization and their relative merits is usually couched in terms of potential or actual efficiency gains with varying degrees of importance attached to considerations of equity. The obsession with privatization however, has revolved around not only the notion of providing an incentive structure through private property, but also the gains in efficiency derived from the competition it is purported to bring about. The assumption that privatization and competition are synonymous dominates most accounts and is virtually unchallenged in the mainstream literature. It follows from this argument that competition will act as a spur to demonopolization and, in addition, bring about improved economic performance at a general level. This ignores the wider context and dynamic of privatization. The crux of the argument is that the internationalization of capital driven by large transnational corporations has forced the pace of privatization and changed the shape of the public sector in all economies, whether they be developed market economies or developing countries.

We must be careful, however, not to confuse the direction and impetus for change. It is not simply that privatization has opened up opportunities for large firms on a global scale as Parker (1993) suggests, rather it is demands from global business for a reorientation of utilities to meet their needs that has been one of the biggest pressures on governments to divest or deregulate this sector. For example, once US deregulation of telecommunications took place in the early 1980s the liberalization dynamic was unleashed and there was pressure on other public telephone operators to open up and follow suit. The increasing trend towards internationalization of production and ensuing global restructuring of markets has not only directly affected utilities, but also other industries that have enjoyed state protection. State ownership or protection represent the most serious obstacles to integrated global capitalism and are viewed as obstructing and frustrating powerful interests. Tobacco is a case in point. In 1980 the US trade department, championing the cause of its giant tobacco companies such as BAT and Philip Morris prized open the previously protected markets of Japan, South Korea and Taiwan with the threat of unilateral commercial sanctions.

We have already observed that a reliance on mobilizing private savings for privatization in Poland is simply not an option, where savings are almost non-existent and 50 per cent of people exist below the poverty line. Neither are there the institutional investors in Poland comparable to those to be found in the West, such as pension and insurance companies. A naive faith in the market coupled with the conditionality of institutions such as the IMF and European Bank for Reconstruction and Development (EBRD), whose lending is heavily biased towards private sector projects, rules out state restructuring in any sort of meaningful way. In short, this points to crucial reliance on foreign investment for privatization and restructuring. In practice it can be seen that foreign investors were involved (in varying degrees) in over 50 per cent of completed capital privatizations. These companies include some of the leading global TNCs such as International Paper and Pilkingtons.

Privatization, rather than having the properties of bringing about competition and demonopolization, opens up these economies to investment by large companies whose activities are inextricably linked to privatization. The effect of this in Central and Eastern Europe is to perpetuate and in some cases strengthen market domination, albeit in a different form. This was discussed at length in the previous chapter. The ability of TNCs to improve the competitive position of privatized companies by updating products and processes should not be underestimated. But perhaps even more crucial is access to the expertise and resources for product differentiation – the key to competition in oligopolistic markets. Privatization, far from bringing about competition has opened up some (not all) markets to a different kind of concentration. There has been a shift in certain sectors from domination by state-owned monopolies to domination by large transnational corporations Further, some firms such as Fiat and General Motors have consolidated their position by successfully seeking state protection from imports, thereby allowing domination of the domestic market.

The Visible Push Behind the Invisible Hand

The drive towards the internationalization of production has not been without its institutional props. A whole range of other organizations have championed the cause of deregulation and liberalization (see Amsden *et al.* 1994 for a full discussion of the Bretton Woods organizations, conditionality and restructuring). Organizations such as the World Bank and IMF, have not had to rely on exhortation alone, the conditionality of stand-by loans and loans for infrastructural development have been inextricably linked to progress on the privatization front. The arguments have not simply remained at the level of propaganda. The United States Agency for International Development (USAID), which has had the task of promoting global privatization, has made large resources available in Central and Eastern Europe to allow direct US investment in privatized assets. For example, the Polish American Fund was set up with a capitalization of $240 million. Its purpose, according to a state department document was 'to take equity or debt positions in new private, joint ventures or recently privatized enterprises.' (Martin 1993: 65).

The link between aid, privatization and foreign investment is not always subtle or covert. Under the 'Stabilization, Restructuring and Privatization Programme' (SRP), the EBRD sanctioned $80 million funding for restructuring forty companies to improve their situation in preparation for privatization, in particular aiming at companies that lack resources for modernization. The goal of the SRP is explicitly to make companies more attractive to foreign investors (*Central European Business Weekly* 20–8 December 1994: 5).

These organizations have not only precluded some paths and narrowly limited choices, but in some cases significantly affected the form of the privatization process. For example, whilst public debates about mass privatization were to the fore in Poland, behind the scenes the World Bank was responsible for back door privatization that circumvented both the Sejm (parliament) and individual firms. This took the form of a joint programme developed by the Polish Government and the World Bank – the 'Enterprise and Bank Restructuring Privatization Programme'. In a sleight of hand, it included this innovation noted by Amsden *et al.* (1994: 114):

> To facilitate privatization as an outcome of enterprise restructuring the EBRD gives credits to state owned banks and others, holding at least 30 percent of a public enterprise's debt the right to convert their claims into shares. In the case of SOEs, this conversion will automatically trigger a transformation into a joint stock company (and the demise of the employees' councils). This provision constitutes nothing less than a breakthrough in the Polish Government's privatization policy since, for the first time, it makes privatization of an enterprise possible without the legal consent of its workers.

This was applauded as something of a coup by officials and advisers who had few qualms about the undemocratic nature of the legislation. Apparently, a short cut to the market justifies all. This meant that, in effect, state-owned banks were now major restructuring agents, because they held the largest share of the debt of financially insolvent enterprises. Thus nine state-owned banks, in existence only since the start of transformation and with little hands-on knowledge, had the task of restructuring roughly 2000 companies (Amsden *et al.*, 1994). The desire to circumvent formally democratic procedures to accelerate restructuring and in particular to privatize individual firms without the consent of the workers is an indication of the way in which organized labour is regarded as a problem by the state. We explore in the next section how the privatization strategy of the state has been a mixture of direct confrontation and compromise with the unions in general and Solidarity in particular.

Control, Compliance and Consent

We saw in the last chapter how the privatization bill adopted by parliament represented a compromise with the employee communities (Skalmati 1992: 53). Subsequently, one of the central tasks of privatization has been to strip or at least minimize the power of the workers' councils reactivated after 1989. These were viewed as having too much say in the fate of individual firms and slowing down the pace of restructuring. The economic justification was that worker control and the hard budget constraint were incompatible, in that workers would resist decreases in employment and wage cuts necessary to improve efficiency. The influence of labour on corporate decision-making is seen by many as fundamentally in conflict with the goals of post-communist restructuring (Lipton and Sachs 1990, Frydman and Rapaczynski 1994). However, as we saw in Chapter 3, Solidarity initially at least had no disagreements with the abolition of the formal structures of workers' self-management.

Privatization attempted to limit the power of organized labour. A tax-based incomes policy (the Popiwek) restricted the growth of the wages fund in all enterprises in 1990 but, after 1991, only applied to state-owned enterprises Popiwek worked by establishing a wage norm for a given firm or sector and then taxing all wage increases above that up to 100 per cent. The result was, firstly, a large-scale redistribution away from farmers and workers in favour of entrepreneurs (Gomulka 1993). It was clear that state employees were going to be expected to carry the costs of transformation (Rosati 1993: 257). The second result was an attempt to lessen union resistance to privatization. The retention of the excess wage tax (Popiwek) on state firms excluded both private firms and those in the process of being privatized. This was meant to encourage privatization and to weaken labour resistance by creating the impression that privatization would mean higher wages.

Crucially, it was also intended to strengthen managerial power and to weaken or eliminate workers' councils, as privatization dissolves such councils in previously state-owned firms (Kloc 1992: 142). Commercialization meant the elimination of these councils and their replacement by boards of directors to manage the enterprise who were answerable to the state. In return for giving up control of the enterprise, employees could purchase 20 per cent of the stock at preferential prices. According to the government, as reported by Alexander and Skapska (1994:

187): 'The preferences guaranteed by the act to employees are extensive. Apart from the considerable price reduction of stock, the right to appoint a third of the supervisory board ensures that employees retain control over the company's development and its fate'. However, a third of the supervisory board hardly guarantees employee influence. Furthermore, we need to examine critically the assumption that the 20 per cent of the stock reserved for workers, even at preferential prices, gives a stake in the company. In practice, employees are only be able to buy 7 to 9 per cent of their company's stock at half price due to the provision in the Act limiting an employee's purchase of preferential stocks to the equivalent of his or her annual earnings. It is also significant that in no firm do non-managerial employees collectively own more than 25 per cent of the total voting shares. This is important because such a bloc would give them the power of veto over certain key decisions. In addition, over a very short period of time even this modest employees' ownership has been diluted. For example, the initial 20 per cent ownership of share capital by the workforce of Philips Lighting, Poland, has been reduced to only 0.18 per cent (Tittenbrun 1995).

It is important to remember that, though the legislation appears to undermine trade-union organization and assumes labour to be antithetical to the process of change, in fact Solidarity viewed themselves as principal agents of change. In the early days of transformation there was no opposition to legislation in so far as the union's policy was to create 'proper' capitalist management structures. Share ownership was viewed as important by Solidarity leaders, in that it gave workers a stake in their firms, but Solidarity itself saw workers' self-management as inappropriate to the new times. However, as we have seen, as the effects of shock therapy proved to be more traumatic than expected, Solidarity, particularly at the workplace level, began to question the nature of privatization and its relation to foreign direct investment (FDI).

The conclusions drawn about the structure of ownership and power in newly privatized companies (capital method) applies, with some modifications to the so-called employee-owned companies (liquidation method). The increasingly publicized examples of employee/management buyouts gives an impression of workers having a significant stake and degree of control in firms privatized by this method. This is, however, misleading and masks the reality of emerging property relations. On the surface, firms appear to be predominantly employee-owned. However, this method converts workers to formal owners on a small scale, whilst the real ownership and control is vested in management. The experience is that management and professional staff hold much higher numbers of shares than blue-collar workers (Tittenbrun 1995). In a case study of such a firm we report in Chapter 9, the new management was a partnership between the previous management and leading, professional members of Solidarity within the factory – the result of a gentleman's agreement struck during the negotiations for privatization. Share ownership was, in fact, only taken up by half of the workforce. The combination of low wages and high share prices precluded large numbers of workers from buying shares and participating in ownership. This throws up a conflicting set of interests, in that for shareholders their interest lies in profitability and the promise of future dividends, whilst non-shareholders want rent in the form of wages.

Behind the façade of so-called employee buyouts lies the opportunity for *nomenklatura* privatization, which can be effected in a number of ways. Tittenbrun (1995) quotes the example of Lodz Chemia whereby management and key employees were lent the 1990 profits of the company through the medium of a non-profit-making organization at a low rate of interest. Another tactic is to simply run down the company in order that it might be bought cheaply. Privatization has thus served to intensify the division between ordinary workers, who have only nominal ownership, and salaried management who have both real ownership of capital and control of the firm. Thus traditional management prerogative is bolstered by the power given through concentration of share ownership. Workers have been stripped of illusions about privatization and myths of share ownership are fast fading in the light of redundancies and the absence of positive changes in traditional workplace relations. This is reflected in a marked change of attitude towards privatization. In 1990 nearly half of the Polish population believed that privatization was good for the economy. Surveys showed, however, that by early 1993 only 5 per cent wholeheartedly supported privatization, with 50 per cent resolutely opposed to it.

Thus it is the case that worker organization and action in a wider sense have been of central importance. The question of labour and labour organization has played a fundamental role in colouring the process and pattern of privatization. It is clear that the Polish government understood the potential threat that unions posed to its policies by adopting a carrot and stick policy to deal with them. The carrot took the form of an incomes policy that discriminated against those working in state enterprises and in favour of those being privatized or in the process of being so. The stick was the abolition of workers' councils built into the privatization legislation, though this was ameliorated by the statutory provision of shares for employees, and worker representation on the supervisory boards of privatized companies. In the early days neither carrot nor stick were vital in promoting transformation, though as time progressed both would assume increased significance.

We can start to bring together various strands of the argument. We have suggested, on the one hand, that privatization is not simply a task that is unique to the transformation of post-planned economies, but driven by global restructuring. This is not to suggest some kind of crude economic determinism, whereby uniform approaches or arrangements will emerge either in Central and Eastern Europe or elsewhere. The particular balance of forces between state, capital and organized labour, contingent on the historical legacy, will significantly influence both the patterns and particular outcomes of privatization. We can therefore begin to explain why the institutional arrangements that have emerged differ enormously from the anticipated outcomes of restructuring and privatization. In terms of either ownership or control it is simply not the case that it involves the simple transfer of assets from the public to the private sector. We explore in the next section how this masks a much more complex array of relationships between foreign and domestic capital, the state and organized labour.

Hybridicity: Between the State and the Market

From the very beginning of the transformation process there has been something of a gap between the rhetoric and the reality of the march to the market in Poland. Despite the apparent abandonment of the economy to unfettered market forces, the sectoral approach to privatization, for example, revealed a high degree of government intervention. The rationale underlying this approach was anything but *laissez faire* and market driven, and was, in fact, motivated by a belief that the market left to its own devices would not necessarily produce the best solution.

The capital privatization route, which would appear to be the most clear cut in terms of transferring ownership from the public to the private sector, also suggests a blurring of the boundary between state and market. A breakdown of the ownership structure of capital privatization reveals a complex picture which falls far short of a straightforward shift from state property to the market. By the early 1990s, 696 companies had been transformed into state treasury companies through the process of commercialization. It is very important, however, to draw a distinction between those that have undergone commercialization (or are in the process of privatization) and those cases where privatization has actually been completed. Out of the initial 696 companies, as of December 1994 only 128 privatizations by this method had been finalized. There are many reasons why privatizations had proceeded slowly, not least because of numerous bureaucratic delays. But there were also companies in this state of limbo simply because no buyer could be found, and given the backwardness and uncompetitive nature of some companies, there would not be likely to be buyers in the future. Thus the state remains a significant holder of assets by default in the large number of companies that have not been privatized and those that are in the process of privatization but remain unsold.

We have pointed to the importance of FDI in restructuring and shaping economies undergoing transformation. This is clearly in evidence in the case of the Polish economy, wherein foreign investors participated in over 40 per cent of the successful privazations. Differences emerge however, in the proportion of shares held and the degree of ownership. In most cases the investors had a maximum of 80 per cent of shares with the statutory 20 per cent reserved for the workforce, and these companies include Unilever and International Paper. Other transnationals participated with a smaller proportion of shares. PepsiCo's involvement with the Wedel plant is on the basis of taking 40 per cent of the shares, the rest being equally divided between public offering, employees and the state treasury. Other large companies such as Asea Brown Boveri and AEG have gone for a minimum controlling share of 51 per cent. The point to stress here is that the state is not simply left with assets by default, but also continues to maintain a share in what are regarded as successful privatizations.

The state, both national and local, continues to play a significant role in other routes to privatization. The local state acts indirectly, for example with the link it maintains with liquidated and small firms through leasing arrangements. The state continues as the owner of assets in the case of liquidated firms until payments are completed over a five to ten year period. Small firms in particular are regarded as the one unqualified success of the privatization programme and indeed small privatization where it has occurred, has been most effective in the retail trade and the service sector. As we have seen a closer examination of this phenomenon highlights the complexity of the term 'privatization'. Earle *et al.* (1993) point out that, in most cases, the privatization of the retail sector does not entail a transfer of ownership rights to the premises, instead the state retains the title and the premises have been merely leased for relatively short periods of time, often with no secure right to renew leases.

The Mass Privatization Programme reveals an even more intriguing web of relationships between the state, market and foreign investors. Critics from the right have suggested that the lead NIF with only 33 per cent of the shares may not provide the same incentive for restructuring as would a controlling or full ownership interest in the enterprise. At present we can only speculate as to whether these NIFs are transitory caretakers of initial restructuring, the womb of entrepreneurship and a stepping stone to the market, or whether they have the potential to become huge state influenced conglomerates.

The question of the state is to the fore in the debate about mass commercialization policy. It is seen by some as the reinstatement of 'enlightened' central management and a restoration of the state's preponderant position in the economy, with firms once again falling under the control of unaccountable and anonymous bureaucrats. This legislation was a product of the post-1993 government, an alliance between the Democratic Left and the Peasant Party. The right-wing journal *The Economist* argued that this was a ploy to keep firms in the hands of the state indefinitely and, further, that because draft legislation gave the government control over appointments to senior posts in commercialized companies, this meant that political contacts rather than management skills would be the dominant criterion. The journal went further, suggesting that the main purpose of the new privatization law of 1994 was to allow those ex-communists who did not get rich in 1989 to do better in the next round of sales (*The Economist* 15 July 1995). This is somewhat ironic coming from a journal that has supported UK privatizations wherein Tory ministers have parachuted out of government and on to the board of companies that they have played a heavy hand in privatizing. Outside of the rabid fantasies of *The Economist,* there is no question of a return to 'socialism', either in rhetoric or substance. The architects of this 'new' proposal see it as undercutting the management–unions–workers' council power triad, which is viewed as a chronic source of the state-run firm's instability. No progressive role for workers' participation is envisaged here. It is an argument about the most efficient way of creating and maintaining capitalism. The current government's view is that the state has a positive role to play in restructuring by creating performance-orientated structures (see *Gazeta Wyborcza* 27 September 1994).

This ambiguity between state and market in the restructuring of the Polish economy should come as no surprise. This mixture is not only evident in other Western market economies, but is present in other countries undergoing transformation. These observations have been made in relation to Hungary (Stark 1993) and Russia (Bim *et al.* 1993), with similar combinations being referred to as recombinant, hybrid or complex forms. Stark writes about the illusory move to the market in Hungary, whereby large organizations have been broken up into between fifteen and twenty satellites around a corporate headquarters. Although registered separately, and each with their own balance sheets and board of directors, in practice they have little autonomy, as the controlling share of the corporate satellite is held by the public corporation itself.

This raises an extremely important issue. Much privatization has taken place not on the basis of the whole enterprise but by the sale of individual property components, where some part of the state enterprise's activity or assets are made available to a private company through sale or leasing. These types of arrangements may, however, be misleading with regard to both the scale and nature of reforms. For example, in our study of HTS, the steelworks (See Chapter 8), employment has decreased from 23 000 to 17 000 over a period of four years. This could be viewed on the basis of the statistics as simultaneously a success in restructuring the state industrial sector and private sector growth. In fact, neither of these things are true. The change in employment came about as a result of a series of activities previously carried out by the steelworks being spun off – for example, catering, a cement works and the design unit. The boundary lines are simply redrawn. Ownership becomes blurred as the steelworks continues to hold a formal degree of ownership in these companies (varying from 3 per cent to 49 per cent), as well as continuing as the owner of the assets which are then leased to the company. In addition, it masks the high degree of dependency between the core company and the spin offs, as their activity is highly, if not wholly, reliant on the continued existence of the steelworks.

So far we have emphasized the relationship between the state, foreign capital and organized labour in the process of transformation. The consolidation of domestic capital has received little attention. The chaos and ambiguity of the previous decade saw the development of powerful blocs of capital that were well placed to take advantage of privatization. A number of holding companies, previously foreign trade companies, have emerged as powerful players in the restructuring process. Participation in the privatization of state enterprises by these Polish capital groups is not only on a much greater scale, but also more complex and far reaching than was originally anticipated, with patterns of cross shareholding and interlocking ownership. These foreign trade monopolies were able to make use of their pension of the past, in that they had greater access to information and knowledge of international markets in addition to having cultivated foreign contacts. Thus foreign trade demonopolization from 1986 onwards coupled with a greater degree of autonomy, placed these companies in an important position as providers of export credits for other Polish companies. The largest foreign trade enterprises thus cames to play the role of quasi banks, engaged in providing credit for exports. Between 1990 and 1993 they played an increasingly important role in financing firms as companies were squeezed by recession and the withdrawal of subsidies.

Two companies have emerged as the leaders, including Elektrim, which controls over 80 domestic companies (see Figure 5.1) as well as 118 foreign firms across five sectors of industry. Some commentators have rather optimistically made comparisons with the financial industrial conglomerates that have been significant in promoting economic growth in the Newly Industrialized Countries (NICs) of South East Asia. It is doubtful, however, whether the institutional position they occupy or the scale of resources they command makes these sections of Polish capital comparable with, for example, the industrial conglomerates (chaebols) of South Korea, Yet they are sufficiently powerful to be incongruent with the rhetoric that capitalism will emerge from below on the basis of the emergence small and medium firms.

The evolutionary and institutionalist schools are able to get behind the rhetoric and make observations that challenge the state–market dichotomy. They produce an analysis that encompasses a number of configurations of state and market, thereby recognizing that the market is not synonymous with capitalism, simply one of a multitude of ways in which it can organize itself. Their second contribution is to emphasize continuity, suggesting that the specificities of emerging property relations and institutional arrangements are contingent on past institutional arrangements and that the present is simply reconstituted or recombined elements of the previous period. This allows us, for example, to understand the process by which new layers of owners are emerging for some elements of old party bosses and managers, combined with, in some cases, leading members of Solidarity, taking advantage of opportunies offered by the liquidation method. However, both the evolutionary and institutionalist approaches are inadequate for the task of analysing the dynamics of transformation. We are not simply pointing to the observable emergence of a mixed economy in post-planned economies, that has shifted along the state–market spectrum by some sort of evolutionary process. More precisely, the form and

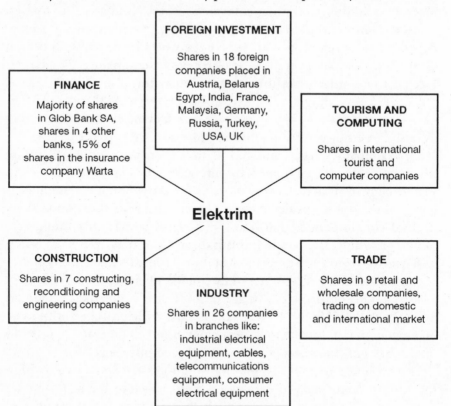

Figure 5.1 *The Structure of Elektrim*

content of restructuring and privatization are manifestations of tensions and compromises between national and international blocs of capital, reflected in different interests both within and outside the state, and of the inherent conflict between capital and labour, as Poland attempts to restructure and fit into the world. We can examine how these tensions and tendencies manifest themselves in particular workplaces if we now turn to the restructuring of the Krakow region and its economy.

SECTION III KRAKOW IN TRANSITION

6 TRANSFORMING KRAKOW

In 1992, the fastest way to reach Krakow was to fly firstly to Warsaw. The taxi from the airport then took us along roads lined with advertisements for Western companies and their products and left us standing outside the station, in the shadow of the Palace of Culture – a gloriously nightmare mixture of 1930s deco and Stalinist realist architecture, by then housing a casino and the new Warsaw Stock Exchange.

The train from Warsaw headed south and about two and a half hours later reached Krakow. As we approached the city, the train passed the enormous chimneys that stood above the old aluminium plant and the power station. As the train wound its way slowly through the largely anonymous outskirts of the town, the environmental legacy of the past became clearer. The allotments were lifeless and the buildings covered in a uniformly grey coating of muck. The station itself stood on the edge of the old town centre and was being rebuilt to house a major east – west transEuropean railway line. We emerged from the station into a run-down area that housed a bus station, the taxi rank and a couple of unprepossessing refreshment stands. Round the back of the station stood the Academy of Economics, dominated by an unfinished concrete tower block, resembling a huge surreal multi-storey car park. This, we were told, remains as a monument to the lunacy of Stalinist planning.

Outside the station, a pedestrian subway dipped under the ring road and we entered a different world. On the far side of the road, passing the Barbican, we went through the mediaeval city walls and into the old town. At first sight it appeared that nothing much had changed here in decades, indeed, just down ul. Florienska was the old art deco bar whose walls were covered with sketches drawn by the artists who drank there before World War II. However, MacDonalds had opened fifty metres up the road, and the smart new shops on either side of the road now stocked clothes in a price range well beyond the means of most of the local inhabitants.

The town square had been tidied up, and most of the buildings have renovated and repainted façades, as has the Sukienice (cloth hall). Under the pillars of the cloth hall clustered the tourist shops selling wood and linen handicrafts and amber, enticing customers sitting at the tables of the restaurants and bars that had sprung up around the square. Four hundred metres outside of the city walls, but still in the sight of Wawel castle and cathedral there was a growing flea market hugging the sides of a covered market area. South from the flea market was the Kazimieriz district, the old ghetto. During World War II, the Jewish population was moved into the new ghetto south of the river, or into the concentration camp at Plaszow. The 'Schindler's List' tour starts just round the corner from the Jewish restaurant in Kazimieriz. Auschwitz-Birkenau is seventy miles west of Krakow.

Krakow grew up during the early middle ages on the north bank of the Wistula, a river that was navigable only by the smallest craft. It is centred on the Wawel fortress and became the seat of Polish kings and the capital city of Poland. For most of its history Krakow was a commercial rather than industrial city. In the nineteenth century it passed into the control of Austria and economic development stagnated. At the turn of the twentieth century, it was a small town of around 85 000 inhabitants that was an important historical monument, but contributed little to Poland's industrial development. Even in 1945, Krakow remained one of the least industrialized and most bourgeois of Polish cities (Pounds *et al.* 1981: 16) However, this was all about to change.

Rapid industrialization lay at the heart of the communist strategy, the policy being not only to increase the production levels of existing industrial plants, but also to stimulate the development of non-industrial regions by the construction of new plants. In Krakow this meant, most importantly, the construction of Huta Sendzimira, HTS, then the Lenin steel works. The motivation for this was not only economic, Krakow had been the cultural and educational centre of Poland since the fourteenth century and represented a possible challenge to communist power. It has been suggested that the siting of the Sendzimira works was a deliberate piece of social engineering, designed to inject an industrial working class into an area seen to be overly liberal and bourgeois. The siting of the integrated Lenin steel works at Nowa Huta on the eastern outskirts of the city eventually added a working-class suburb of around 100 000 people to the city's now extended boundaries. Other large production facilities constructed in the Krakow region during this period included aluminium works, telecommunications assembly works, concrete and ferro-concrete works. Expansion of existing facilities occurred in tobacco, cable industries and meat processing plants (Bednarczyk *et al.* 1992: 2).

The outcome was a growth in industrial employment running at nearly twice the national average in the 1950s. By 1990, industrial employment accounted for 37 per cent of the region's workforce, compared with a figure of 29 per cent for Poland as a whole. Extensive growth meant typically that increased output resulted from increasing the scale of production units, predicated on increasing quantities of labour transferred from the land. In the case of Krakow this involved 200 000 people migrating from the land between 1948 and 1965. The role of technological growth in the region's development was negligible, which, coupled with a fall in investment in the 1980s, left industries with depreciating plant and equipment.

Krakow, with 750 000 inhabitants, is the third largest Polish city and is also the capital of the Krakow voivode (administrative unit), a region with nearly 1.2 million residents. The area provides a typical example of the way in which Soviet-type economies were developed in the period following 1948.

This chapter starts by putting Krakow into the context of the development of regions in Soviet-style economies. We examine the experience of foreign direct investment (FDI), privatization and small and medium-sized firms (SMEs) in the region before outlining the development of a new institutional framework in the form of local government structures. We conclude by outlining intervention in the local economy both by the new local government structures, and crucially by Solidarity.

Regions and Regional Development

Although it is difficult to find a coherent definition of a region in the West that is logical in any economic sense, it has been argued that there are important general characteristics that differentiate regions in Western economies from regions in Central and Eastern Europe. Zon (1992: 15) argues that communist rule largely dismantled local society and economies, with the Polish version of Fordism leading to an almost total liquidation of the local economy. Regions in the administrative sense are weak and underdeveloped in Central and Eastern Europe and administrative units at a regional level often did not coincide with cultural or historical regions.

At a local level, welfare was linked to employment in large state owned enterprises (SOEs), which were responsible for social assistance, day care centres, community centres and higher education. In effect, responsibility for the productive and reproductive aspects of the state function were assumed by large employers at the regional level. For example, HTS support for health services centred on the Nowa Huta health centre, serving around 75 000 people. The centre employed 150 doctors and an equal number of ancillary staff, with wages being met by the voivode, whilst HTS covered premises, equipment and mainte-nance costs. In the field of education, HTS provided part of the premises for the centre for vocational training and itself provided training for more than 400 students from the centre and the metallurgi-cal training school. The HTS centre of culture provided the focus of cultural life in the Nowa Huta part of the city, as did the 'Hutnik' sports club for sporting and recreational pursuits. HTS is increasingly hand-ing responsibility for these centres to the municipal authorities. Between 1991 and 1993, HTS spent Zl. 70 000 million (over £2m) on social support and more than Zl. 110 000 million (nearly £4m) from the housing fund. Employees and their children were given subsidized holidays, and support was provided for employees in need as well as loans for housing coming from the housing fund. HTS did not con-struct houses itself, but rather the HTS housing co-operative built a number of housing estates and single family houses. These several thousand 'steelworks' flats constitute a major proportion of all flats built in Krakow in recent years.

Local government (such as it was) was simply a transmission belt obeying directions issued from ministries or party officials, with high ranking party officials regarding local councils as official safeguards for national interests at the local level (Jensen and Plum 1993: 574). Between 1945 and 1990, town planning was basically an exercise in accounting and management, serving largely as a diagnostic tool in drawing up an inventory of a region. Municipal governments made their plans without the co-operation of large enterprises in their local-ities, and these plants made their own plans, usually ignoring local plans. In turn, both local plans and and those of large enterprises were ignored by central government when taking investment decisions. Krakow, for example, was not informed of the decision, taken in 1958 to triple the size of the steelworks. The municipal plan had assumed a stable output (Ryder 1992).

The legacy of the pre-1989 industrial structure posed as many problems as that bequeathed by the institutional framework. Central planning had focused on the development of particular industrial sectors or branches with little thought for 'balanced' regional development. Local economic structures in Central and Eastern Europe were the complete inverse of those generally found in the West, resembling an inverted pyramid with a tiny base of SMEs supporting a structure top heavy with medium and large-sized enterprises. Due to centralization, capital cities attracted more resources than in most comparable Western countries. At a regional level, resources were siphoned off at the expense of rural areas. Rural areas are still more backward and lacking in infrastructure than is generally the case in the West. Social and economic life was organized vertically and highly controlled, generally through large organizations or the Communist Party. However, it would be simplistic to suggest that all regions in Central and Eastern Europe exhibited all these characteristics with exactly the same weighting. Zon (1992) goes on to suggest that five general types of region can be identified, each having different prospects for further development:

Firstly, there are regions, including the capital city, generally having a diversified economic structure and comparatively well-developed infrastructure. In the case of Warsaw, this is reflected in relatively low unemployment and a disproportionately high share of national FDI. Secondly, there are regions with a diversified economic structure. In Poland, examples would include Gdansk and Poznan, which it is argued are emerging as new regional growth centres, perhaps due to their relative proximity to Scandinavia and Germany respectively (Stryjakiewicz 1995). Thirdly, there are backward regions heavily dependent on agriculture – for example, North East Poland – and in the Polish context this is particularly important given that Polish agriculture remained dominated by private ownership, principally in the hands of peasants on small holdings. Fourthly, there are regions heavily dependent on former CMEA markets, producing – for instance – so-called high tech goods, but the most obvious example is armaments. Finally, there were regions dependent on heavy industry, such as coal mining, steel and basic chemicals. These regions were often dependent on just one industry, and collapse would be particularly deeply felt as heavy industry was a source of relatively well-paid employment.

Development of the Krakow Regional Economy

As we shall see, with some important local peculiarities, it could be argued that Krakow most closely resembles the dependent type of region and has all the problems that are associated with such structures. The local economy was dominated by large state-owned heavy industry with a high degree of vertical integration characterized by plant sizes much higher than those prevalent in the West. Only 30 per cent of plants in the region employed less than fifty people, a low figure even by Polish standards. HTS accounted for 40 per cent of all industrial employment growth between 1950 and 1965. The first blast furnaces came into operation in 1954 and steel production began in 1955. As Table 6.1 shows, both employment and output grew rapidly.

Table 6.1 *Output and Employment, Huta Sendzimira, 1955–1978*

Year	Employment	Steel production ('000 tons)
1955	16,090	324
1965	24,331	2,651
1978	40,000	6,800

Source: Pounds *et al.* 1981

As the steelworks grew in employment and output, so Nowa Huta, the new town built to house the influx of workers for the steelworks, increased in importance in the population of Krakow. Between 1950 and 1977, the population increased ten fold to a figure of 217 000. By the mid-1960s, Nowa Huta accounted for nearly one in four of the city's population, with this figure rising to almost one in three by 1977. Unsurprisingly, the steel works came to dominate the investment portfolio of the region. In 1990, for example, the plant accounted for

65 per cent of industrial investment allocated to the region, a figure only 5 per cent lower than the high point of 70 per cent in 1950 (Bednarczyk *et al.* 1992: 7).

Despite its dominance of the area, Sendzimia steel works has brought little regional development with few local linkages being scarce. In 1980 only 1.6 per cent of the supplies purchased by the steel works came from the Krakow region, and these were mainly non-essential supplies (Bednarczyk *et al.* 1992: 12). Similarly, with regard to consumption local linkages were few, with most of the output sold to enterprises outside of Krakow, 12 per cent being exported and only 2 per cent sold to buyers located in the Krakow region. Although isolated, yet dominant, HTS had further malign influences on the locality. By 1983, machinery within the plant was old and the technology outdated, with less than 2 per cent of the processes described as fully automated. Furthermore, the workforce were suffering with over 20 per cent of them regularly off sick with work-related illness. High levels of depreciation, obsolete equipment and lengthening cycles of repair were reflected in increasing environmental problems. By the early 1980s, Krakow had the second highest pollution levels in the country. In the city centre dust falls exceeded safe limits by a factor of two, and in some parts of the city it ranged from ten to fourteen times those limits. Levels of sulphur dioxide were between fifteen and twenty-five times higher than already high safe limits, and levels of fluorine were seven times higher than recommended levels. In 1980, 162 200 tonnes of sulphur dioxide and 632 600 tonnes of carbon monoxide entered the city's atmosphere. Whilst HTS was not solely responsible for Krakow's pollution problem, it was a significant contributor.

Although we have pointed to the dominance of HTS in the local economy, it is not the only sector of major importance. Table 6.2 shows a large degree of concentration of Polish production of certain goods within the Krakow region, in particular meat processing and cigarettes. ZPT Krakow, one of our case study organizations, accounts for 40 per cent of Polish cigarette production, employs over 3 000 people and is one of the top thirty companies in Poland. With eleven university level colleges, and around 50 000 students, by the late 1970s, educational and cultural sectors were the second most important source of employment in Krakow, constituting some 11 per cent of the workforce.

Though the local economy was not fully dependent on HTS, nevertheless it lacked diversification, with both its infrastructure and service

Table 6.2 *Percentage of Polish Output Produced in Krakow Region, 1992*

Coke	14.0%
Electricity	3.1%
Crude steel	21.0%
Rolled steel products	25.0%
Pharmaceuticals	8.0%
Meat products	92.0%
Cigarettes	42.0%
Telephone cable	18.0%

Source: Atkins 1993: 2–2

sector (excluding education) underdeveloped. In 1992 metallurgical production accounted for over 25 per cent of the Krakow region production, with HTS accounting for 93 per cent of the workforce in this sector. However, the number of employees in metallurgy had fallen from 23 000 in 1991 to 19 800 in the first quarter of 1993. As we shall see in Chapter 8, the restructuring of HTS, initially relatively slow, accelerated after 1993 which will have important implications far beyond the employment levels in the plant itself. Spinning off non-central concerns will have implications for employment and the provision of social and welfare services, and the path of restructuring will have an effect on SME formation.

Even though in 1992 heavy industry still accounted for the majority of the region's output and employment, Table 6.3 shows that the dominance of Sector II (manufacturing broadly defined), so obvious in 1975, had waned. See Table 6.6, for example, for an indication that just over 4 000 people were employed in tourism related industries in 1994. This figure will rapidly increase as Krakow becomes a major tourist centre, and

Table 6.3 *Structural Change in Employment Patterns, Poland and Krakow, 1975–1992**

Year	Sector I		Sector II		Sector III	
	Krakow	Poland	Krakow	Poland	Krakow	Poland
1975	24.0	29.3	40.0	39.6	36.0	31.1
1985	21.7	28.9	35.3	35.9	43.5	35.2
1990	22.7	29.4	34.4	33.3	42.9	37.3
1991	22.6	28.1	32.4	31.5	45.0	40.4
1992	22.9	28.6	31.4	29.9	45.7	41.5

* Table shows the percentage of workers in Krakow (or Poland) employed in each of the three sectors: Sector I = agriculture; Sector II = metallurgy, light industry, electromachinery, food processing, chemicals, construction; Sector III = Local government, trade, finance and insurance, administration and justice, education.

Source: Atkins 1993: 2–4

employment levels are likely to be higher than official figures indicate as much current activity is undertaken by very small and often unofficial firms. Although agriculture has not been as important in the region as in Poland as a whole, it would appear to be the case that agriculture has acted as a shock absorber for redundant industrial workers with the proportion of people employed in agriculture reversing its long-term decline in the early 1990s. Finally, it is important to note that the largest proportion of the structural changes in employment patterns that took place in the years prior to 1992 occurred between 1975 and 1985, reinforcing our contention that many of the post-1989 changes are simply accelerations of tendencies already under way.

So far we have painted a picture of the economic, organizational and institutional legacy that the 1989 'jump to the market' was supposed to transform. The agenda for transformation of the local economy was exactly the same as that being applied at the national level. The recipe combined privatization and FDI with the re-emergence of the small firm sector.

FDI and Privatization

Privatization has been taken as the centre piece of the move towards a market-style economy. However, far from being a speedy and comprehensive process, the Polish experience has been protracted, tortuous and fraught with contention. The national experience is reflected at the Krakow regional level with a 1993 report on the local economy concluding that there had been no major examples of privatization in the region (Atkins 1993). Interviewed in the spring of 1994, an official from the regional ministry of transformation stated that seventeen firms from Krakow were to be included in the national investment funds of the Mass Privatization Programme. Ninety-three enterprises remained in the control of the voivode, compared to 130 at the beginning of the process. It would appear then that whilst around forty enterprises were in the process of privatization, only twenty organizations had been actually privatized by the beginning of 1995.

By the beginning of 1995, there were a growing number of privatizations, including the Wawel confectionery plant, which had taken the worker/management buyout option through the liquidation route. Other significant examples of privatization, either completed or under negotiation, have all involved foreign firms. These would include an 85 per cent stockholding in Skawina (confectionery) by a German firm, Bahlsen, and a 35–40 per cent share taken in the Okocim brewery. In mid-1995 Philip Morris were in the process of negotiating an increase in their interest in the local tobacco plant. The American company had a long-standing licensing agreement with the Polish cigarette maker whereby 10 per cent of the plant's production and 20 per cent of profits are derived from the production of Marlboro.

This relates to two themes developed in Chapter 4: firstly, that FDI has been crucial to the privatization process; and secondly, that FDI that has arrived in Krakow reflects national patterns, with a high concentration of acquisitions in the food processing and soft drinks sectors. The most significant example of greenfield investment is a Coca Cola bottling plant.

It has been claimed that there has been a growth in the area of Joint Venture Companies (JVCs). In December 1991, there were around 190 JVCs in the Krakow region, over half of them involved German or American partners, with other countries including Austria, France and Italy. However, this should not be taken as indicating a strong surge in foreign direct investment, as many will have been speculative, small, and often in the retail sector, for example, the opening of one branch of Benetton would be included in this category. By 1994, the ministry of transformation was suggesting that there were 130 joint ventures registered in the Krakow region, which were made up of a large number of small joint venture enterprises involving small amounts of capital investment. Table 6.4 suggests that the average capital contributed by JVCs in Krakow is a paltry figure of between £30 000 and £35 000. Again this reflects the national picture whereby a small number of large transnational corporations (TNCs) account for the majority of investments with a large number of small FDIs contributing little or nothing. At the factory level, as we shall see in Chapter 9, both the presence, and indeed the absence of FDI, have important, though complex effects on the process and pattern of organizational transformation.

Table 6.4 *Joint Ventures in Poland, by Voivode, 1993*

Voivode	Number	Foreign capital (zl.m.)	Total capital (zl.m.)	Foreign capital as % of total capital	Average foreign capital per JVC (zl.m.)
Warsaw	1222	3 873 240	4 574 203	84.7	3169
Poznan	177	347 018	613 286	56.6	1960
Katowice	141	167 225	299 325	55.9	1186
Krakow	135	164 846	331 688	49.7	1221
Lodz	132	104 037	156 780	66.3	788
Gdansk	128	52 937	102 278	51.8	413

Source: Kot *et al.* (1995)

Table 6.4 shows that whilst the region is lagging behind voivodes such as Warsaw, Poznan and Katowice in the level of JVCs in the region, Krakow is ahead of regions such as Lodz and Gdansk. Furthermore, Krakow's failure is only relative, in that both FDI and privatization at a privatization at a national level have, as we saw in Chapters 4 and 5, been markedly unspectacular.

Small and Medium-sized Firms

One fact about which most commentators are agreed is the apparently successful re-emergence of the private sector in general, and SMEs in particular (Rostowski 1993). The number of private sector units in Krakow rose from 2652 in 1990 to 78 203 by the end of 1994, with growth being the most dramatic in firms employing less than five people. The number of these small, private enterprises rose from 9271 in 1991 to 71 411 in 1993 (Kot *et al.* 1995).

A picture of the re-emergence of the private sector and the rebirth of small firms can be gleaned from Table 6.5. Krakow, like most Central and East European regions, was heavily reliant on a small number of very large organizations, and though the situation started to change in the 1980s, the size distribution of enterprises bore little resemblance to the pyramidal structure of most advanced capitalist economies. However, it is worth noting that Krakow stands forty-third out of forty-nine voivodeships in terms of the share of the private sector in total regional GDP. In Krakow this stood in 1993 at a figure of 40.6 per cent, compared to Leszno with a figure of 71.8 per cent. This can be explained, at least in part, by the relatively low share of agriculture in Krakow's regional GDP, coupled with the fact that 70 per cent of production (as opposed to services) is still carried out by state-owned enterprises, at a national level.

It is also important to note that there has been significant growth, in relative terms, in private sector firms employing between 101 and 499 people, and in those units employing more than 500 people. We suggest that an explanation may be sought in the restructuring of large firms, spinning off non-core activities as new medium-sized firms. We illustrate this phenomena in some detail when we examine the restructuring of HTS in Chapter 8.

Wisniewski (nd: 10) suggests that SMEs that emerged in regions such as Krakow in the early 1990s could be divided into three categories: firstly, those with no strategy whatsoever, beyond sheer survival, mostly in the traditional craft sector, and the emerging street and market traders and kiosks; secondly, firms aimed at avoiding 'punitive' tax structures, either by inflating costs of production, or by formally closing down extant organizations and opening new ones to take advantage of tax relief for new SMEs; thirdly, innovative SMEs or those concerned with exports, usually involving some element of foreign capital. The first two categories are unlikely to be significant sources of growth in either production or employment terms, whilst the third category is potentially more dynamic in terms of innovation and growth. We would add a fourth category, where often one-person firms are the outcome of large organizations spinning off non-core elements of their activities, thus creating new SMEs. For example, Rostowski (1993: 8) attributes some of the growth in the

Table 6.5 *Number of Enterprises in the Krakow Region, by Numbers Employed, 1991–1993*

Year		Number of employees					
Sector	Total	Less than 5	6–20	21–50	51–100	101–500	More than 500
1991							
Total	11 050	8 419	1 394	466	330	300	141
Public	1 779	142	532	365	309	290	141
%	16.1	1.7	38.2	78.3	93.6	96.7	100
Private	9 271	8 277	862	101	21	10	0
%	83.9	98.3	61.8	21.7	6.4	3.3	0
1993							
Total	73 243	66 617	4 581	925	480	490	150
Public	1 832	208	554	367	306	281	116
%	2.5	0.3	12.1	39.7	63.7	57.3	77.3
Private	71 411	66 409	4 027	558	174	209	34
%	97.5	99.7	88.9	60.3	36.3	42.7	22.7

Source: Kot *et al.* (1995)

transport SMEs to cash-strapped state enterprises selling off trucks they no longer needed to fetch scarce inputs from distant suppliers.

Few of these small firms will be sources of growth or employment, with the exception perhaps of the third category, examples of which are few and far between. This has led one analyst to explain the dynamics of the SME formation process in Central and Eastern Europe as moving from the second economy to the informal economy (Stark 1993: 7). In addition, a high degree of turbulence is typical of this sector with over 150 000 firms liquidated in 1992 in the Polish economy as a whole, but around 500 000 firms were created, mostly in trade (and often street sellers). Bankruptcies of SMEs came about for a number of reasons including inefficiency, the effects of recession, collapse of subcontracting from the public sector, increased rents and simple tax avoidance.

Privatization also contributed to the growth of 'new' SMEs in at least two ways. Hitherto, the voivode had been responsible for most small-scale enterprises in their region. Therefore, the so-called 'small privatization' at the beginning of 1990 meant that a large number of shop premises, service sector organizations and handicraft or manufacturing premises were either rented or sold. Secondly, privatization by the liquidation route in a number of cases led to manager or employee buy outs. In many cases, as we have seen, these are not genuine independent small firms, as the voivode simply leases the premises.

Labour Market Change

The three major changes affecting employment structure are the shift to small firms, the rise of the service sector and the associated emergence of the private sector. However, it is important to note that many of these changes were already under way when the former regime collapsed. The share of manufacturing and construction in Krakow's employment declined from 40 per cent in 1975 to 34 per cent in 1990 and 31 per cent in 1992. The private sector's share of employment had risen to 57 per cent by August 1994.

However, it must be realized that the process of shift from manufacturing to services, from public to private sector has not been without its problems. As Table 6.6 demonstrates, within the Krakow voivode in the year to August 1994, only trade and repairs showed any increase in employment. Although the unemployment rate in Krakow remains low compared to other voivodes, this still left 46,600 people unemployed in August 1994. Of this number, 26 600 were women, 10 800 of the unemployed had never had a job, and 23 500 unemployed workers in Krakow had no rights to unemployment benefit, mainly due to the effects of the 1991 Employment Act, as we saw in Chapter 2. In August 1994, 3256 people came off the unemployment register, of which only 444 were women. However, of this total only a third took up employment, whilst two-thirds simply lost the status of being 'unemployed'. In the same month, employment agencies had 5176 jobs on offer, of which 4414 were in the private sector and 2168 were full time jobs. During the same period, 52 enterprises announced 2410 redundancies, with over half of these companies being in the private sector and accounting for more than 50 per cent of the jobs lost. Overall then, it would appear that women are suffering disproportionately from unemployment and finding it increasingly difficult to find work if they lose their jobs. Non-standard (i.e. other than full time) employment was on the rise and

Table 6.6 *Average Employment in the Krakow Voivode, August 1994*

Sections	Krakow voivode	
	(thousands)	Aug. 1993 = 100
Total	190.9	97.2
Industry	96.3	99.6
Construction	36.8	85.2
Trade and repairs	24.4	100.8
Hotels and restaurants	4.3	99.2
Transport, storage and telecommunication	8.8	93.0

Source: Regional Statistical Office, Krakow, September 1994.

although the private sector was rapidly re-emerging, it was also contributing significantly to the ranks of the unemployed.

The workers of Krakow are obviously beginning to pay a heavy price for restructuring even before the process gets fully under way in workplaces such as ZPT Krakow, Wawel (the confectionery company) and HTS. However, it has been a central element of our analysis that workers must be viewed as active participants in shaping the future, not just the victims of impersonal economic forces. This is evident at the local level where Solidarity in particular has played an important though complex and contradictory role in the process of workplace restructuring. In Chapter 8 we examine the case of HTS and in Chapter 9 we look at tobacco and confectionery factories and demonstrate the way in which workers and their organizations have had an important role to play in influencing the pattern and process of restructuring at a workplace level. However, before we examine the role of Solidarity, it is important to understand the changes that have taken place in the nature of local government.

Towards Local Intervention

Under the auspices of shock therapy, regional economic policy was subordinated to macroeconomic policy and, further, it was felt that if markets were given free rein then regional disparities would automatically narrow. After 1991, there dawned a realization, even at central government level, that increasing integration into the international economy was creating a series of tendencies and problems that had a clear spatial dimension. Growing regional variation in levels of FDI, privatization, small firm formation and unemployment were leading to the socioeconomic marginalization of large areas of the country (Central Office of Planning 1994, 1995). It was argued that the only areas benefiting from the process of transformation were those that had multifunctional and diversified economic structures, good transport connections (particularly to other countries), a good business environment and a highly skilled workforce. Krakow, as we shall see, would seem to fit this picture however, even here the prognosis is not overly optimistic.

In general, current transformation processes have revealed a tendency towards petrification if not increasing polarization of the regional system. We explored in Chapter 4 the way in which increased integration with the international economy in general and the EU in particular through trade and foreign investment has been uneven, between and within Central and East European economies. This is reflected in an increasing regional inequality in Poland with polarization increasingly evident along two dimensions: firstly, the poorly developed eastern regions versus the more advanced western ones; and secondly, rural versus urban areas, particularly large agglomerations (Stryjakiewicz 1995: 2).

A growing disillusionment with the increasingly obvious failures of the free market philosophy led to the emergence of a consensus around the notion that regional disparities were based on a deep infrastructural gap in both physical and institutional terms. Furthermore, the consensus now recognized that intervention would be necessary to overcome the apparent infrastructural gap. What was needed, it was now agreed, was policy to develop local infrastructure, necessary for and capable of attracting and retaining the FDI that was seen as the major carrier of local economic development. We will examine the prescriptions being applied to Krakow in Chapter 7.

The May 1990 elections introduced a new form of local government. The old system of the local state (commune) was replaced by a new system of self government (gmina). The councillors from the gmina then appoint representatives to the voivode (regional government). However, the heads of the voivode remain appointed by central government. In theory at least, the gmina are now charged with providing the community with the range of welfare functions previously provided by regional organs of the state. This extends to education, roads, water, housing, health service, public transport, environmental protection, culture, parks etc. But there is a major problem and that is the ability of gmina to raise revenue to provide these services. Jensen and Plum (1993: 579) argue that costs greatly exceed revenues from the letting of housing and the provision of public services. The only genuine sources of income are state subsidies and various local taxes, although for most gminas these contribute only to a very limited degree to current budgets. In fact, revenue and expenditure patterns of central and local government reveal an interesting but disturbing picture. Whilst central state expenditures have remained slightly above revenue for the period 1989–93, local revenues and local budgets have declined by approximately 50 per cent (Kosek-Wojnar 1995: 73). Therefore, the ability of local government to provide an alternative source of local welfare provision, as large state-owned enterprises withdraw from the field, is highly limited. It also follows that the gmina's ability to intervene in the area of local economic development is going to be equally circumscribed. This was the economic and institutional framework that confronted Solidarity in the early 1990s.

Solidarity in Krakow

The Krakow voivode is a part of the larger Malopolska region within which Solidarity had around 150 000 members in 1200 workplaces. The majority of members are in large workplaces in larger towns and cities, and the union's organization reflects this concentration with the headquarters being in Krakow, and offices in ten other large towns. The union's largest single concentration of membership is in HTS, the steel works on the outskirts of Krakow. Early in 1994, Solidarity claimed 6500 members or around one in three of the workforce. In general, the union has its largest concentrations of members in large workplaces in heavy industry. As we have already seen, Solidarity sees itself as an agent of restructuring, placing a protective umbrella over successive governments administering shock therapy. This role had brought about an increasing tension between national and local union organization, and between the union's role as an agent of restructuring and that as defender of workers' terms and conditions of employment.

During the course of 1994 the terrain on which the union organized changed dramatically at both national and local level. That change was brought about by the September 1993 election, which brought to power a coalition government made up of the SLD (the Democratic Alliance comprising the reformed Communist Party amongst others) and the PSL (Peasants Party). Although the Solidarity vote had held reasonably well in Malopolska, in the country as a whole the movement was electorally routed. This was to have a significant effect on the attitude of the regional officialdom. Hitherto the union had tried to resolve major disputes through parliament, before considering strike action, but with little meaningful representation in the Sejm this was now defunct as a tactic. This might suggest that Solidarity would revert to a more orthodox trade-union function, but herein we discover the implications arising from the complexity of the union's multifaceted nature.

The new strategy was based on the fact that, though demolished at national level, Solidarity in the Malopolska region still had significant leverage at the local level in negotiating with local government in the 130 gminas. The trade-union law giving the union a right to be consulted over laws passed by the gmina affecting work conditions, standards of living and levels of employment was, however, not considered to be enough. Attempts were made to create greater possibilities for intervening in local government and the local economy by participating in the 1994 local elections. They would, therefore, not campaign as Solidarity alone, but rather in coalitions, although rejecting partnership with either the PSL or the SLD.

Solidarity had also signed agreements with a number of, mostly larger, gmina. The aim had been to reach consensus over issues such as co-operation in the process of transformation of enterprises owned by the gmina on the basis that this has a direct influence on the level of local employment. The union wanted to negotiate guarantees for employees of local organizations in the process of being transformed. However, here the many roles that Solidarity plays come potentially into conflict. For the union's regional officers there are two issues in the negotiations: the first is the interests of the workers in any particular organization; and the second is the interests of the local community. The result of Solidarity at a regional level attempting to act both as a quasi political party and as a trade union, was that regional officials increasingly took on the mantle of managers of discontent. The outcome was intervention to mediate in disputes between Solidarity representatives and managers at workplace level, and at a more general level intervention to diffuse discontent at the regional level. For example, in the case of the provision of water, sewerage facilities and public transport, all under the control of the gmina, the union intervened to try and argue that wage increases should not be passed straight on to the consumer in the shape of price rises. The major problem emerging for Solidarity regional officials was how to act as managers of discontent at a regional level without appearing to be divorced from the workplace.

According to union officials, co-operation at the level of the voivode was being blocked by the legacy of the past history of Solidarity in that the resurgence of the union *qua* social movement brought in many people in the late 1980s who would later have little sympathy for the organization's union activities. This is a phenomenon we pointed to in Chapter 3. Co-operation between the union and the voivode was described as unsatisfactory. It was argued that Solidarity had been given little chance to have an input into the development of the Krakow labour market strategy, and blame for this was laid firmly at the door of the director of the voivode labour office. This man had been a colleague of the regional Solidarity officials in the underground movement, but had become unwilling to listen to the union, according to Solidarity officials.

In 1994 Solidarity faced three major problems across the region: the first was simply coping with rising unemployment amongst the membership, and the union had created a labour office to assist in the task of finding jobs for people. Although Krakow itself had been relatively unaffected by unemployment, levels of 20 per cent and above were not uncommon in gminas that were heavily reliant on one employer that had been run down. In particularly extreme cases half the jobs in a locality disappeared when the major employer had closed down. The second cause for concern was the growing necessity of defending workers from attacks on their wages. This took a number of forms, varying from firms paying below the legal minimum to avoidance of social security payments by new firms, and included protecting workers' guaranteed wages when firms went bankrupt. The third issue was that health and safety at work was becoming an increasing problem, and it was getting increasingly difficult to get companies to provide items such as special clothing or protective glasses. In other words, restructuring was generating a series of problems across the region.

Early in 1994, regional Solidarity officers said that the union's lowest levels of representation were in new small private enterprises. The union officers hoped for recognition in co-operation with managers in such firms, however, co-operation was not going to be simply or readily achieved, as in many firms Solidarity faced recognition problems. Polish labour law guarantees the right to recognition and the right to form a workplace committee only in workplaces with more than ten employees and the union was finding great difficulty in representing workers in small firms. The problem usually only became manifest when workers who were no longer members of the union turned up at the union office, having been made redundant. It then transpired that conditions had usually been abysmal and wages low, often below legal minima. The difficulties of organizing in small firms and the problems faced by people who worked in them are not limited to Krakow. A survey of the social and economic conditions of Polish workers (Gardawski and Zukowski 1993: 36–7), reported that about half of the Polish workforce, outside of agriculture, worked in private enterprise, mostly in SMEs. The report concluded:

> The working conditions in these enterprises provide little basis for optimism. But it is in these small private enterprises . . . that the new economic structure of Poland is being created . . . 'The work in private enterprises is much harder,' one of the workers told us. 'For a start, we have to work longer hours. The eight hour day is gone; we do not even talk about it anymore. The ten hour day is now the rule.' . . . There is also widespread concern about the poor and unsafe conditions of work; 'I worked on a lathe in one such enterprise. The machines are so close together and the working space is so constricted that the filings are flying all around you.' Another worker on a similar theme; 'The machines we work with are so old. I do not know where they buy them, maybe at some auction or junk sale, who knows. Then the whole lot is banged together here and they get it turning over. The cog wheels are completely worn out and the machines are noisy, but they turn over somehow and the owner rakes in the profit.' . . . One of the consistently expressed fears of the workers we interviewed was the fear of sudden and completely arbitrary lay offs. In this context, it is worth mentioning that in none of the newly established private enterprises was there any kind of worker representation . . . When asked if there was any possibility of establishing trades unions in their private enterprises, these workers treated the question as a joke.

At the end of 1994, the new Secretary of the Regional Council was attempting to set up an organizational form which would allow workers in SMEs to join the union, despite the fact that they had no legal right to recognition. Furthermore, they were looking to help workers in SMEs who were not members of the union. A case in point was hairdressers whose wage levels were around a tenth of the national average. A victory here would be important in so far as it would demonstrate that Solidarity could intervene in SMEs even when they had no members in those companies. The tactic adopted was to lodge a complaint with the state labour inspection office (broadly similar to the now defunct UK wages councils). However, this was a tactic which was dependent on having workers from SMEs who are willing not only to complain, but also to take their employers to court.

It was not just SMEs that were causing Solidarity problems. Although the nature of the problems arising in large organizations depended on the form of transformation, there were usually serious implications for salaries and conditions of work in companies that were being transformed. Regional officers of Solidarity reported problems in nearly all enterprises in the process of transformation. When a state enterprise was privatized all workers were entitled to retain union membership on being transferred to the newly privatized company. There were examples of workers' councils being told that privatization not only led to the abolition of the Councils, but also to the abolition of union membership rights. Management in the new companies appeared not to want unions in their organizations, despite the fact that some of them will have been members of Solidarity in the late 1980s.

The role of foreign direct investment in local privatizations was also contentious. Regional officers of Solidarity no longer believed in privatizing all state owned enterprises, they now favoured a mixed economy of public and private sector firms. Part of this slight change of heart can be put down to attitudes to foreign direct investment. In the case of Wawel, one of the four major Polish confectionery plants, the union backed a worker management buyout in the face of attempts by Suchard to take a controlling interest in the firm. There is a strong nationalistic streak in the union that wishes to see strategically important enterprises remain under Polish control. This was evident in the case of a local power station where Solidarity representatives had prevented a foreign investor from buying the facility by convincing other employees that the financial status of the foreign investor was dubious. Despite the fact that the ministry of ownership transformation wanted the purchase to succeed, Solidarity's position was based on the firm belief that the power station was modern, profitable and most importantly a local monopoly, and therefore should remain in local hands.

In general, there had been little trouble negotiating union recognition in large firms with significant levels of foreign direct investment in that recognition, in major cases of FDI, was usually negotiated prior to the company coming to Poland as part of a total social package. Most companies coming to Krakow had been found to be willing to discuss pay, conditions and fringe benefits, but this need not have been out of any sense of altruism. Rather it is the case that if there is to be a competitive tendering process, then having the support of Solidarity can, at the very least, remove a potential barrier to entry, and at best swing the workforce behind the bid of a particular organization. The concerns of Solidarity stretched beyond whether a particular firm could meet any negotiated package of pay and conditions, to whether they could adhere to their investment agreements and business plans. To that end the union had set up its own business information centre and conducted research for themselves. Co-operation with the union in the early stages of establishing a presence in the locality had not always lasted, with problems arising when companies had attempted to limit the activities of the union after the company had arrived in the locality, for example by denying use of office facilities or simply charging high rents for such facilities. Although, according to Polish law, companies cannot restrict the activity of Solidarity, the reality was that both foreign and Polish firms had attempted to do so, with companies, according to the regional union officials, always able to find a way round legislation.

Conclusion

By examining the transformation of the region in general, and organizations within it in particular, we are able to analyse the process of transformation in microcosm. In Chapters 8 and 9 we will examine the restructuring of three major workplaces within the locality, highlighting the interrelationship between FDI, privatization and the role of organized labour. Further, we analyse the connections between restructuring of SOEs and the re-emergence of the small firm, as well as the effects that restructuring is having on the provision of welfare in the region. However, we begin in Chapter 7, by critically evaluating prescriptions that have been offered up by Western practitioners and academics for transforming localities in Central and Eastern Europe in general, and Krakow in particular.

Prescriptions for the restructuring of regions such as Krakow, usually emanating from the West, assume that the legacy of the past is a total institutional void. Therefore the whole edifice of local governance and thus economic development must be constructed. This is misleading in that although new local government structures came into existence in 1990, institutions dating from before 1989 had a vital role to play, particularly Solidarity, the voivode and HTS. This is not to say that rapid changes are not taking place in the local economy. Small firms are emerging, and large firms are restructuring, but the transformation is far more problematic than was first envisaged.

The restructuring of dominant organizations such as HTS, only just getting under way in the mid-1990s, will have ramifications for years to come. The implications, as we shall see in Chapter 8, are not only increasing unemployment levels, but also detrimental effects on the net social and welfare provision available in the locality. With unemployment high, and likely to continue to rise, Krakow's workers, particularly women, are faced with a series of acute problems inside and outside of work. However, two potential sources of help have proved to be a mixed blessing, in so far as SMEs are re-emerging but the number and nature of jobs being created is problematic. Yet the role of Solidarity both as an agent of transformation and as a defender of workers' interests is increasingly being called into question. As the Utopian dreams of the free marketeers turn sour, attitudes towards ideas, organizations and transformation itself, have started to change. A major theme running through the following chapters is the way that workers in particular have experienced the realities of transformation and in so doing have changed their own attitudes to that process, their organization's approach to transformation and thus the process of transformation itself.

7 LOCAL STRATEGIES: RUSHING TO FILL THE VOID?

As we saw in the previous chapter, disillusionment with unfettered free market solutions to Poland's regional and national transformation problems surfaced in the early 1990s. The idea that a new market economy would rapidly and naturally emerge collapsed in the face of high and rising unemployment, deepening levels of poverty and the apparent failure of foreign direct investment (FDI) and privatization to produce rapid results. At a local level, a consensus began to coalesce around the idea that widening regional disparities were due to institutional and physical infrastructural inequalities. Furthermore, it was now recognized that intervention would not only be necessary to overcome regional disparities within Poland, but more fundamentally that there existed an institutional void in all regions within Poland, compared to their counterparts (or competitors) in the West. What was now deemed to be necessary was policy at the local level designed to develop local infrastructure capable of attracting and retaining FDI as well as developing indigenous small and medium-sized firms (SMEs).

The importance of this as far as Krakow, and other regions are concerned is that no well-developed institutional framework existed. Local government reform had created the gmina, but there remained a void at the regional level with the voivode remaining an appointed representative of central government. However, the notion of an institutional void extended beyond the underdeveloped state of local government to include the lack of strong local representation of employers' associations. Further, as Stryjakiewicz (1995: 9) argues, it is held that well-developed institutions of the business environment are a precondition for developing regional potential. However, such institutions (chambers of industry and commerce, agencies of regional development, consulting agencies, business support centres and business incubator units) did not exist before 1990 and their development has been highly uneven since. Stryjakiewicz noted that the quantitative growth in these institutions in Poland has apparently been impressive, given that most regions were starting from scratch; however, growth in numbers has not been accompanied either by an increase in the quality of institutions or by the emergence of the appropriate financial base for these institutions. He suggests that although the aims and tasks of the growing network of agencies for regional development are similar to those of their Western counterparts, what makes them substantially different is their legal situation and the means at their disposal. The agencies are not supplied with budgets and thus act as commercial companies, with the consequence that profit is treated as the main criteria of their effectiveness, relegating the agencies to the level of being yet another consultancy or training firm.

As we shall see shortly, policy prescription for local economic development in Krakow, has been based on varieties of local micro-corporatism. However, given the lack of a developed local state and little in the way of development agencies or employers' associations, it is unsurprising to find the director of the labour office of the voivode, interviewed in the autumn of 1993, arguing that the local institutional framework did not yet exist capable of sustaining highly developed local regulation. Despite these apparent handicaps, it is worth noting that Krakow is considered to be second in national rankings of regions (after Warsaw and above Poznan and Lodz) ordered by the development of their local business infrastructure.

It would, however, be a mistake to suggest that there existed a total institutional void at the local level. From 1990 onwards there were organizations seeking to influence local economic development. A fledgling local democratic state was emerging, and Western academics, consultants and governments were promoting varieties of prescription that varied little from the emerging consensus. In this chapter we look at two prescriptions that are currently being promoted in Krakow, both seeking to rush to fill what they see as a local institutional void. The first prescription has been applied in Krakow since the early 1990s, and represents the conservative consensus on local economic development that emerged in the UK in the late 1980s, tailored to meet the perceived needs of Central Europe in the 1990s. The second prescription, just beginning to find an audience in Poland in the mid-1990s, purports to be a more radical approach to democracy and locality, and emerged from the flexible specialization school outlined in Chapter 1.

Bootstraps

Foreign participation in the transformation process has been much wider than that of the (albeit small) transfer of foreign capital. Intervention has also taken the form of advice and consultancy from government and non-government sources at a regional as well as a national level, and this can be seen in operation in Krakow. For example, through the auspices of the Know How fund, the UK employment department has been active in the Krakow region since early 1991. Three out of four Know How funded projects in Krakow have concentrated on HTS, the steelworks. An early project, aimed at providing retraining and work experience for workers threatened with redundancy, was held up because of disagreements with the unions over redundancies. A later project had supported senior management in developing strategic and business plans for each department, in preparation for a major restructuring of the plant prior to privatization. A mission statement and objectives for the plant as a whole had been developed by the end of 1994. The third project focused specifically on HTS was designed to win union support for the proposed restructuring of the plant, with the aim of demonstrating that a new development agency could identify and create jobs for workers who were to be made redundant. We will examine these initiatives in some detail in the next chapter. A more general element of the UK employment department's approach involved the recognition of the need to support the Krakow regional labour office and other local institutions in developing a regional strategy.

Early in 1992, consultants W.S. Atkins were commissioned by the UK employment department to undertake the project. The stated aims were to assist Polish 'partners' to develop the institutional infrastructure assumed to be necessary to support regional development. In particular, this meant producing a labour market strategy for the Krakow region, developing the skills of senior staff in areas such as strategic planning and programme evaluation and finally strengthening the institutional framework for implementing the strategy and subsequent action plans (Atkins 1993).

The core team of Polish officials was drawn from the voivode administration (regional government), the regional labour office, the central labour office and the European training policy section of the UK employment department group. There was little involvement of members of either OPZZ (the official union federation) or Solidarity linked trade unions; indeed, according to the Western consultants, the unions had kept themselves at arm's length from the process. As we have already seen, Solidarity believe that officials of the voivode have kept the union at a distance from policy-making in the field of local economic development.

In July 1993, W.S. Atkins, in conjunction with their Polish partners, produced an eleven-point list of strategic objectives. These were:

(1) promoting active labour market measures
(2) improving the operation of the employment services
(3) encouraging employers to train and upgrade the skills of their staff
(4) improving the skills base in the local labour market
(5) encouraging employers to develop and implement manpower and training plans
(6) improve support to small and medium-sized enterprises (SMEs)
(7) establishment of a local enterprise agency for the Nowa Huta region
(8) promoting inward investment
(9) promoting exports from the Krakow region
(10) undertaking strategic investments in local infrastructure to generate job promotion
(11) promoting technology transfer

The central government and local state were to be active participants in developing SMEs, investing in infrastructure and labour market development. This list, though wide ranging, would be instantly recognizable (with the possible exception of the emphasis on privatization) to anyone involved in local economic development in the UK in the 1990s. For example, a Coopers and Lybrand report (April 1992) concerned with the promotion of Hertfordshire, stressed the importance of three elements: firstly, indigenous growth (including expansion of existing firms and new starts); secondly, UK relocations; and thirdly, foreign direct investment. Proposed initiatives included action on technology

transfer, SME development and a customized skills enhancement programme. In other words, the prescriptions are virtually identical.

This should not surprise us. Eisenschitz and Gough (1993) have
provided a compelling analysis of the way that the burgeoning local
economic development initiatives of both the left and the right in the
UK, in the 1980s, have collapsed in the 1990s into an enterprise-based
pragmatism. Consensus has emerged around what is aptly called the
'bootstraps' approach, within which local economic development institutions and initiatives emerge as the 'commonsense' of the age. It is
worth examining the ideas and assumptions behind 'bootstraps' in a
little more detail as they have important implications for Krakow.

Totterdill (1989) suggests that interventionist local economic development strategies in the UK followed a path from 'traditional' through
'reconstructionist' to 'reconstructing for labour'. Totterdill's categories
track the emergence of, and subsequent retreat from, radical local
economic development strategies. However, Totterdill goes on to argue
that the 'reconstructing for labour' approach is inappropriate for the
conditions of the 1990s. The collapse of the radical Greater London
Council and the abolition of the other metropolitan authorities in the
mid-1980s, coupled with the ideological shift to the right in the Labour
Party, led to an abandonment of radical interventionist strategies at
both local and national level. As a result, and echoing the majority of
commentators, Totterdill suggests that what is now suitable is a form of
pragmatic interventionist local corporatism. This is the bootstraps
approach.

What emerges is a prescription based on centre–local partnerships,
increasingly involving a non-elected local state (for example, urban
development corporations and training and enterprise councils
(TECs)), to which the increasingly limited and financially constrained
local government devolved powers. The main agenda items are SME
promotion, and labour force and infrastructure development designed
to attract foreign direct investment. However, the continuing and
deepening inner city crisis in most major towns had led to a questioning
on the political Right of a simple reliance on the free market to solve all
problems. Emerging out of the recognition of the necessity of some
degree of intervention came the quangocracy of the 1990s, represented
by TECs, regional health agencies, and development corporations. In
other words, the same institutional structure as the deradicalized interventionist strategy. 'Bootstraps' had become the dominant ideology of

local economic development, the common sense of the age. Although dressed up in an image of democratic local microcorporatism, the reality of this approach in the UK has been the emergence of a business dominated quangocracy. In the name of local control, what has actually emerged are instruments of the non-elected local state increasingly bent to the wishes of an increasingly centralized state machine (see Bovaird 1995). In effect, the collapse of opposition to central government at the local level meant that an urban Left was replaced by urban managerialists, at the same time as local government itself was increasingly being replaced by small scale, semi-representative bodies increasingly responsible to and controlled by central government (Cochrane 1993). This model, if exported unaltered to Krakow, has obvious implications for the pattern of local economic development. Furthermore, questions are raised regarding the implications for local democracy and the involvement of organizations such as Solidarity.

Radical Alternatives: The New Localism

'Bootstraps' represents the 'common sense' approach to local economic development, viewed from the UK in the early 1990s. It is conservative, and relies on small business development, encouragement of FDI and the creation of an appropriate supportive local infrastructure. It is not, however, the only item on the local economic development menu. Despite the fact that 'bootstraps' represents a retreat from the more radical prescriptions of the 'restructuring for labour' type approaches, there has not been a wholesale retreat into the conservative common sense of the day. In the 1980s and 1990s an analysis was developing centring on the re-emergence of regions as significant actors on the economic stage that not only claimed a more radical garb than bootstraps, but also claimed to be relevant to the emerging regions of Central and Eastern Europe. It was further claimed that democratic structures lay at the very heart of the emerging prescriptions.

This approach leans heavily on a body of work variously described as flexible specialization or flexible accumulation and initially associated with Piore and Sabel (1984). Jessop (1994), in a paper published by the Krakow Academy of Economics, applies this analysis explicitly to regional economic strategies in what Jessop describes as post-socialist economies. Common to all these writers is a belief that the crisis of the 1970s and 1980s resulted from the limits being reached of a model of industrial development – Fordism – founded on mass production. We are now assumed to be crossing the industrial divide from Fordism to post-Fordism. As we saw in Chapter 1, post-Fordist analysis suggests that an economy dominated by mass production is being replaced by more flexible production systems, with important consequences for state structures at both national and local level. Regulation will be central to the new world, promoting local micro-corporatism on the basis of the perceived necessity of balancing co-operation and competition between capital and labour, as well as between competing production units. Two major organizational changes are associated with this trans-formation: the first is the re-emergence of small firms in regional networks resembling Marshallian industrial districts; and the second is the decentralization and vertical disintegration of large firms so that they increasingly come to resemble networks of quasi SMEs. This obviously has important implications for small firms, industrial re-structuring and local economic development. Jessop (1994: 5) argues that what is emerging is a complex dialectic between regionalization and globalization in the world economy, to which the newly emergent post-socialist market economies must adapt. That adaptation seems to involve a belief in the necessity of a local micro-corporatism in areas such as Krakow.

This approach is largely derived from analyses of regional develop-ment in the US and Western Europe in the 1980s. Common to these approaches was a belief that emerging structures would not only enhance local democracy but also serve to act as a countervailing force to the power of large firms in general and transnational corporations (TNCs) in particular, in an era of increased globalization. This has obvious relevance for regions reliant on FDI for transforming their economies whilst simultaneously attempting to construct local demo-cratic structures. In the last section we followed Totterdill in tracing a development, in the UK, of economic development policy at the local level from 'traditional' through 'reconstructionist' to 'reconstructing for labour', the latter being commonly associated with the radical interventionism of the Greater London Council (GLC). Totterdill rejects the reconstructing for labour approach and argues that the conditions inherent under post-Fordism allow for policy to be devel-oped along the lines of pragmatic, interventionist local corporatism.

This would lead to a strategy 'aimed at the development of a highly socially regulated local micro-capitalism ... perceived as a means of attacking the power of large scale capital, thereby reestablishing a form of community control over local economies' (Totterdill 1989: 518). This is possible because under flexible specialization small firms come in from their peripheral role under Fordism to a more central role 'where they may well be in a strong position to challenge conglomerates' (Totterdill 1989: 498).

Writers in the same school have suggested that in some sense the mode of production has gone back to the future, in so far as small firms are becoming integral to the functioning of economies. Furthermore, local economies can develop along different trajectories, and national economies become little more than the sum of their (separately developing) parts. Therefore, cities and localities are now the obvious entities around which progressive growth and justice coalitions can be formed (Cooke and Imrie 1989: 326, Cooke 1988: 198), an encouraging thought for regions newly emerging and acquiring the institutional framework deemed necessary for economic development. The policy implications are seemingly obvious, at least as far as local economic development is concerned (see Hirst 1989: 277):

> Good local networks in which local councillors and local government officials, local economic policy specialists, business people and representatives of labour can fruitfully interact are crucial ... the aim of such local strategies ought to be to sustain or recreate thriving 'regional economies' based on manufacturing districts with networks of small and medium firms in a mutually supporting but diversified cluster of industrial lines ... Local authority interventions should put industrial success first, and other policy goals should be adapted to whatever interventions that primary goal requires.

In general, it is suggested that what is required is intervention in the local economy to control the worst excesses of the market. As Jessop (1994: 9) argues, the transformation of the regions of Central and Eastern Europe requires simultaneously both the liberation and the restriction of market forces:

> [Market forces] must be articulated to specific ways of organising production, specific mechanisms for matching production and consumption

so that expanded economic reproduction can occur, and specific ways of regulating economic activity so that the dilemmas, conflicts and contradictions of capitalism do not become so acute that further accumulation becomes blocked. If the emerging market forces are not embedded in appropriate non-market relations, they will produce catastrophic disequilibrium and reinforce the systemic vacuum in eastern Europe.

In a more detailed and prescriptive contribution, Cowling (1992) argues that in order to avoid a transformation from state socialism to monopoly capitalism, privatization in Central and Eastern Europe needs to be a planned process: part of a strategic industrial policy requiring the reorganization and redirection of industry. This is problematic in so far as these countries are left with a state apparatus they are trying to disengage. This emphasizes the need for a new, relatively autonomous strategic planning institution responsible directly to parliament, staffed with people from outside the existing state apparatus – a different sort of planning by a different sort of people. We have explored at length the problems of the institutionalist approach in Chapter 1.

Meaningful regional economies need to be created, which are not just sites for the branch plants of the giants, but which should provide a durable and dynamic industrial structure for well-defined communities. It is vital that the size distribution of firms be decisively altered in favour of the creation of a strong small and medium-size enterprise sector, the big hole in Central and Eastern Europe and the former Soviet Union. Generally, the big monopolies need to be broken up, but in an organized way – that is, within an overall strategy. Networks of smaller enterprises should be created to provide mutual support; a collective entrepreneurialism comprising a careful mixture of co-operation and rivalry, perhaps with international links. A multiplicity of types of organization, as well as a multiplicity of types of firms, should be allowed for to enable experiments with the way forward to take place – including capitalist organization with a broader definition of membership, together with non-capitalist organizations, for example co-operatives and municipal enterprises. These forms may not necessarily accord with conventional definitions of privatization, rather they represent alternative ways to begin to establish community control (Cowling 1992: 14–15).

Cowling's concentration on, and prioritization of, the concept of democracy is refreshing, and is couched in terms of the construction of a countervailing power (rather than a successive power) to the concentration of private power brought about by privatization. Small firms are assumed to have a vital role to play, not only as dynamic innovative organizations but also collectively as constellations of organizations linked in a complex division of labour not only between themselves, but also with large (international) organizations. It also views the locality as an important organizational focus of democratic intervention in economic development. However, as we shall see, policy cannot deliver what it promises.

With specific reference to Poland, Zon (1992) argues that policy must be driven by the need to mediate a shift from competitive rule to co-operative relations. This can only be done by social structures that are inevitably and inextricably bound to specific regions, with the aim being to 'valorize the given cultural specificity and cultural diversity' of any particular locality. As far as public authorities are concerned, apart from traditional instruments of economic policy at local and regional level, four instruments for deblocking economic development are emphasized:

(1) the foundation of innovation centres, business incubation centres and technology parks;
(2) the organizing of self help training courses to further economic development, eventually with the help of external experts;
(3) the furthering of cross-border inter-regional and twin city co-operation;
(4) the reorganization of public services in the direction of a service infrastructure conducive to innovation and technological change (Zon 1992: 93).

The theoretical and empirical structures of post-Fordist analysis, upon which the new localism is based, have come in for much concerted criticism (Williams *et al.* 1987, Callinicos 1989, Rainnie 1991b), however, two points are worth noting at this juncture: the first is that the prescription that emerges from the new localism, a supposedly radical form of analysis, differs in only small matters of degree from 'bootstraps'. Policy distils down to little more than support for SMEs, encouraging FDI and providing a local infrastructure. The second point is that the approach has been described as a Utopian myth 'hinged upon partial truths, obscured realities, discontinuities with the past and unattainable panaceas' (Amin 1988: 1). In the following chapter we explore in more detail the discrepancy between rhetoric and reality in so far as the restructuring of HTS is concerned. For the time being, it is worth noting that the new localism is reliant on a mythical version of Marshallian industrial districts, which as we have seen stresses inter-firm co-operation. In fact, the whole network structure is predicated on co-operation, not only between small firms and quasi small firms, but also between workers and management. In other words, it is suggested that the fundamental divisions that lie at the heart of our analysis – capital–capital, capital–labour – can somehow be controlled, if not actually abolished (Rainnie 1991b).

There are a number of problems associated with the new localism and the bootstraps approach, beyond the obvious Utopian idealism, including the fallacious equation of local ownership with local control, and the belief that institutions at a local or regional level are powerful enough to activate and control an effective form of action (Eisenschitz and Gough 1993). Equally, it assumes that as Central and Eastern Europe cannot wait for institutions to emerge, that there must be off-the-shelf models available from the West that can be simply and unproblematically transferred (Casson 1993: 8). However, we wish to point to two further problems. The first problem is that small firms are treated as an homogeneous mass and are also imbued with an almost talismanic entrepreneurial status in the drive towards a market economy. We are asked to accept a view that sees current economic development as simply swapping one crude dualism for another. Under Fordism contracting relationships are competitive and dependent and all small firms are in subordinate positions. In other words, small is brutal. In the emerging new times, contracting relationships are long-term, high trust, symbiotic and co-operative and the inherent flexibility of small firms allocates them a priority position. Small is beautiful. The second problem is that not only are privatization and FDI treated as separate categories, but they are also divorced from questions of organizational transformation and the re-emergence of the small firm. We have already seen that both FDI and privatization are not only thin on the ground but also problematic. The same turns out to be true for SMEs. Furthermore, all three elements that lie at the core of the restructuring process were not only creating problems for Solidarity, as we have seen in Chapter 6, but also differ hugely from the image to be derived from the new localism.

Restructuring Large Firms

The restructuring of large firms causes problems, and can take two forms: firstly, change in the nature of ownership; and secondly, change in the nature of intra- and inter-firm relationships. Changes in the nature of ownership in Poland either takes the form of the state transforming ownership patterns through privatization, or of FDI setting up greenfield sites or, more often, setting up joint ventures with existing firms as part of the privatization programme.

According to the flexible specialization/new localism hypothesis, an important element tying together small and large firms is the fundamental restructuring that large firms are supposed to be undertaking. Inter- and intra-firm restructuring takes the linked forms of deverticalization, and the restructuring of subcontracting relations. In essence, it is argued that large organizations must be more flexible to meet the challenge of rapidly changing markets in a post-Fordist world. According to this view, this requires large organizations to restructure themselves, internally, to resemble a federal structure of quasi small businesses. Internal restructuring along the lines of just-in-time systems requires a transition from competitive, dependent subcontracting relationships to a new world of symbiotic and co-operative relations. In this new world, small firms, being innovative and flexible, are particularly well placed to benefit from the structural changes under way. If we examine the dynamics of organizational change in large organizations in Krakow, a very different picture emerges. The major actors in the local economy, as we have said, are either significant examples of FDI, or institutions such as HTS. We will examine the restructuring of HTS, in detail, in the next chapter.

Echoing the Polish experience generally, there are few significant examples of FDI in the Krakow region. However, even if there were, we have reason to doubt that any significant local multiplier effect would fundamentally prioritize local small firms (see Chapter 4). In fact the opposite may be the case, for example, if Philip Morris increase output of Marlboro at ZPT Krakow, and diminish production of Polish cigarettes, then there will be a drastic pruning of the ranks of small tobacco growers in Krakow and beyond. In general, in the 1980s many SMEs appeared to be operating in and around the interstices left by large state owned enterprises. Any significant restructuring of the SOEs could have the effect of pruning that SME base.

More fundamentally, there is little reason to believe that the restructuring of buyer–supplier relations. JIT driven or not, will benefit local small firms. Evidence would seem to suggest that the relationship between large firms and their primary suppliers is increasingly coming to resemble relationships between very large firms, a restructuring of oligopoly, rather than the re-emergence of the small firm. Quality, price and delivery rather than size or locality are vital. In these circumstances primary suppliers of FDI in Krakow need not even be in Poland, never mind Malopolska. Small firms do fit into the new supply chains but are dragged very much as junior partners almost inevitably into a position of dependency. Alternatively they may be left hanging around major FDI companies picking up intermittent specialist, one-off or low level service contracts. The implication for Krakow is that even if significant examples of FDI arrive, armed with JIT production processes, there is no reason to believe that their primary suppliers will be local SMEs. Indeed it is more likely that primary suppliers will be equally large companies with no particular need for geographical proximity. Thus if FDI companies have an established supplier network, there will be little drive to restructure or relocate that organization. We have already pointed to the examples of General Motors and Ford setting up what are little more than screwdriver operations, reliant on existing non-Polish supply networks. Local SMEs fit into this picture, but only as marginal or peripheral actors (Rainnie 1991a, 1993). FDI will remain largely as cathedrals in the desert, significant but isolated, hardly embedded, providing development in the region, but not of the region.

SMEs and Uneven Development

The restructuring of large firm–supplier relations and their implications for small firms and local economic development, provide a specific example of a general point. We have already argued (Rainnie 1989, 1991a) that small firms cannot be understood in isolation from the activities of large organizations (be they large firms or the state). We argue that, at any one time, small firms will find their relationships with large firms determined primarily by one of four sets of circumstances:

(1) dependent – complementing and serving the interests of large firms, e.g. through subcontracting;

(2) dominated – manufacturing and service firms that compete with larger firms by intense exploitation of machinery and labour;

(3) isolated – operating in specialized and/or geographically discrete markets, niches of demand, that may remain untouched by large capital: this often entails a hand-to-mouth existence;

(4) innovative – operating in (often founding and developing) specialized/new products or markets, but remaining vulnerable to the potentially fatal attractions of large firms (Rainnie 1991a: 188).

In essence, we are arguing for a form of analysis based on the notion of combined and uneven development (Lowy 1981, Rainnie 1989, Smith 1990). This takes us far away from the crude dualisms on which the new localism relies, particularly the idea that small firms are necessarily beautiful, innovative and havens of industrial peace. However, by taking such an approach, the question of small firm formation and the relationship between small and large firms in Krakow's development becomes more problematic.

An examination of small firms in Western Europe, and the UK experience in particular, is instructive. Increased small firm formation rates in the West, particularly at a time of recession, can be as much a measure of severe structural problems in the local economy as an indicator of entrepreneurial vitality. Foreman-Peck (1985) has tracked an increase in the formation rates of small firms in all the major advanced economies in the 1930s. These, however, he describes as 'chaff' rather than 'seedcorn'. Two-thirds of small firm set-ups were in service sectors with low barriers of entry and high ease of exit, with the same sectors dominating the small firm death league. As we have already argued, Krakow's regional economy has all the problems of declining regions in the West, within which an examination of the experience of SMEs takes us even further away from the new localism. Examining the recession hit North East of England in the 1980s (Storey and Johnson 1987, MacDonald 1992), research suggests that small firms, though increasing in number, will not be an answer to unemployment. MacDonald argues for an analysis of the structural, ideological and cultural factors which shape the patterns and experiences of self-employment and SME formation. In the context of the North East, he suggests that most SMEs will be 'plodders' or 'fallers', and Storey and Strange (1992) argue that in these circumstances, few SMEs are likely to grow.

The importance for Krakow is that the local economy, on one reading, represents an extreme version of the North East of England, with a historic lack of SMEs, high rates of unemployment and over-dependence on single, large, declining industries. Most SME formation in Krakow, as we have already seen, took place in the commercial and retail sectors, and is likely to exhibit the same tendencies as the SMEs portrayed above. They will tend to exist in the 'isolated' or 'dominated' categories, operating in geographically discrete markets, or competing against incoming or emerging large companies (for example, Benetton in retail). Most will never create new jobs and will be based on low wages and low skill, surviving on sweat equity.

Bootstraps and the new localism assume the importance of, and the controllability of FDI as well as unquestioningly supporting small firm formation. Equally, both assume that restructuring of large organizations will be of benefit to local economies in general and SMEs in particular. Both approaches retain their adherents despite the fact that most research suggests that small firms contribution to both the quantity and quality of job creation has been vastly overstated (Storey 1994), and that SMEs are embedded in their local economies to only a marginal degree, and have little contact, for the most part, with large firms (Curran and Blackburn 1994).

Conclusion

We have suggested that there is an emerging consensus in the field of local economic development that consists of a number of factors: firstly, the major carriers of local economic development will be FDI, privatization and small firms; secondly, that a local infrastructure consisting of, *inter alia*, local governance institutions and trained workforce are necessary to attract and retain FDI; and thirdly, that those local governance structures must be based on a variety of local microcorporatism that can ameliorate the worst tendencies of competition by promoting co-operation at a regional level.

For institutionalists in the flexible specialization school, historical evidence, it is argued, demonstrates that evolving national industrial orders have influenced the technological and organizational competencies of both small and large firms (Lane 1991). Support systems can be provided by the state, both local and national, and societies can be classified by whether they possess densely organized institutional structures (Germany) or whether they were institutionally impoverished (Britain). The important point is that the support system can be constructed, and it is argued that the German social-institutional framework has been conducive to the creation of a particularly strong and self-reliant sector of SMEs with favourable access to the factors of production (Lane 1991: 522). Such a structure can also act as a countervailing force to the power of incoming FDI.

The prescription is being applied to Poland, with Johnson and Loveman (1993) suggesting that the choice is between the German and the US/UK models. The US/UK model allows SMEs to compete on the basis of who pays least, resulting in low cost, standardized products (the low road), rather than competing on the basis of the more highly skilled, higher paid labour and higher quality more specialized products (the high road). The dilemma for Poland is how to balance the need for employment and output growth with a desire for SMEs to follow the high road strategy.

However, we suggest that the position is not as straightforward as this. We have already presented evidence that all three central pillars of the restructuring process – FDI, SMEs and privatization – are causing problems for Solidarity. In the following chapters we will examine in more detail how the restructuring of large workplaces, and the re-emergence of SMEs reveal a reality that departs significantly from the myths of the new localism. We can, however, already see that for the majority of Krakow's working population the central pillars of the restructuring process hold out little hope for significant improvements in their standard of living. The problem goes deeper even than this. Bootstraps and flexible specialization amount, in effect, to little more than variants on a theme of 'place marketing' as local economic development, aimed at securing elements of mobile capital, usually parts of TNCs. The region then becomes subordinated to the demands of TNCs, reshaping itself in a vicious beauty contest that amounts to little more than dog-eat-dog competition with other equally desperate regions.

Krakow itself may be relatively privileged in terms of the regional development dog-fight between Polish regions. However, Polish regions are now increasingly drawn into competition with regions across Europe. In that context Krakow remains on the periphery of European urban hierarchies within which there has been a growing divergence between core and periphery since the mid-1980s in favour of the core regions of London, Paris, Brussels, Amsterdam, Cologne, Frankfurt, Munich and Milan (Budd 1995).

If we pull together the strands of the argument so far, it is clear that strategic decisions about location, production, process and product mix will increasingly be made and co-ordinated at the centre of a small number of ever larger organizations. Production location, by contrast, will be decentralized, but in units that are increasingly monitored and controlled from the centre (Harrison 1989). The implications for small firms are that they will exist largely in the dependent, dominated or isolated elements of our typology. There is little that local government can do to control TNCs. They can take part in the dog-eat-dog competition to attract FDI, but control is a myth. Equally, promotion of SMEs in these circumstances will not result in the Utopian delusions of the industrial districts, but rather the reality of the sweatshop economy.

We do not question the fact that small firms will emerge in significant numbers in regions such as Krakow, fundamentally altering the size distribution of local economic structures. However, the majority of new SME owner/managers will be reluctant entrepreneurs, press-ganged into the ranks of small firm formation by poverty, redundancy and unemployment. These same forces will dictate that most new SMEs will be in sectors with low barriers to entry, and extremely high death rates. Most will be in the service sector, competition for the business provided by a population sinking ever deeper into poverty. Competition will be based on hyper self-exploitation. The experience of SMEs in other depressed areas in the West is that little can be done at the local level to prevent this. The new localism will simply usher in old fashioned poverty.

8 From the Lenin Steelworks to Lean Production

Catch a tram out of the centre of Krakow heading east towards the Huta Tadeusz Sendzimira steelworks (HTS) and the landscape changes swiftly and dramatically. From the polluted beauty of the town centre through the solid, stone built if unexciting older suburbs the architecture transforms into a serid ranks of tower blocks. These are the first indications of Nowa Huta. The tower blocks are thirty to forty years old, soulless and showing exactly the same signs of decrepitude as their counterparts in any rundown new town development in the UK. The monotony is now punctuated by the occasional fast food outlet such as Pizza Hut. Eventually you arrive at the centre of the new town, a circular tram interchange surrounded by four-storey blocks of flats, built over the top of shops. Sweeping round, you pass a new 'post modern' orange, blue and white office block and turn eventually into a long avenue, absolutely undeviating, which drags your eye towards a monumental collection of buildings at the end of the road. This is the entrance to the former Lenin Steelworks, now renamed 'Huta T. Sendzimira' (HTS), and the new name is displayed on an enormous sign dominating the entrance. The long avenue is now called ul. Solidarnosc and brings to mind the photographs pinned on the wall outside Solidarity's offices. These are pictures of steelworkers, taken in the early 1980s, fighting running battles with the military and the police along the length of the avenue.

The entrance is dominated by two mock castle-like structures standing on either side of the road and containing the management's offices and union premises. Inside, huge, wide winding staircases in shabby 1950s decor lead you to badly lit corridors, with threadbare carpets. Outside one, the offices of Solidarity 80, you find photographs of the hunger strike of the early 1990s. Having collected our guide, a retired steelworker, and clutching our special passes we cram into our hire car, a tiny Polon. We need a car because HTS covers twenty square kilometres. The guard on the entrance looks slightly bemused at our approach, tells us that photographs are forbidden and expresses surprise that 'distinguished visitors' should be crushed into such a small car.

The site is enormous and is populated by a whole series of derelict or semi-derelict buildings. The precipitate decline in output and the imminent arrival of the continuous casting process has left most of the former buildings redundant and the land polluted and unused. Drive past yet another massive building containing only broken windows and we stop beside the oven-like structures that defrost the train loads of coal that arrive frozen solid in the depths of the Polish winter. Up an iron staircase and into a building belching steam and smoke, we walk round a gantry encircling a scene from a lunar landscape. Men in incomplete sets of protective clothing are clearing a channel through sand. At that moment, the furnace is opened and molten steel cascades down the channels and into the giant vats lined up on a train on the level below. The men in the protective suits stand aside, letting the molten metal flow, clearing the way through. A thin haze of metallic dust catches the light from the molten metal as the winter sun pours through the broken windows. A little while later, and in another building, we cram ourselves, our guide, translator and taxi driver into a small control booth. Two buttons are pressed and oxygen floods into the convertor. A steel plant is instantly converted into the gates of hell. Just before we leave, we are taken up into one of the control rooms overlooking the furnaces. Dials monitoring temperature and content line the wall, and there is a fairly primitive computer screen on a table in the middle of the room. We are asked how modern we think the plant is, and how it compares to the British steel industry. We avoid the question.

Huta Sendzimira dominates the local economy in a way that reflects far more than simply its size. In the 1980s it was not only the largest steel works in Poland, it had the highest paid workers (Kennedy 1991) who were of central importance to the activities of Solidarity. Although there have been some reductions in the workforce, the large-scale running down of the plant is a highly politically sensitive issue. Although Krakow has a relatively low level of unemployment (8.1 per cent in June 1993, compared to a national average of 14.6 per cent), this may reflect as much the impossibility of rapidly and radically restructuring HTS as any particular vibrancy in the local economy. Some estimates have put the degree of dependency at enormous levels, suggesting that around a quarter of a million people rely, directly or indirectly, for their employment on the steelworks. It is not surprising then to find that plans for restructuring the works have concentrated on issues of re-deployment, and have been handled with a degree of delicacy. As of 1994, it was generally accepted that 7000 to 8000 jobs were surplus to requirements.

Until 1989 steel production in Central and Eastern Europe was substantially insulated from the rapid changes that had taken place in the world market in the post-1974 period. These changes were charac-terized by significant shifts in the global distribution of steel consump-tion, production and trade, coupled with, and in part driven by, changes in technology and competition. More than any other industry the steel industry has epitomized the often painful process of re-structuring that has been experienced within industries in Western Europe over the past couple of decades. Therefore, in order to under-stand the problems and possibilities of restructuring the Polish steel industry and in particular HTS, it is necessary to understand develop-ments in the global steel industry.

Global Restructuring of Steel

Hudson (1992) suggests that it is erroneous to perceive steel-making as a technologically obsolete 'smokestack industry' and points to consider-able technological changes that have taken place. Although he high-lights innovation in the production of small batch, special steel produc-tion, technological innovations in electric arc furnaces and 'mini mills' as an alternative route to cheaper ordinary steel, the biggest and most significant changes have been in the bulk production of ordinary steel. The introduction of basic oxygen steelmaking in the 1950s revolution-ized bulk steel-making, reducing the labour time to convert iron to steel from eight hours to forty-five minutes. By 1974 over 60 per cent of European crude steel was already produced via the basic oxygen route and by the end of the decade had virtually displaced open hearth and other bulk steel-making technologies. The introduction of continuous casting (concast) techniques, eliminating the need to cast semi-finished steel as ingots, greatly increased efficiency cutting costs by up to £20 per tonne. This was achieved through the reduction of energy inputs by avoiding the need to reheat steel prior to the rolling stage. Continuous casting expanded rapidly from the early 1970s so that by the mid-1980s 75 per cent of steel was produced in this way. At the heavy end there has been a growing use of computer control systems and increasing automation in rolling mills, allowing more precise specification of standards, quality control, fuller use of capacity and a reduction in wastage and production costs.

From the mid-1970s, production declined significantly in Western Europe and North America, though less so in Japan, but grew markedly in the Newly Industrialized Countries (NICs) of South East Asia. By the mid-1980s an estimated overcapacity of about 30 per cent on the world markets led to fierce competition for markets in countries which did not produce steel and were net importers. Competition centring on bulk produced low value added ordinary steels had two effects: firstly, an increase in covert or overt protectionism; and secondly, price competition, which resulted in prices falling by an average of 30 per cent in Europe between 1989 and 1992 (Hudson 1992). Competition manifested itself differently in the market for high value added special alloy steel with increased emphasis on quality rather than price. Much of the decline in Western production can be traced directly to falling consumption by bulk ordinary steel consuming industries. However, decline in the demand for steel is also due to technological changes within industry leading to a lower demand for steel for a given volume of output.

There have been a number of strategies pursued to deal with the new competition and changing global circumstances. Firstly, cutting back on capacity, output and employment has involved the closure of older technologically backward capacity at long-established inland sites. However, such has been the intensity of competition that not even the coastal or quasi coastal locations have been immune from the pressures of capacity cutbacks. Secondly, firms have aimed to reposition themselves in the market in a number of ways, for example by moving out of lower value ordinary steel production to the production of high value added special steels. Thirdly, selective mergers have taken place on two fronts. This strategy has been aimed at centralizing capital in order to realize scale economies in production and creating local monopolies in particular products or segments of the market. Hudson (1992) points to examples of mergers involving companies abandoning some products areas in return for a greater share of the market in others, with a view not simply to producing national monopolies but also to becoming internationally competitive producers. In addition, the search for international competitiveness has extended to cross border mergers, though these have usually involved small or medium-sized acquisitions relating to the finishing capacity of special steels. A strategy of particular importance that many companies have pursued is vertical integration by extending their operations downstream into distribution by purchasing steel stockists both within their national market and internationally.

The market has not been left to restructure the steel industry. The way in which steel within Europe remains intensely sensitive to political influence, with state involvement evident at a variety of levels, is most obviously the case where steel companies are nationalized or in public ownership. However, state influence extends to private sector producers who have, to a lesser extent experienced pressures through having to work within a national framework. Until 1988 the steel industry in Europe was truly a 'command industry' based on domestic production quotas and protected by strictly binding trade barriers. Exports of steel from Central and Eastern Europe were subject to quotas and basic minimum prices which kept their share of the market to 3 per cent of steel consumption in the European Union (EU) (Messerlin 1995). Despite the rhetoric of trade liberalization and a more market orientated approach between 1988 and 1992, quotas on steel remained firmly in place although at increased levels.

The Association Agreements between Poland (with Hungary, the Czech and Slovak Republics) and the EU were originally intended to eliminate quotas and state protection and were based, in theory, on moderate and declining tariffs. In reality this trade liberalization was short lived lasting only from March 1992 to August of the same year, since when a whole range of protective measures have been introduced as a result of lobbying by European steel producers in response to the increase in steel imports from Central and Eastern Europe, which reached 4 per cent of the market. Protective measure included anti-dumping duties, automatic surveillance of a long list of steel products, quotas and minimum prices. Steel imports to the EU subject to regular tariffs are limited, with additional tariffs of between 25 and 30 per cent according to product. This has serious implications for Poland in developing and expanding markets in the EU. As far as steel production in the economies of the EU is concerned (with the possible exception of the UK) the market and trade liberalization have their limitations and protection and managed trade are the order of the day.

Restructuring, efficiency and technological progress have neutral or positive connotations in conventional economics and these words are often used to suggest the inexorable march of progress. As Hudson (1992: 11) spells out, however, under capitalism the outcomes and consequences of restructuring are that tens of thousands of jobs have been lost, entire works closed and communities decimated across Europe as the economic rationale of these places is dissipated: 'In sum, "old" industrial regions aren't so much becoming "new industrial" regions as locations that are marginal to the main currents of the accumulation process, their residents literally redundant and marginalised as a consequence, part of a surplus population that is dependent on the state transfers for its survival.' It is important to bear this in mind when we turn to examine and discuss how the Polish steel industry, and in particular HTS, is going to fit into this emerging pattern of international production.

The Steel Industry in Poland

Poland is, therefore, seeking to integrate with a global market where there is a continuous drive to seek competitive advantage via technological innovation and the introduction of new production techniques. In short, falling output, growing overcapacity and mounting financial losses have intensified competition between steel producers and companies in Europe in the context of increasingly competitive world markets especially for bulk steel. From the mid-1970s onwards we have witnessed competitive restructuring in which nation states were often visibly involved and into which the supranational European Union was seemingly inexorably drawn. Companies were striving for competitive advantage via changes in what they produced, how they produced it, and where they produced it.

Poland's attempt, via the Balcerowicz Programme (1990), to jump to the market resulted in an immediate and sharp fall in the overall level of economic activity, with a disproportionately large fall in the level of industrial output which had particularly severe repercussions for the steel industry. Steel consumption fell even faster than the average level of industrial output due largely to the fact that heavy engineering and machine building had been the most severely affected industrial sectors, along with steel consuming industries such as armaments.

In 1989 the steel industry in Poland comprised 26 mills with a capacity of 15 million tons annually. In 1992 a restructuring strategy for the Polish steel industry, designed by Canadian consultants, was adopted. This proposed a 40 per cent reduction in capacity including the liquidation of all or part of eight mills and departments. The estimated cost of the restructuring was $4.45 billion over the ten year period for financial restructuring, new investments, environmental protection and 'employment reduction schemes'. Most of these funds were to come from internal or private financial sources, although for 1994 the government agreed to provide up to $90 million in loan guarantees for three mills. A major part was spent on the liquidation of obsolete open-hearth furnaces and broad implementation of continuous casting technology. As part of the restructuring, those steel mills already commercialized will be transformed into joint stock companies, but there are no short-term plans for full privatization. The process was to be managed by a co-ordinating council, which would include representatives from the relevant ministries and regions, led by the ministry of industry. The restructuring of the industry was expected to result in a decrease of employment by 80 000 jobs to 43 000 workers. Only about half of this change would result in net job loss, as the rest is associated with spinning off non-core operations and associated social, cultural and educational institutions.

The three largest steel plants are Huta Katowice, HTS at Krakow and Huta Warszawa with a small number of special steel producers. The steel plant at Katowice makes long products and HTS makes mainly flat products and tubes. Overall capacity utilization (somewhere between 40 and 60 per cent) is low. An accurate assessment of costs is difficult as little hard information is available and costs are in any case changing rapidly as input prices are adjusted. Some general points, however, can be made. The cost of producing steel in Poland is generally lower than in its Western counterparts, with the source of this comparative advantage lying specifically in low wages and not productivity. For example, it takes HTS fourteen labour hours to produce one ton of steel compared with the EU average of four. Thus the steel industry in Poland (and other Central and Eastern Europe economies) started restructuring with a number of problems. Other than the advantage of low labour costs, the Polish steel industry was manifestly inefficient in terms of productivity with high unit consumption of ferrous metals due to obsolete and inadequately maintained equipment and poor quality iron ore producing high levels of pollution.

Restructuring HTS

HTS is a full cycle steel works with coking plants, sintering plant, blast furnaces, and hot and cold rolling mills and is the only producer of hot rolled steel, cold rolled sheet zinc and tinned sheet in Poland. It has a virtual domestic monopoly in these products and is protected from international competition by the existence of customs duties likely to be in place until the end of the 1990s. Technical conditions vary with recently installed modern machines such as a modern electrolytic coating plant alongside obsolete installations dating back to the 1950s. This is illustrated by the age of the works' machinery. In 1983 56 per cent of the machinery dated from between 1951 and 1960, 33 per cent from between 1961 and 1970, and 11 per cent from between 1971 and 1980. Some 27 per cent of the operations in the works were described as manual, 65 per cent as mechanical, 5.8 per cent as partially automated and only 1.8 per cent as fully automated (Ryder 1992). The problems of the company were exacerbated by the pressure to increase output. Although they were designed to produce only 5.5 million tonnes, at their peak, the works were producing 6.8 million tonnes of steel annually. They were also hampered by shortages of labour, domestic and imported materials, a lack of transport, poor labour productivity, high turnover and high absenteeism. Thus in 1989 HTS exhibited all the problems faced by the Polish steel industry, such as obsolete methods, high energy usage and pollution. Furthermore, sales were generally inefficient with orders taken long before they were realized and deliveries usually overdue.

The initial restructuring proposal was the result of a study carried out by a Canadian consortium in 1992 which recommended combining the HTS and Katowice steelworks. It was proposed that concast slabs would be taken from Katowice and rolled at HTS, until such time as a rolling facility could be built at Katowice. In effect, this would have meant the almost complete, though gradual, closure of HTS. The consultants proposal came in the middle of a policy hiatus at a national level, a situation which was exacerbated by the fact that the two plants were the responsibility of different ministries. Strong opposition from within HTS ensured that this proposal was never implemented.

The next stage in the restructuring process came in 1992 when the HTS became a state treasury company leading to the dissolution of the workers' council. The preliminary stage of restructuring involved the building of a new continuous casting process which was designed to come on stream in 1996 and produce 2.05 million tonnes of steel per annum. This has been financed by supplier credit supported by a government guaranteed loan. The second element was to spin off sections of the previously highly vertically integrated plant into quasi independent units, which were to be sponsored to 'independence' by the parent company, HTS. Examples have included the majority of the former welfare function (catering and hotels, for example) as well as design units and scrap reprocessing functions.

Although modernization and rationalization were under way the most difficult issue relating to restructuring had yet to be confronted. Modernization, a process which would move the technical process closer to that of HTS's Western counterparts, was located within the context of a debt-ridden state owned enterprise (SOE) with wide ranging social commitments. It was symptomatic of the scale of the problem facing the locality that HTS has a full-time 'Know How' funded UK consultant, based in the plant, working with the new strategic management department, focusing almost entirely on these issues. The dilemma faced by the Western consultant was how to 'downsize' the workforce, concentrate on the profitable core concast operation, and shed the social and welfare commitments in the face of workforce opposition to job loss. An earlier Know How scheme to retrain displaced workers proved to be unworkable because the unions would not accept the idea of redundancy.

As we have already seen, employment in the works has declined from a high of around 40 000 to approximately 17 000 in 1994. Although there had been early retirement programmes since 1989, there had been no compulsory redundancies. The vast majority of the reduction in employment has been achieved by spinning of non-core functions, but with an average workforce age of 39 years there is little further scope for early retirement.

The process of restructuring has involved attempting to change management style and practice. In the same way that HTS is being advised to divest itself of its social and welfare function, so management were encouraged to become more cost conscious, and divest themselves of any lingering notion that HTS was anything other than a profit driven entity. Management were trained in methods of identifying, analysing and controlling costs within departments, and the senior management team were encouraged to produce a mission statement for the new company, more fitting with its new lean outlook. This had been an only partially successful experiment, insofar as managers had become more cost conscious, but the emerging mission statement still carried echoes of HTS's commitment to the region, not only in terms of the provision of jobs but also of welfare.

The restructuring package eventually accepted appeared to be an attempt to construct not only a lean core production unit, but also a means whereby workforce concerns with redundancy could appear to be addressed. Pacifying the workforce by deflecting concerns about job loss was an essential element of the programme. The core operation with the continuous casting facility would become lean and profitable and, most importantly, a separate company. In essence, the remainder of HTS would remain as a shell organization with all the liabilities and debts of the old HTS. Debtors would be offered shares in the new core enterprise, HTS SA, which would eventually employ only 10 000 workers and would be involved with the continuous casting process. The new company would be more flexible in its structure and management style and, therefore, more able to search for foreign partners. Job creation schemes would be set in process to employ 'surplus' workers with the suggestion that HTS's redundant land and buildings could be used to attract inward investment. The spin offs would remain associated with the old HTS, as does the new East Krakow Development Agency, set up to encourage small firm formation amongst the soon to be redundant HTS workforce. We now examine each of these elements of restructuring in turn: firstly, the spinoffs; and secondly, the prospects for the plethora of agencies engaged in job creation.

In Orbit: The Spinoffs

On the surface at least then, there are superficial similarities to the

Table 8.1 *HTS Spinoffs, 1994*

Enterprise	Activity	Employment	HTS shareholding
Belmer	Maintenance and repair	1000	49%
Hutpus	Social service	750	49.5%
Metal Odlew	Foundry	330	45%
PMO	Production of refractories	1000	49%
PTS	Road transport	550	49%
ZD-Project	Design	150 +50 part-time	–
Zlomex	Scrap processing	200	40%

Source: HTS (1994)

vertical disintegration hypothesis, with the added bonus that, by definition, the spinoffs will be local. Indeed examination of the firm's strategy
indicates that restructuring and privatization are designed to transform
the large, complex company into a holding of smaller, more flexible
and competitive ones. Table 8.1 contains details of seven spinoffs,
although there are around twenty in total. HTS's share in the companies ranges from nearly 50 per cent in the major, direct spinoffs to
less than 1 per cent in the new East Krakow Development Agency.
Although there have been spin offs from the steelworks, in no sense can
any of them be described as small firms, and the problems are even
more deeply rooted than this would suggest. In order, to investigate
how far vertical disintegration can be equated with competitiveness and
flexibility we examine in detail the experience of two of the spinoffs.

Hutpus was formerly responsible for some of the social functions of HTS, specifically catering and holiday houses. The company is now converting five holiday houses to tourist hotels located in some of the most attractive parts of the mountain regions of Southern Poland. The company also provides 13 000 meals a day to HTS workers, prepared at a central catering facility. The organization employed 750 workers in 1994. Belmer covers a wide range of services including construction, mechanical engineering and the installation and maintenance of electrical and chemical installations, and had over 1000 employees in 1994.

Both firms were spun off in 1993, under a process which was described to us as 'a kind of privatization' and now they both appear in the statistics as independent private sector organizations. Like most of the spinoffs, Hutpus and Belmer are organizationally ambiguous. In both companies HTS had retained 49 per cent of the share issue, with 51 per cent going to the workforce. Both Belmer and Hutpus have similar management structures with a board of management, half of whose members were nominated by HTS. The Director of HTS appoints the chief of the board that determines the strategic direction of the company, leaving the managers in charge of operational concerns. In Hutpus six hundred workers had taken up share options and in Belmer employees bought over 90 per cent of the share allocation, in bundles of five shares. Different views emerged as to the merits of the arrangement. The new management at Hutpus argued that fragmented ownership meant that the shareholders had no influence on strategic decision-making. But the management of Belmer were more positive about the changes that had taken place, arguing that the new management board now had more freedom than in the past, and in particular no longer had to consult with the HTS management board. Furthermore, worker share ownership, they argued, meant increased commitment on behalf of employees, for example in monitoring use of raw materials.

Early in 1994 all the assets and real estate in both companies remained owned by and leased from HTS. A major preoccupation with the managers we interviewed was to own and therefore control the assets themselves. Neither company had the capital with which to buy its own assets and the possibility of buying out the leases was further restricted by the lack of a capital base amongst small shareholders. Furthermore, high interest rates ruled out the possibility of borrowing from banks. Belmer recognized that the capital required to buy out the leases would be enormous and therefore had a strategy to buy it incrementally over a period of five to ten years. Both companies referred to the necessity of finding a strategic investor, in the case of Hutpus to update production and in the case of Belmer to develop new products. On the other hand there are firms such as ABB stalking these firms with the prospect of cherry picking the most efficient and profitable divisions.

However, questions of dependency go far beyond simple issues of share ownership and advisory board appointees. In 1994, Hutpus provided 13 000 meals a day to HTS employees and their families. Each HTS worker was allowed to claim meals for immediate family members on a regular basis. However, this seemingly captive market could come under threat from two different directions: firstly, the number of people employed at the plant is set to decline by a further 7000 in the next few years, and whilst it may continue to provide meals for employees, there is no guarantee that that HTS will continue to extend this provision to family members; and secondly, HTS currently subsidizes the price of a meal to the extent of 60 per cent of cost. Any reduction in this subsidy would probably have a detrimental effect on demand for meals and, under these circumstances it is hardly surprising that the company is seeking out markets beyond HTS.

One of the major problems perceived by Hutpus in pursuing this strategy was the cost of investment in new technology deemed necessary in order that meals could be served at a competitive price. The company was not envisaging using cook-chill technology, still intending to serve warm meals, and therefore saw a market restricted to a 100 km radius around Krakow. However, even this level of technological development, it was suggested, would require investment that ran into millions of dollars. Similar problems are faced in terms of developing the hotel sector. Hutpus now leases five large hotels from HTS, and the capital necessary to buy out the leases would be enormous. The hotels also have a problem of market placement, in that management see the hotels as being in the low to middle class range and thus unable to compete with chains such as Orbis. Continued concentration on the HTS market has also meant that Hutpus has failed to develop connections with the main tourist agencies in the same way that Orbis, Granada and the Holiday Inns have, with the result that market surveys suggest that, even in Poland, there was little knowledge of the existence of Hutpus.

In general, the question of labour costs was causing problems. Although productivity growth had been below the level of wage rises, wage levels at the point of transition had been below the legal minima, although counterbalanced to some degree by subsidies for services such as catering. If subsidies are to be abolished, then wages would have to rise above the minimum level. Hutpus still employed the same number of people, and management argued, about seventy people (around 10 per cent of the workforce) would have to be sacked to bring productivity up to acceptable levels. However, this would not be easy because of social pressures and redundancy costs (three months wages). In the tourist section of Hutpus, wages and salaries accounted for over 40 per cent of all costs. Furthermore, working patterns were very different from the private sector. Private companies, it was argued, only opened during the season and only hired workers for the duration of the season, whereas Hutpus was open all year round and employed permanent full-time employees. Therefore, there was increasing pressure not only to reduce the company headcount, but also to introduce seasonal, and perhaps part-time, working.

Belmer appeared to have more potential for diversifying into new markets. Employment levels had increased by 25 per cent since the new company started as a result of bidding for new work outside of HTS rather than a growth of work from the steelworks itself. In general, there was an attempt to break the links with HTS, with a new marketing branch to be physically located off site. However, for the time being at least the rest of the plant would have to stay physically within HTS. Belmer saw its current strength and future development being based on the size and diversity of the organization and was planning to divide the company into divisions which would concentrate on specialist areas. The strength in diversity was seen to be the ability to provide work across branches, as a successful bid in one area was likely to provide work in related fields, thereby enhancing their ability to win contracts by offering a complete range of services. This was in contrast to their competitors, who, particularly in the construction field, were smaller and more specialized.

It is clear then, that the relationship is between one very large firm and several other large to medium firms. If small firms are to fit into this picture, it will be once again as junior partners in the supply chain, if the spinoffs ever reach the stage of developing their own buyer-supplier relations. Although relinquishing formal control, to a greater or lesser degree all the units are dependent on HTS in a number of ways. Firstly, in terms of ownership, the spinoffs are joint stock companies where HTS holds between 40 per cent and 50 per cent of the stock, and the remainder is owned by employees. They are then dependent on HTS in a very real sense and HTS has been known to take advantage of its seniority in this relationship. For example, some of the spinoffs were involved in taking HTS to court in an attempt to get it declared technically bankrupt as part of a desperate strategy to get the company to pay bills that were overdue. Degrees of dominance range from some firms who were completely dependent on HTS to others who had had a significant part of their market outside. As we have seen the possibilities for diversification either in terms of product or market are limited, but not impossible. However, although the terms of the leasing arrangements makes further borrowing to aid restructuring problematic, 'successful' spinoffs may have the option of ploughing back profits into purchasing plant machinery and real estate. For the foreseeable future these firms are inextricably linked to the steelworks. In the medium to long term, their health and vitality will depend on the continued existence of HTS or the ability to diversify in terms of markets or products.

HTS, Small Firms and the East Krakow Development Agency

We have already argued that a major problem for HTS management was what to do with the workers who would be 'surplus to requirements'. The plant employed 17 000 people in 1994, but that figure was expected to fall to around 10 000 by the turn of the century. Solidarity expected about 4000 people to take early retirement or permanent sick leave, but that would still leave 3000 people as potential candidates for redundancy. Others have suggested that around 70 per cent of the 7000 would be forced to leave involuntarily, although the union has no objection to those workers leaving the steelworks. In fact, with the active encouragement of both management and Solidarity, workers leaving the steel plant will be shepherded in the direction of setting up their own small firms. The new East Krakow Development Agency had been set up precisely for this purpose, and within HTS a small number of prototypical small firms had been set up, targeted at sectors related to the steel industry, for example construction. The importance of these organizations lies not in their numbers nor indeed in the number of jobs created, but rather in the crucial importance of a demonstration effect, generating the idea that ex-HTS employees can set up successful small firms.

Within the plant itself, pilot projects have been created employing between thirty and fifty people, working in areas related to the steel industry such as mine roofing systems, and building products. The importance of the projects was to show that spunoff small firms could succeed, to take away what management described as the fear factor. More important in this respect was the East Krakow Development Agency, a joint venture set up in conjunction with Krakow itself and the voivode, designed to create new businesses in what was described as a special economic zone. According to senior strategic managers in HTS, the purpose of the development agency was two fold: firstly, to create new small firms on the basis of the strengths and assets of HTS and its employees; and secondly, to create firms that would act as subcontractors demolishing or reconstructing the HTS site.

However, interviewed in 1994, the manager of the newly formed agency had a slightly different view of the function of the organization. The purpose of the agency was seen to be two fold: firstly, to utilize redundant premises, property and land; and secondly, the creation of new jobs. However, for the agency management, small firms were not considered to be part of the agenda, especially not ones formed by ex-members of HTS workforce. Echoing the HTS management's complaint that there was no government financial support for restructuring, the agency had been told not to expect any government funds to aid its development. It would have to rely on the voivode and Krakow, but principally on HTS itself.

The development agency's strategy had two elements: firstly, the development of an industrial park for job creation; and secondly, investment, to get large redundant buildings converted into storage or warehouse facilities. The industrial park would require eighteen months work to get land flattened and ready for development. The park would provide administrative support in a central facility, but incoming business would be expected to build their own factories or workshops. Neither HTS nor the voivode could provide grant aid for redundant steelworkers and the banks would not lend on the basis of steelworkers low wages, therefore the only job prospects for redundant steelworkers would be in companies set up by someone else. The converted large buildings were specifically not aimed at SMEs, rather they were aimed at trading companies requiring large warehousing space, such as construction companies.

Desperately Seeking Polish Capitalism

The management concerned with the strategic planning of the organization have seen union support for the restructuring plans as crucial, this concern having been heightened by the poor industrial relations at the steel works at Warszawa Lucchini which led to several weeks of strike action in 1994. Management of HTS have been largely successful, in so far as none of the three unions opposed the general thrust of restructuring, viewing it as something of an inevitability and recognizing that the works based on old technology would go bankrupt without modernization. However, the attitudes of the three unions in HTS are slightly at variance and are revealing in their difference.

Organized labour within the plant reflects many of the problems that face union organization at a national level. This is manifested in particular in attitudes towards restructuring of the plant itself, and the relationships between Solidarity, Solidarity 80 (the radical offshoot) and the OPZZ (official federation) affiliated union within the plant. Solidarity claimed to have 6500 members, OPZZ claim 4100 though this figure rises to 6500 if retired members and union members in the spin offs are included. Solidarity 80 claimed to have about 500 members, though they were, it was claimed, mainly in strategic positions where industrial action would quickly paralyse the operation of the steel works. This left roughly a third of the workers in the plant being members of no union at all.

Solidarity's representatives in HTS viewed their central role as changing people's attitude to restructuring, suggesting that workers would not readily accept the tough message of restructuring coming from management. This is hardly surprising given that, in the past, workers had no commitment to or involvement in the plant. The hangover is, according to the union (Solidarity) leadership in the steel works, that people did not care about the condition of the works in the past, and even now many people did not understand the implications of the fact that the works could be threatened with bankruptcy. If attitudes were to change, workers would be more receptive if the message came from Solidarity. The process of restructuring would appear to be fairer and more just than if the message came from management. As a consequence, the union became actively involved in setting up courses for its members which were quite specifically designed to change the way that people viewed restructuring. These dealt with the economics of the free market in general, and more specifically the union ran courses in management for people who wanted to leave the steelworks and set up their own firms. Solidarity has no objections to people leaving the works. The attitude of the union leadership was that the work in the plant was hard and pay was not high, furthermore 7000 jobs have to be lost; therefore, if workers wished to leave voluntarily, the union had no objection.

Solidarity in the steelworks had not opposed the spinoffs, indeed they had been involved in setting up two of them. Solhut and Statbusiness, which dealt with renovating the works and marketing. The spinoffs were seen to be important not just as a source of employment but also as a means of changing workers, attitudes towards restructuring. The Solidarity president argued that because the workers had shares in the new companies, a stake in ownership resulted in a relatively rapid change in attitudes. The problem, however, lay with those those workers who remained employed in the core business. Because these workers still had jobs, union officers claimed that it was difficult to convince them of the necessity of change. Workers did not want to consider privatization because, it was suggested, they knew that the process would necessitate redundancy and they were afraid of losing their jobs. Equally there had been antagonism initially to the idea of foreign investment, though this had declined as the realization had dawned that there was no alternative.

Historically, of course, there have been bitter differences between Solidarity and the unions that fall under the OPZZ banner, and there are still grievances emanating from the confiscation of Solidarity property which was passed over to OPZZ during martial law in the early 1980s. It was still the case, as one of the OPZZ vice presidents in the works made clear, that it was difficult for the unions to reach a consensus before negotiating with management. Despite the fact that all the programmes of the unions were very similar, and some attempts by the unions to work together, generally they negotiated separately. OPZZ argued that, for them, the situation had been particularly difficult under the Solidarity dominated governments, and the union had sent many delegations to Warsaw to talk to ministers, but after the election in 1993 of a new government led by the former communist party the union was not active any more in fighting with the government. This is not surprising, given that the union president and one other member had both been elected as MPs.

The OPZZ approach to restructuring the works was very similar to that of Solidarity, in that they supported the plan, but acknowledged that the union had not been particularly involved in the process of developing it. The only obvious point of departure from the Solidarity line was opposition to the spinoff of social and welfare functions into a quasi independent unit, based on the claim that, once spun off, services such as canteen meals became very expensive for workers. Opposition may also have something to do with the fact that the union's membership was concentrated in social and welfare services. Furthermore, the union's propaganda proclaimed itself as being left-wing, the point of departure from Solidarity, and this appeared to mean supporting claims for free social services. Again, the union saw its role as convincing its members of the necessity of restructuring and the demonstration effect, like Solidarity, included setting up and taking shares in spinoffs. The union had been active in setting up two joint stock companies dealing with scrap from the plant. The rationale behind this was job creation to alleviate workers fear of unemployment arising from restructuring. However, the organizational and attitudinal legacy of its past revealed itself in the union's attitude towards its own members and their fear of job loss. The vice-president of OPZZ in HTS argued that there was little awareness of the threat of unemployment amongst the workforce, though there was amongst the union leadership, largely because the leaders did not tell the workers what the full implications would be, in an attempt, as they saw it, to protect the workers.

Both OPZZ and Solidarity in HTS described Solidarity 80 as very small and very loud, as well as impossible to co-operate with. Solidarity 80 retaliated by suggesting that neither of the other two unions were actually real trade unions. In fact officers of Solidarity 80 argued that there were three directors of the steel works, these being the official director and the leaders of Solidarity and OPZZ. OPZZ is viewed simply as a remodelled version of the communist unions whose only task was to transfer management's ideas to the workers. This was evidenced, it was argued by Solidarity 80 officers, by the action of the OPZZ MPs in the new government, who had supported the continuation of Popiwek (incomes policy) despite the fact that this in effect held down wages whilst the price of basic goods increased. Furthermore, both OPZZ and Solidarity were viewed as being compromised by their share ownership in the spinoffs, in that this type of involvement meant that they could not properly represent workers. Solidarity 80 claimed that they were the only union not financially dependent on HTS. They produced a bulletin intermittently for their members when finances permitted, whereas Solidarity, they claimed, produced a weekly bulletin financed by HTS.

Solidarity 80 had emerged in the plant in 1991, growing out of industrial action organized against the threatened closure of the plant. Arguing that Huta Katowice was being favoured against Huta Sendzimira for purely political reasons, despite government promises that restructuring would take place on purely economic criteria, a small number of Solidarity 80 members initiated a hunger strike. Starting two days before Christmas in 1991 with four people, the action quickly escalated drawing on support from other parts of the steel works as well as from other companies all over Poland. Whilst many members from other unions supported the action on a personal basis, the other unions themselves in the plant supported the strike in what was described as a 'moral' way, providing no official support or solidarity.

In general, Solidarity 80 argued that it was radical, active in pay and labour disputes, whilst the other unions were much less willing to confront management. Furthermore, both Solidarity leaders from the 1980s and OPZZ members in recent times had become MPs, and it rapidly became clear that they were more interested in their own careers rather than defending the interests of union members. Rather than seeing themselves as a social movement, political party and quasi managerial trade union running courses on the market economy, Solidarity 80 argued that the role of the union should be concern with the day-to-day problems of workers. Radical though they may be, the union, however, does not oppose restructuring, and neither do they view loss of jobs as a real threat. Whilst it is acknowledged that new technology would lead to job loss, they are sanguine about the ability of the spinoffs to create jobs. The union had its own proposals for dealing with redundant steelworkers. Solidarity 80 suggested that many workers in HTS came from family farms in the small towns and villages that surround Krakow. The farms are so small that they cannot support a family; therefore, agriculture has to be combined with work in the HTS. The union suggested a voluntary redundancy package for these workers comprising a payment of twenty times their monthly salary which could be invested in their farms.

Into the Future

Although the restructuring of HTS bears superficial similarity to the reorganization of large firms postulated within the flexible specialization hypothesis, the reality is far removed from the myth of the new localism, though none the less important as far as implications for the locality are concerned. The concentration of HTS on a core process of continuous casting has involved a process of restructuring, which as late as 1995 had not involved any compulsory redundancies. The spinoffs had accounted for the bulk of the decline in core company headcount. This situation was set to change. Redundancies were now envisaged at the core operation and the setting up of the East Krakow Development Agency, as well as the demonstration projects within HTS, were recognition of this fact. However, there appeared to be a divergence between the rhetoric of SME development for redundant steel workers coming from company management and the reality of the strategy of the agency itself, which saw no place for such firms. If redundant steel workers are going to create SMEs then they are likely to be in the vulnerable and dependent end of our classification (see Chapter 7), closer to the flea market. More likely, redundancy will simply result in the short or medium term in unemployment.

The spinoffs themselves are faced with imminent restructuring. However, their freedom of manoeuvre is severely circumscribed, firstly by their continuing dependency on HTS, and secondly by their inability to access significant financial resources either through internal generation or external borrowing. It is impossible to predict the future for the spinoffs in general, largely because they are very different forms of organization operating in contrasting sectors; however, drawing on the examples of Hutpus and Belmer, a few tentative conclusions can be drawn.

For Hutpus, particularly in the hotel section, working relations are moving towards part-time and temporary contracts. Furthermore, jobs were being threatened by the search for increased productivity. Therefore, restructuring has implications not just for the number of jobs that will survive, but also for the nature of jobs that remain. For the catering section, the future of HTS is vital, but the drastic decline in the numbers to be employed have important implications for the future of Hutpus. Belmer shows that, in the short term at least, spinoffs may be a source of new employment but also that a limited ability to finance their own restructuring makes them vulnerable to predatory transnationals.

By 1996, the core concast operation will be largely comparable with its counterparts outside of Eastern and Central Europe improving both yield and efficiency in slab production. There are, however, a number of questions as to whether this will enable the new lean and streamlined company to compete on world markets or even maintain its position in the domestic economy, particularly as import protection will be gradually lifted by the end of the century. In the first place the modernization process is not complete and it is generally agreed that the hot rolling mill needs completely rebuilding. In addition, without major investment the plant will be unable to meet environmental regulations, even taking into consideration a fall in emission pollution. The plant is, therefore, dependent on the continuing tolerance of the authorities.

Government financial help is highly unlikely. Even if it were regarded as desirable, debt constraint would preclude government intervention on anything like the necessary scale. Thus the white knight on the horizon, as far as unions and management are concerned, is a foreign investor encouraged by the current progress who will invest the capital necessary to complete the modernization. An optimistic scenario might be that changes in the international division of labour will leave Western Europe as producers of high value added special steels and Poland (and other countries in Eastern and Central Europe) as producers of bulk ordinary steel. This does not seem to be a likely outcome. Current trends within Europe point to the consolidation of national steel industries' often underpinned by active state involvement, with limited forays across national boundaries. It may be that the large number of delegations from other European countries that have visited HTS are motivated more by a desire to size up the competition than any serious intention of investing. The fact that the steel industries of Central and Eastern Europe are regarded more as a threat than an opportunity is evidenced by the way in which intense competition and the relative success of these economies in exporting to the EU has resulted in a series of skirmishes on the question of dumping. Whilst the Association Agreements (1992) between the EU and Central and East European economies purported to open up trade, this did not extend to 'sensitive' areas such as steel which have been subject to quotas and anti-dumping duties.

Neither can it be assumed that an upturn in the Polish economy will revive the prospects of a flagging steel industry, in that growth has brought and will continue to bring about a structural shift from manufacturing to services. Furthermore, the experience of Europe is that any increase in growth manifests itself in technical and product innovation, with new investment promoting the rapid substitution of steel products and the development of less steel intensive products. In emphasizing the continual change in both the demand for and technology to produce steel Hudson (1992) suggests that there is no guarantee of profits in any one particular sector.

The implications for Krakow go far beyond the nature and number of jobs that remain in HTS itself and the spinoffs. The concentration of HTS on its core activity has implications for the social and welfare functions it previously provided. As these are spun off, or simply disappear, there are implications for employees of HTS and in particular their families. Operating on a commercial basis means that it is unlikely that Hutpus will continue to provide subsidized meals for extended family networks, nor indeed that HTS will continue to provide the subsidy. In general, the gmina have been charged with the responsibility of providing the functions previously delivered by organizations such as HTS. However, this is likely to be beyond their means. In effect social and welfare provision will be thrown back on to the family, either to be absorbed informally (for example, childcare and the provision of meals) or in a more commodified form, in that services will be privatized and then purchased on the market, with important and severe implications for women workers in particular.

The changes that restructuring is bringing about in working practices, and wider social relations, is creating a tension between Solidarity's role as an agent of restructuring and its function as a defender of workers' rights at workplace level. The problems faced by Solidarity in HTS are not specific to the plant or the region. With varying degrees of severity, the same situation has confronted most of the steel producing regions of Europe in the last two decades. The outcome, in most cases, of unions acting as collaborators with, rather than opposition to, the process of change, has been far from encouraging, as Hudson (1992: 11) points out:

> Whilst trades unions, steel workers and their communities in some cases initially resisted plant closures and job losses, opposition was uneven and unions and communities became active collaborators rather than resistors of the process of change. It then seemed that the only hope of some employment . . . was to compete with other steel works and communities. Those who lost out became deindustralised ex-steel towns, in turn the foci of state policy intended to attract new industries and jobs via competition in the place market for new firms and mobile investment. Typically such policies failed to produce their intended results, raising profound questions as to their futures as communities and places.

9 GLOBAL STRATEGIES, LOCAL FIRMS, WORKING LIVES

In this chapter we bring together the various elements of the analytical framework that we have developed in previous chapters, and use them to develop an analysis of the transformation of individual firms. We use the concept of combined and uneven development to examine the integration of particular units of capital into the global economy. We have argued that it is essential to go beyond simple economic determinism, and therefore the changing nature of the capital–labour relationship forms a central element of our analysis. However, competition is the motor that drives the process of accumulation, but the nature of competition itself is for ever changing, and this has important implications for the firms that we examine. Finally, we stress that not only are capital–capital and capital–labour relationships critical and continually in flux, but also that the state–capital relationship is crucial and also undergoes the same process of metamorphosis.

In the last chapter we argued that it was only possible to understand the process of restructuring of HTS (the steelworks) by placing the firm into the context of the Polish steel industry and then examining the dynamics of development of the industry at a European and global level. Only within the context of heightened competition, driven by overproduction can we understand the problems and possibilities of change in HTS. Chapter 8 focused on the dynamics of organizational change and the trade-union response, but only just started to open the black box. In this chapter we take the analysis one step further and look at the process of change, the trade-union response and, in particular, the implications for the lives of workers within two more major employers in the Krakow region: ZPT Krakow, the cigarette producer; and Wawel the confectionery plant. We put each plant into the context of its sectoral trajectory of development within Poland and then analyse the process of integration into the world economy through the twin drives of FDI (foreign direct investment) and privatization. In so doing we examine the change in the nature of competition that integration brings with it. These changes can only be understood by developing an analysis of the changing role of the state, not only within Poland, but also within the process of economic development generally, following our analysis of the decline of late industrialization as a model of development.

These forces simply lay down the parameters of the field of play, and the rules of the game in which organizations such as Wawel and the tobacco factory are involved. In essence, they simply take us to the factory door, and cannot by themselves explain the particular pattern of development within an individual organization. For example, both Wawel and the Tobacco Factory have in common that they operate in sectors that are dominated by large TNCs (transnational corporations), which operate globally; however, the process and outcome of transformation are very different in each case. An explanation for individual trajectories of organizational development requires global, regional and local factors to be hooked into the actors and activities within a particular firm, in a particular town at a specific historical conjuncture. We begin by examining the changing nature of the market in which the Wawel confectionery factory operates.

Confectionery: Global and National Context

The food processing sector in general has been subject to massive restructuring in the past decade. Between 1985 and 1992 the food and drink industry was one of the most active sectors in Europe, in terms of acquisitions and mergers, surpassed only by the financial services sector. In particular, high activity in the area of mergers and acquisitions in the chocolate sector over the past five years has led to a significant pan-European concentration. Several significant factors have been driving this consolidation: firstly, the existence of a single expanded European market has allowed for further economies of scale. More importantly, the food and drinks industry is a mature industry, thus the demand for products grows significantly more slowly than the rise in incomes. Therefore, there is a continual drive to produce more value added and upgraded products and thus, branding and product differentiation are critical to competition. Costly advertising and marketing have the effect of establishing high barriers to entry for newcomers. Given the high risk and costs involved in launching new products and building new brands, it is simpler to acquire a company with established brands and market positions than to build a market position from outside. When asked if it was necessary to have spent $8 billion on major new acquisitions over the past seven years, Helmut Maucher, spokesperson for Nestlé, explained that it would have taken the company twenty to thirty years to build a similar position.

There is also a change in the nature of competition. In 1994 the European food and drink industry, particularly on the continent, comprised a large number of privately held or family controlled businesses. The 1990s, partly as a result of moves towards the single market, saw competition dominated less by national boundaries and more by product categories. This has led to a tendency for firms to restructure, concentrating on core products and divesting themselves of peripheral ones, thus leadership of a product category becomes crucial. Restructuring has therefore been based on reinforcing strong core products and building a critical mass to compete in chosen markets. Philip Morris built a European chocolate business after the acquisition of Jacob Suchard in 1990, following this move with acquisitions of Freia Marabou in 1992 and Terrys in 1993. These were seen as important moves in filling strategic gaps in Suchard's product portfolio and geographical coverage. It is possible then to see the move of companies such as Philip Morris into Central and Eastern Europe as an extension of these strategies and trends.

By January 1994, food processing in Poland had attracted the second highest amount of foreign direct investment (see Table 4.2), and confectionery had been the subject of particular interest and competition. Large TNCs such as Nestlé and Kraft Jacob Suchard (part of the Philip Morris group) have been active in making acquisitions across Central and Eastern Europe. KJS for example, the third largest food manufacturer in Europe, has made acquisitions in Hungary, Slovakia, the Czech Republic, Lithuania and Bulgaria, as well as Poland.

As we have seen in Chapter 4, the scramble for acquisitions and joint ventures in Central and Eastern Europe has been driven by a number of factors. Firstly, the desire for new markets is critical given the maturity of the industry and the low income elasticity for food in general. There is also a specific demand for Western consumable products such as chocolate and cigarettes. However, it is not simply new markets, but domination of those markets that is driving development in this sector. The strategies employed by these companies, particularly in confectionery and food processing sectors, exhibit classic oligopolistic characteristics of collusion and rivalry (Cowling and Sugden 1987). Rivalry is evidenced by the degree of competition in acquiring companies, not paralleled in other sectors. As we saw earlier, Nestlé won effective control of Poland's second largest chocolate factory, 'snatching' Goplana away from a UK commodity broker who had been working for two years with an Israeli food processing company to win control of the factory. This offer was rejected by Goplana employees when Nestlé used local radio and representatives at the factory gates to explain the merits of their offer (*Financial Times* 7 January 1994).

The explanation as to why these companies have chosen joint ventures and are buying into existing companies, rather than serving the market through exports or developing greenfield sites, can partly be explained by their desire to inherit informal trade contacts cultivated under the old regime to smooth exports to other countries within the former bloc. More importantly, they wish to take over popular and well-known existing names of companies and brands as well as producing new products tried and tested in established markets. One legacy of the former planned economies was that many large plants were, in effect, monopoly producers, both within these economies and the bloc as a whole. The starting point for foreign entry into the confectionery industry in 1989 was a high degree of market concentration. Although there were, in total, 145 firms in the confectionery sector, 63 per cent of production and 34 per cent of the workforce was concentrated in eight firms. Three of the most important firms, characterized by renowned brand names, good quality and expertise, now have a high degree of ownership by transnational corporations, as we can see in Table 9.1. It is also worth noting that in 1994 Cadbury Schweppes was building a new plant near Wroclaw.

Wedel and Goplana between them account for 25 per cent of the market. This has implications both for existing firms which have been privatized by worker/management buyouts (Wawel and Jutrzenka) and the entry of new firms. Questions are raised about the ability of domestic firms to compete in a market dominated by these transnational companies. Potential entrants are not kept out so much by

Table 9.1 *FDI in Polish Confectionery*

Plant	FDI
Wedel, Warsaw	PepsiCo
Goplana, Poznan	Nestlé
Olza, Cieszyn	Kraft Jacobs Suchard
San, Jaroslaw	United Biscuits
Jutrzenka, Bydgoszcz	Employee share ownership
Wawel, Krakow	Employee share ownership

Source: Privatization News (various) 1994

economies of scale relating to production or research and development, but by market experience and large advertising budgets, where product differentiation is the key to competition.

Wawel: Buyouts – More Management than Workers

Wawel is one of the largest confectionery firms in Poland, employing 1900 people in 1994 (second only to Goplana). Offers of investment from foreign firms were rejected by Wawel on the grounds that whilst they were willing to consider a limited partnership, they did not want to be taken over by what they regarded as a large foreign investor. This left Wawel as one of only two major confectionery firms which, in 1994, had not received significant FDI. Overtures had come from a number of foreign firms including KJS, part of Philip Morris, largely because up until 1948 Suchard had owned the plant. However, Suchard had wanted to take over 100 per cent of the share holding, and both management and Solidarity, although prepared to consider foreign investment did not want this to exceed 50 per cent. This has echoes of the emerging desire for a capitalism with a particular Polish hue exhibited by Solidarity (see Chapter 3).

Long negotiations led to the worker/management buyout, an option supported by the leadership of Solidarity in the factory. The buyout involved a seven-year leasing arrangement with the voivode. Only 800 workers took up the option of owning shares, most of whom were the more senior professional, technical and managerial staff. A senior (male) member of Solidarity explained that this was because most of the manual workforce were young women who were not interested in the future of the plant, only in how much was in their pay packets on pay day. A strong streak of sexism ran through the union approach to the potential membership. Union activity, we were told, was not high because most of the workforce was made up of young girls.

In fact the relatively low take-up of shares can be better explained by the terms of the share issue. Each worker was entitled to a maximum of 200 shares at Zl.1 million per share, and the company would give each worker a loan of up to Zl.50 million (at a 10 per cent interest rate) to facilitate taking up their share option. However, in 1994 the average wage in Poland was approximately Zl.4 million per month, and un-skilled women workers in Wawel would earn less than that. So, even for a worker on the average wage, taking up the full share option would cost nearly four years' salary. The maximum loan therefore represented more than twelve months salary and with a rising proportion of Po-land's workforce on or below the poverty line, such expenditure would be out of the question. Even if they could afford to take up the loan offer, it is unlikely that most workers would have access to sources of capital to finance the final 75 per cent of the share option. Although both Solidarity's factory leadership and senior management argued that people chose not to take up their option to buy shares, the reality for a large proportion of the workforce was that they had no choice. What on paper appeared to be a worker/management buyout in fact turned out to more closely resemble a management buyout. This was reinforced by the changes in management that took place as a result of the restructuring. The management structure consists of the managing director and four directors with responsibility for trade, technical matters, finance and production. Two remain from pre-change days, and in theory all have been elected. The reality is that there was a gentlemen's agreement prior to the change, between management and senior members of Solidarity as to who would be directors in the future.

This arrangement would overcome the generally perceived problem of *nomenklatura* capitalists remaining in control and failing to modernize plants. However, the arrangement also contributed to the fact that a *de jure* worker/management buyout became a *de facto* management/ technical/professional worker buyout. This, as we have seen in Chapter 4, is consistent with the experience of worker/management buyouts throughout Poland (Tittenbrun 1995). It would appear that such buyouts, for much the same reasons as Wawel experienced, are temporary and transitional forms rapidly assuming more 'conventional' capitalist structures.

The new structure was not without its problems. The company was profitable in 1994 and a meeting was scheduled to decide the division of resources between wage increases and dividend payments. A growing split was emerging between shareholders and non-shareholders as to how profits should be allocated which was increasingly coming to resemble a division between unskilled shopfloor workers and more senior employees and managers. There have been significant changes in management structure and emerging differences between shopfloor workers and the management, as well as between shareholders and non-shareholders. As yet these tensions have not been accompanied by significant changes in the organization of the production process itself.

Making Chocolate

Wawel operates on a number of sites, in and around Krakow. Visiting one site in 1994, located in the middle of a residential area in the south east of the city gave some clues to the issues and problems that have to be confronted. The factory had a brand new facade, with a plaque on the wall commemorating a strike that took place in 1980. The white and red, newly painted entrance leads you into a lobby with stairs up to the new office suite and a small canteen leading off the main lobby. Ushered through the lobby, out of a door and into the central court-yard, the picture changes dramatically. The square courtyard is surrounded by three storey buildings of venerable vintage in an apparent state of disrepair. The courtyard is full of large tin drums full of oil and wooden boxes crammed with sacks of cocoa beans. There is an acute shortage of storage space, we were told. Just-in-time obviously has not yet arrived.

Picking our way around a large tank of chocolate, seemingly abandoned, open to the air at the bottom of a flight of stairs, we climbed to the second floor. Here we found a man in industrial trousers, heavy boots and a vest, pouring sacks of cocoa beans into a machine that smashed the husks and, using gravity as the main propulsion system, dropped the whole lot into a machine on the floor below that separated the kernel from the husk. On the ground floor the various elements of the production process combined to produce either cocoa butter or large bars of chocolate itself. The machinery was East German, of unknown vintage, and in processes such as packing it was largely electromechanical and reliant on large amounts of female manual labour. We walked past the refrigeration unit that cooled the chocolate bars just before they reached the packing section. The production line snaked its way round the ground floor of the factory with no perceptible division into separate departments. We ate the chocolate as it came out of the coolers. The flow line then turned through a ninety degree angle to a section where six women, dressed in white coats were taking wrapped bars off the line and putting them into cardboard boxes, piled high by the side of what appeared to be a fairly primitive packing machine. The machine itself was out of use as it could not cope with anything other than the standard size bar of chocolate. Every once in a while one of the women would wander off to the toilets, just off the main production area, for a smoke.

The main products of the company are chocolate bars, filled chocolate, hard sweets and wafers. Although the management structure of the company has undergone a radical restructuring, the production process has remained essentially unchanged. Two new production lines were being introduced but the technology remained the same. However, the new machinery was felt to be more reliable, which had helped to improve consistency and quality. Products, it was argued, now looked better and the packaging was more attractive. Employment had risen from 1600 to 1900 since the organizational change and it was mainly unskilled workers that had been taken on, whilst existing skilled workers have been transferred to the new production lines. There remained a major problem, as far as management are concerned, with employees' attitudes towards work in general and quality in particular. As we have seen, management believe that their unskilled women workers were only interested in the contents of their pay packets. Management were intending to prepare for ISO 9000 in 1995, but suggested that there would have to be a major change in the mentality of their workforce, many of whom did not feel quality assurance to be either necessary or important. Further it was doubtful whether the factory had either the expertise or the resources to get such a certificate, particularly as only twenty firms in the whole of Poland were in possession of one in 1994. The leisurely pace of change was partly explained by a management belief that they did not want to upset the workforce in the light of all the other changes that were taking place. However, survival in a rapidly changing market threatened to remove the protection that allows a softly-softly approach.

The largest Wawel plant employed around six hundred people and made filled chocolates and chocolate covered jelly sweets. The factory itself stands on the site of the original Piasecka factory, which opened in the 1920s. The main building was, in fact, the original 1920s factory. Most of the machinery was electromechanical, with little evidence of computerization in sight. Most importantly, the relatively simple technology was heavily reliant on large numbers of unskilled female workers. Three women with short wands sorted out sweets emerging, inadequately covered, from a chocolate coating process. The sweets themselves were sorted into lines prior to coating by two women sitting either side of a wooden frame structure.

The wrapping process is illustrative of many of the problems Wawel confronts. The process involves two women per wrapping machine. The first worker, wearing white chocolate stained gloves, took chocolates, one at a time, and loaded them onto a carousel that held eight chocolates in all. The second worker loaded wrapping papers on to the top of the machine. As the carousel turned and wrapped chocolates, one at a time, so the first woman replaced chocolates in the gap vacated on the carousel. Every variety of sweet that required wrapping was dealt with in this way, so a large area of the second floor of the factory was taken with groups of these machines arranged in lines. Management explained that investment in automated wrapping machines was not possible for two reasons: firstly, the cost at around $400 000 was beyond the reach of the company; and secondly, wrapping and packing systems were now integrated. New technology would replace most of the women in the section we currently stood in. However, the demands of competition and the necessity of investment had been the material basis for changing the company's attitude towards involving foreign investors in the plant.

Closer to the World

Quality was believed to be important, being seen as the passport to the export markets deemed to be vital as the home market was currently stagnant. There appeared to be an awareness that competitor Polish firms now linked with FDI were causing problems because of access to advertising budgets and expertise, but the management appeared to believe that their own marketing strategy would allow them to compete and survive. Competition, the management believed, was on the basis of quality, though tradition and customer loyalty was important. Their prices, however, were roughly 60 per cent of those of Nestlé and Lindt.

In 1992 they had instigated an export drive, which had raised the share of exports in output from 3 per cent to 25 per cent, and a presence had been established in the USA, Australia, South Africa and Western Europe. However, this had been achieved by contacting members of extended families or personal contacts in major cities in these countries and asking them to contact local shops to take Wawel products. A second major line of attack was Eastern Europe in general and the Ukraine and Bielorussia in particular, which accounted for a major share of increased exports. Despite the fact that these countries are poorer than Poland, apparently there was significant demand with Russia constituting one of the world's largest markets for confectionery.

The concept of marketing itself was problematic, as the company's attitude to the home market demonstrated. Management were aware that conditions in the home market were difficult, but professed not to be overly concerned. In 1994 they had two sales staff with refrigerated transport to maintain contact between the company and their 200 partners (outlets), but planned to increase the sales staff to sixteen over the following twelve months. A special shop had been opened in the centre of Krakow, selling nothing but Wawel products and it was hoped to open similar outlets in other towns. These initiatives were accompanied by special displays in shops and participation in international fairs and exhibitions. It was hard to believe that it would be sufficient, faced with the might of Cadburys, Suchard, PepsiCo and Nestlé.

An important element of Wawel's survival strategy was that they saw themselves as operating, in Poland, in a quality-defined niche market and indeed in 1994 won a national award for one of their products. A senior manager described the company as being a tiny monopolist in a special section of the Polish market. There are competitor firms, such as Wedel, but not many. However, the possibility of defending a position in this niche market is reduced by the two-pronged approach of TNCs. For instance, PepsiCo has taken over Wedel, on the one hand gaining the advantage of a well-established and traditional firm; and on the other hand, enhancing their capacity to produce and promote products well established in the West. Even within the perceived niche, the nature of competition is profoundly affected by the influx of TNCs. Viewed from the outside competition still appears to be on the basis of quality between two old-established Polish companies. The reality is that competition is now between one small, undercapitalized, under-developed Polish firm with limited expertise and resources in areas such as marketing, and TNCs that bring expertise, finance and an extended product range. This is not only an unequal struggle, but also a state of affairs that is likely to deter new entrants to the market. We have emphasized the presence of large TNCs in the confectionery sector and suggest that they have radically reshaped the nature of the market to which firms such as Wawel must adapt and compete if they are to survive. These large TNCs have promised to commit significant investment to update processes and products as a condition of their entry, negotiated by the state. Access to such resources is simply not a possibility for Wawel. Equally, if not more important are the resources for, and expertise in, marketing and advertising, which result in the erection of barriers to entry for new firms and to certain product markets for existing firms. Thus, even if Wawel had perfect knowledge of the new circumstances in which they are operating, they are con-strained by a lack of resources to which other companies have access.

Tobacco: Global and National Context

The tobacco industry globally has undergone massive restructuring and internationalization over the past decade, reflecting closely the trends outlined in Chapter 4. In particular, the end to state monopolies and the opening up of competition in national markets have provided opportunities for entry into new markets through new ventures or the acquisition of existing plants, resulting in the penetration by TNCs of markets that were previously closed. It is not simply that liberalization has opened up opportunities for these global firms, but that the home states of these large TNCs have lobbied and jostled for markets to be opened up. The US trade representative, for example, threatening unilateral commercial sanctions, has forced the opening up of new markets in Japan, South Korea and Taiwan that previously protected domestic monopolies by limiting imports. In 1990 the US challenged Thailand under a clause in the GATT agreement which upheld the principle of free and open markets. The effect has been to allow substantial penetration of these new markets. For example, in Japan tobacco firms gained entry into the market in 1987 under the leadership of Philip Morris, who then proceeded to increase their market share from zero to 16 per cent by 1993.

The US market is dominated by six firms, with three – Philip Morris, R. J. Reynolds and America Brands – accounting for 90 per cent of sales. Although world growth had been predicted to grow by 7 per cent (1.3 per cent per annum) between 1993 and 1997, the trend in the US market was downwards with sales falling by 2.7 per cent between 1986 and 1990. This was compensated by only a small growth of 1 per cent in the West European market in the same period. Thus, expansion into and development of new markets is now critical, with the most significant areas of growth being in developing countries, Central and Eastern Europe and the Newly Industrialized Countries of South East Asia (NICs).

The extension of competition policy to the tobacco sector within the European Union (EU) in the 1970s led to the opening up of state monopolies to competition, with individual countries losing control over imports from other European countries, particularly US brands produced in Europe. The opening of European countries to more competition has not led to Europeanization of the tobacco industry driven by the pursuit of economies of scale and competition as predicted by the Cecchini Report, but rather a penetration by US multinationals. The accession of Spain and Portugal to the EU in 1986 illustrates the effects of opening up national markets to international competition. The result has been, as elsewhere, that Spanish and

Portuguese brand names have lost ground to US brands, such as Marlboro, Lucky Strike, Camel and Chesterfield, despite their higher price, largely as a result of marketing and advertising. Between 1980 and 1990 the tobacco industry in Europe underwent a period of large-scale restructuring characterized by closure, modernization and concentration with the result that employment fell in this period from 124 000 to 83 000. This was reflected in the decisions taken by major companies with Rothmans, for example, deciding to concentrate production in three factories in Europe and BAT's closure of plants in Liverpool and Amsterdam.

The tobacco industry in Poland is highly concentrated with three major plants accounting for about 85 per cent of domestic cigarette production. Domestic cigarette producers accounted for about 75 per cent of the market in 1994. Six private producers, principally RJR Nabisco and the American Cigarette Company, account for 15 per cent of the market. The remainder is assumed to be accounted for by black market activity.

The tobacco sector employed about 10 400 people in 1993, and was generally regarded as being profitable. The industry made a significant contribution to the state budget through the turnover tax on cigarette production. Initially, the strategic importance of this industry and its monopoly position led the government to exclude it from the privatization programme. However, the perceived necessity of foreign investment to update processes and products and, it was suggested, the primacy of short-term revenue concerns over longer-term monopoly considerations led to a change of policy, with the state beginning negotiations over linking FDI and privatization. It may also be reasonable to speculate that IMF conditionality, always linked to the question of continuing privatization, may have brought some pressure to bear to open up sectors hitherto excluded from the privatization process.

The situation was further complicated by the election in 1993 of a coalition government that included the Peasant Party, whose policy favoured maintaining the exclusion of the industry from privatization as a means of protecting the interests of Polish tobacco growers, a sector which accounts for approximately 70 000 families. However the Peasant Party opposition was overruled by other partners in the coalition. The change in the nature of the domestic market has already led to a decline in Polish tobacco production from 125 200 tons in 1986 to 36 100 tons

Table 9.2 *Polish Tobacco Companies, 1994*

Company name	FDI	Sales Zl. bn.	Net profits Zl. bn.	Employment	Sales per employee Zl. mn.	Average wage Zl. thou.	Investments Zl. bn.	Total share of production %
Zaklady Tytoniowe, Lublin	Rothmans	661.30	24.10	713	×	2530.0	0.70	
ZPT Augustow		464.20	8.50	832	37	3206.4	33.30	4
ZPT Lodz	House of Prince	304.00	1.60	×	×	2837.0	36.60	5
ZPT Krakow	Philip Morris	9152.90	495.70	4020	400	5062.5	351.40	34
ZPT Radom	Tabacalera	2317.80	34.00	2313	114	3765.3	48.60	28
ZPT Poznan	Reemtsma	4013.90	208.00	2406		3489.0	131.60	25
R.J. Reynolds Tobacco		756.00		149				

Source: British News from Poland 1994.

in 1993. This is reflected in a growing concern that the Polish tobacco content of cigarettes had fallen from 92 per cent in 1990, to 80 per cent in 1991 and 50 per cent in 1994.

However, the state cannot be said to have abandoned the industry to the exigencies of the international market. Import controls to prevent producers from lowering the Polish tobacco content of cigarettes, allegedly to maintain quality, were motivated by a desire to protect Polish tobacco growers. Concern with tobacco growers arose from their numerical importance and their influence on the Peasant Party, but also crucially from the highly integrated nature of Polish cigarette production. Any move towards restructuring factories such as the Krakow Tobacco Company, particularly a move towards milder tobaccos, would have disastrous consequences for an important element of the agricultural population of the Krakow region. Thus the importance of the tobacco growers was reflected in proposals for privatization of the factories.

Capital privatization was the path selected which involved turning the tobacco firms into joint stock companies and then selling them. It was envisaged that foreign investors would be allowed to buy between 10 per cent and 60 per cent of the shares (40 per cent being reserved for employees and tobacco growers). In the case of the Krakow plant, a portion would be sold by public offering and later traded on the stock exchange. Negotiations with potential investors were not only intended to cover the price, investment intentions and social packages with particular regard to employment levels, but also measures to aid tobacco growers associated with the plant. In October 1994, the Polish industrial lobby (mainly state industrial sector management) proposed that 25 per cent of the equity of the three largest plants (Krakow, Poznan, Radom) would be put into a national holding and offered to investors, including overseas investors. Fifteen per cent would be offered to employees, 30 per cent to growers and 30 per cent would be retained by the treasury. The equity of the rest of the plants would be offered to investors without restriction. The final outcome was still unclear in 1995.

The Krakow Tobacco Factory – ZPT Krakow

ZPT Krakow is the largest cigarette producer in Poland, accounting for 40 per cent of Polish production. Since 1973 the factory has produced Marlboro under licence for Philip Morris, which accounted for 10 per cent of production and around 20 per cent of profits in 1994. The factory occupies a large site on the outskirts of Krakow. To reach Solidarity's offices it is necessary to go past the laboratories and the new block of flats the company has built on the site. They have been offered at market rates to employees to buy with a loan repayment period of ten years, but the cost at $500 per square metre would exclude most normal shopfloor workers. The path leads past the kindergarten to a single-storey building that houses the offices of Solidarity. The union has one small office and a large meeting room with fax and telephone installed.

We had just finished a meeting, our third in eight months at the site, and were about to be taken on a tour of the plant. We were to meet the production manager of the section of the factory that produced Polish cigarettes – Klubowa, Caro and Caro Lite. We walked along the path of a pavement in the process of being laid and into the portals of a brand new building. The manager took us into the tobacco treatment section. Here tobacco from all over the world, as well as Poland was being prepared for sending to the cigarette production section. Machinery, almost brand new and made in Italy, was heating, sorting, mixing and shredding the tobacco. The machinery, the manager said, was not the absolute state of the art but was as good as anything to be found in most other companies. It was during this process that the various blends of tobacco were put together that eventually went into different varieties of cigarette. Not only the machinery was new, the floor was newly tiled and some pot plants were distributed in apparently haphazard fashion around the place. Both these, we were told, were introduced on the demand of the union. Overall the unit was clean and spacious and, though suffused with the smell of tobacco, far from the oppressive and outdated image of an outmoded system of production.

Through the massive double doors and across a road covered in mud – a proper surface was just being laid – we entered the recycling plant. Here are gathered together all the parts of the leaf not used in the tobacco processing operation. Alongside stalks and tobacco dust, rag-tag bits of tobacco leaf are collected and soaked, heated and pulverized until they re-emerge as a dark brown thin cellulose. Torn into shreds, it has a vague resemblance to damp tobacco leaf, and its destiny is to act as just that, forming part of the tobacco mixture for lower grade Polish cigarettes. The machinery is Italian and made by the same firm that produced the units for the processing plant. It seems to be a fairly sizable investment, which, the manager claims, saves the firm a large amount of money each year. However, if the cigarette market moves in the direction of Western-style cigarettes, as appears likely, then this whole section could be under threat.

Back over the road and into the main building once again, we reach the third floor and the cigarette production unit. The room is long, well lit with yellow lines painted on the floor to mark out routes for the fork lifts. Groups of workers, women in white coats and men in blue overalls, attended working units or gathered in small groups around a machine that, for whatever reason, was not functioning. Everybody looked up to see who had come into the section, but work dictated by the pace of the machine meant that only the men could stop what they were doing for any length of time. There is a mix of machinery, old and new, but all of it is English, manufactured by Molins. The oldest machines are around twenty years old and the newest have been installed in the last eighteen months. There is obviously significant ongoing investment. The new machinery is almost identical in operation to the old, producing a long cigarette tube which is then cut to the appropriate length and the filter added, but on the newest machines computers have been added to control and monitor the operations. The old machines were organized in groups of two, with two women working each machine and a mechanic assigned to each group of two machines. Despite the new computer attachments, for most women work appears to be unskilled, simple, dull and repetitive. The manager told us that the new machines produced 1.5 million cigarettes per shift compared to 800 000 for the old ones. Furthermore, the new machines only required one attendant. The employment effects of further investment, which hitherto had been incremental, are obvious and potentially devastating. The problem though, according to the manager, was that because the machine operated at a much higher speed than the old systems, it had a much higher wastage rate.

The mechanics, we were told, were on a 30 per cent premium in comparison to the wage levels of the women production workers. The explanation for this was that mechanics were required to have finished technical high school, and then do at least two years on the line. We asked whether any women ever applied to become mechanics, but this apparently had never happened. The gendered division of labour, the manager informed us, was traditional in the Polish tobacco industry. The union official did not disagree.

On the floor below, the finished cigarettes reached the packaging department. Large rolls of paper stood by machines that produced soft packages, and one of the newer lines produced a hard pack for Caro Lite. Once again a semi-automated flow line production system required large numbers of white-coated female workers to sort, order and monitor both individual cigarettes and packages. New machinery, once again computer aided, was in evidence without apparently fundamentally altering the system of production. The major improvement, we were told, was that now the correct number of cigarettes went into each package, and the cigarettes were not damaged either before they went in, or in the process of packaging.

Creeping FDI

FDI is often associated with change in both products and processes over a short time scale. Although there has been continuing and important investment in ZPT Krakow, this appears to have produced incremental rather than fundamental changes in the production of Polish cigarettes. A partial explanation for this phenomenon might lie in the concern that the factory's Solidarity branch had initially expressed in Philip Morris becoming a majority stakeholder in the firm. There is obviously no incentive to modernize in the face of intransigent opposition. However, by the end of 1994 the union had withdrawn its opposition, and with certain guarantees regarding employment and investment, now supported increased Philip Morris involvement. Yet it is worth pointing out that senior management in the factory saw foreign involvement as inevitable, largely on the basis that sector trends, as they saw them, heralded the demise of nationally based companies in an era and sector dominated by TNCs. For senior management, the logic of such a development was the eventual cessation of production of Polish cigarettes accompanied by a concentration on the production of Marlboro. Solidarity officials, however, believed that the best strategy, acknowledging that the influx of foreign cigarettes was effectively segmenting the market, was to concentrate production on a small number of leading Polish brands alongside continuing and growing production of Marlboro. There is evidence of an emerging third way, so-called 'middle-class cigarettes', made of a mixture of Polish and foreign tobacco and priced in between Polish brands and high quality ones.

These are being produced both by state sector companies and firms such as RJR Nabisco.

As in the case of Wawel, Solidarity was not opposed to privatization *per se*. Initially, the union organization had wanted a leasing arrangement similar to Wawel, but it proved to be prohibitively expensive. The union officials were desperate to modernize management practices, and viewed their own management as a fundamental block to this process, particularly in areas such as personnel, investment appraisal and marketing. Equally, they recognized the necessity of resources for modernizing production. Apparently, ZPT Krakow had been anxious to buy eleven machines for their Caro Lite department, but with one machine costing $3 million they could only afford three. Thus without the capital support promised by the licensee they were unlikely to be able to modernize capacity. Though the factory union committee thought that privatization was an absolute necessity, it did not want Philip Morris to acquire 100 per cent of the shares. Once again, we have evidence of a desire to construct capitalism with a Polish face, demonstrating the ambiguous attitude of the union to the increased involvement of Philip Morris. On the one hand, they argued that their deal represented the best agreement with a foreign partner negotiated by any Polish tobacco company. But, on the other hand, they were concerned with other examples of foreign partnership where the experience had been, they argued, that marketing was done elsewhere and profits transferred out of the country, leaving only production in Poland. Concerns about the transfer of profits out of Poland evidenced in other examples of FDI had to be offset against the fact that Solidarity believed that further co-operation with Philip Morris would guarantee access to improved technology, capital and new management practices and work systems.

By 1994, conditions were ripe for Philip Morris to expand its ownership of the tobacco company. Although there were ambiguities in government policy, opposition from Solidarity had virtually disappeared and a business plan was agreed and a letter of intent signed, but Solidarity believed that the investment intentions were less than impressive. The letter of intent, we were told, called for $200 million investment over ten years, with 75 per cent to be committed in the first half of that period. However, Solidarity pointed out that in the light of the fact that the company was already making around $35 million per year profit, and that experts had stated that the company needed between $100–110 million investment immediately, then $200 million spread over ten years was not impressive either in terms of quantity or velocity. We would speculate that the initial figure of $200 million allows Philip Morris to open up the door to creeping takeover of the Krakow tobacco factory. Gradualism allows Philip Morris flexibility and adaptability at a time when the sector as a whole is undergoing a complex global restructuring of both markets and production. For the time being a low-wage, low-technology production process will remain, at least until such time as a degree of stability has emerged.

Joint ventures have been the most popular form of FDI in Eastern Europe, largely because they hedge against a whole range of uncertainties. The advantages to be gained from a gradual takeover process more than offset the fact that negotiation of takeover can be a time consuming and convoluted processes. Gradualism has the additional advantage of undermining some of the more xenophobic oppositional elements because of limited initial visibility. Solidarity believes that the possession by the ministry of transformation of a 'golden share' provides some protection for the workforce, and the best guarantee that the terms of the business plan will be adhered to. However, there are already danger signs. By the autumn of 1994, Solidarity officials in the tobacco factory, whilst acknowledging that the business plan required employment to stay at existing levels for two years, intimated that Philip Morris would be looking for voluntary redundancies. They believed there was little they could do to combat this, as anyone accepting redundancy terms wanted to leave the job anyway.

However, even if Philip Morris were to reach or exceed these investment targets, this will not guarantee the continued existence of the plant, at any level of employment. The future of the Krakow plant will depend on where, if at all, it fits into Philip Morris's global plans for development. Within Europe, as we have seen, opening up national markets led to a scramble for investment closely followed by restructuring, closure and redundancy. We have suggested elsewhere that the exclusion of Poland from the European Union may have a detrimental effect on its ability to attract FDI, ironically in this sector it is largely the existence of Polish trade barriers that has led to interest by foreign firms in penetrating the domestic market. Membership of the European Union (although unlikely in the short term), might trigger another bout of restructuring by these companies as the internal market became larger.

There are issues around the structure of production, in particular the division between Polish and US cigarettes. The plan currently is that production will concentrate on leading Polish brands such as Caro and Klubowa. In a market undergoing rapid change and restructuring, one might question whether this is a short-term palliative measure with a longer-term plan to switch to Marlboro. The Spanish experience suggests that with the aid of advertising, there is a decisive change in taste towards milder US brands. This switch has implications for the future of Polish tobacco growers as this would mean more imported tobacco. The factory is well placed as the licensing arrangements means long-standing co-operation, and it may be that ZPT Krakow gains at the expense of other Polish factories and co-operation with a foreign investor may give them a decisive competitive advantage. However, the enormous potential for restructuring within Poland and Eastern and Central Europe as a whole must not be underestimated.

Solidarity and the Organization of Work

Solidarity as a workplace organization was not simply passively waiting for Philip Morris to reorganize the plant, as in other organizations they see themselves as active agents of restructuring. By the end of 1994, Solidarity in ZPT Krakow had 1538 members out of a total workforce of around 3600. Membership had grown by 180 in 1994 alone, and 360 since the beginning of 1992. OPZZ (the official union Federation) had members in the factory, but Solidarity claimed to be recruiting from their membership. As in the case of HTS, there is no formal co-operation with OPZZ, the reason given being that no one can forget the confiscation of Solidarity's property during the period of martial law. OPZZ are still viewed as being little more than a service unit for management. The growth in union membership was surprising, on one level, given that in common with HTS, Solidarity in ZPT Krakow had a policy of not actively recruiting people, preferring to wait for them to express a wish to join the union. This, as we have discussed already, arises from a desire to establish difference from and distance between Solidarity and the OPZZ type unions. Under the old regime, union membership was to all intents and purposes compulsory, Solidarity therefore want to emphasize the personal choice element in membership of their organization.

The union officers in the plant argued that the organization of work was outdated, and saw a lot to be admired in the Philip Morris management style. The union viewed high costs of production influencing the price of the product and therefore they had approached sociologists at the Jagiellonian University in Krakow with a view to designing and implementing a modern human resource management (HRM) strategy. This, along with initiatives in the field of marketing and investment strategy, was viewed as being the most pressing restructuring needs. The union officers argued that they were aware of the large gap between Polish and Western firms. However, the development of HRM, deemed by the union to be fundamental to the process of bridging the perceived gap, was proceeding too slowly and could only be accelerated if a younger and more dynamic management cadre were to be introduced. The task of the Solidarity factory leadership, as they saw it, was to convince their membership of the necessity of change. This meant convincing workers that they would not lose their jobs as a result of restructuring but instead would be transferred within the company. This argument was based on the assumption, common to many Solidarity representatives, that successful restructuring and increased profitability would secure current employment levels, or even provide for increased employment.

The first change that Solidarity had demanded in ZPT Krakow was in the pay structure. Previously pay had been linked solely to performance, that is to the number of cigarettes produced per shift. The old system had been dangerous and caused enormous waste of raw materials, according to women who worked on the line, and health and safety, it was claimed, had been a serious problem. Therefore, demands for a new pay system were driven by the related issues of safety and waste management. After consulting Solidarity, experts from the Jagiellonian University had recommended the introduction of performance related pay to be determined by assessment sheets. This reflects a general tendency encountered in interviews with Solidarity representatives, a profound and unshakeable belief that, under capitalism, a 'good' worker will necessarily and inevitably be rewarded with something other than redundancy. Linked to this was another common theme, a belief in the importance of performance-related pay. If good workers will necessarily be rewarded, then it is obvious that what is needed is a payment system that can identify and reward deserving individuals. Such a reaction is not surprising given that the old system was regularly described to us as 'they pretend to pay us, we pretend to work', reinforced by the barrage of Western propaganda linking reward with individual effort.

Pay in ZPT Krakow was reconstructed to consist of two elements: firstly, a basic pay rate linked to job classification; and secondly, a premium for production per shift, with an upper and lower limit. Each worker was assessed by a supervisor twice per year, but problems arose from the failure of management to provide adequate training in assessment techniques, so the system still appeared to be arbitrary and unfair. This is a complaint common to PRP schemes across inter-national boundaries. At least with the new pay scheme, the unions desire for restructuring in general, and specifically an HRM package, could appear to be squared with improving the conditions of the membership. Women on the line said that the new scheme meant that they could slow down and concentrate on the quality of output. This meant that the pace of work was not so frantic but improved quality had meant no loss in acceptable output figures. However, the women also reported that the new machinery being introduced was leading to a greater intensity of work because of a need to concentrate harder. This was reflected in complaints received from women workers on the new lines that the production system was causing headaches and pain in workers' legs. Experts from the Jagiellonian University were called in who suggested that the problems were largely psychological though the brightness of the new working areas and their slippery floors may have contributed. The women's complaints according to these experts had little to do with the perceived greater intensity of work. In general, the union argued that people were not prepared for the changes that privatization would bring. The demands that punctuality, discipline and productivity brought were leading to greater stress in the work-force, to the extent that some people were leaving. Officially there had been no redundancies but in the autumn of 1994 there were around 600 fewer people working in the factory than in the previous year, with little union resistance to this process of 'downsizing'.

We have already seen that Solidarity's strategy had altered from uncritical support for restructuring, to a search for Polish capitalism, involving a mixed economy. This is a complex phenomenon, and the change has been largely driven by the continuing and growing social problems arising from transformation, particularly poverty and un-employment. On the one hand, there was still a largely uncritical approach to Western management practices within organizations. On the other hand, there is evidence of a growing discontent with restructuring, with important implications for Solidarity and the other unions. Solidarity is being pulled in opposite directions simultaneously. On the one hand, it has to protect its members from the increasingly obvious adverse effects of transformation. On the other, it remains at the forefront of the advocacy of change. This can be illustrated if we look at the experience of women workers.

Disillusion and Discontent: Women Workers

Regional Solidarity officials argued that women over the age of 40 had been the main victims of unemployment in Malopolska. Therefore, a major problem for the union was that for a rising proportion of its members unemployment was becoming a permanent fact of life. Furthermore, the number of work-related accidents was rising. The conclusion that Solidarity reached was that the average active working life span was falling, as was life expectancy itself. It is now widely accepted that women have suffered disproportionately from unemployment, and the fear of losing their jobs loomed large in the minds of the women workers we talked to in both ZPT Krakow and Wawel.

All the workers we talked to pointed to the new freedoms that individuals had acquired since 1989. Women in ZPT Krakow said that the most important thing was to have real freedom, not to be afraid to say things, to be able to express dissatisfaction. Now it was possible to speak out loud, to fight for your rights officially and ask others to help you if you wanted to. Secondly, transformation had increased the availability of goods and services. One woman said that transformation had made many goods and services available twenty-four hours a day. Competition, she continued, had led to freedom of choice, in so far as whenever things were needed they could be acquired without having to rely on personal connections or bribery. If you had money, you could get what you want, therefore life was easier, and less time was now spent on acquiring everyday necessities. And finally, most of the women workers we talked to said that it was now possible to gain respect for the work that a person did.

However, change for the women in the chocolate and tobacco factories was not an undiluted blessing. The problems that arose provided a stern challenge to the Solidarity organization in the region. As one woman put it, survival is now enormously expensive. Under the old regime, people had money but no goods to buy, now there are goods in the shops in abundance but people do not have money to buy them. In particular, it was argued, that in former times the cost of basic goods such as food, gas and electricity were kept low, now prices were rising continuously, and, according to the women in the tobacco factory, housing costs soaked up around 50 per cent of total household income. All the women worked full time (40–48 hours per week) out of necessity. One of the tobacco workers said that in a market economy work was not optional. She couldn't imagine women staying at home because everybody in a family had to work. Even if two parents were working, it still did not bring enough money into the house to cover even basic costs. In these circumstances, it is hardly surprising to find that unemployment, or the threat of it, was also creating a climate of fear. Under the old regime work was guaranteed, now unemployment was high and rising. In former times, we were told, there had been a high rate of labour turnover, with people seeking better work and higher pay. However, it was now the case that if a woman had a job, particularly a relatively good job such as those in ZPT Krakow, then a decision to leave would only be taken under duress.

Childcare had always been a problem, though under the old regime some workplaces such as Wawel had provided a kindergarten and although ZPT Krakow still provided some childcare, Wawel no longer did. It is worth noting that under the old regime only the better-off members of the staff (management) had been able to use these facilities. Now, though the state still provided some kindergarten places, prices were rising. In the autumn of 1994, a place for one child in a state kindergarten cost around a fifth of the average weekly wage. There are private kindergartens, but the women described them as expensive and very snobbish. Transformation is a double-edged sword for the women in the Krakow factories. On the one hand, change has bought freedom, but, on the other, the free market has brought poverty, the threat of unemployment and increasingly the loss of the social infrastructure.

There were, however, long-standing grievances with the system of work organization that, in the process of confronting, forced Solidarity to act more as an orthodox trade union and less like a restructuring agent. Around half of all the ZPT's workers are women and all workers work a three-shift system on a one-week rotation basis. Shifts are 6–2,

2–10 and 10–6 and a worker does a five-day week on afternoons and nights, but a six-day week (that is, including Saturday) on mornings. There is no such thing as part-time work. This system is not uncommon, a similar practice operates in Wawel where around 80 per cent of the workforce are women. This, as the women pointed out, plays havoc with family life and no one can ever say that they get used to it. Childcare is managed through using grandparents and organizing shift systems with partners so that husband and wife are never on the same shift. Greater stress arises as workplaces abolish factory kindergartens and the cost of state and private childcare moves beyond the reach of ordinary workers. Solidarity had surveyed 500 workers about the night shift after a flood of complaints. Ninety per cent reported hating the night shift, preferring that it did not exist at all. The argument was that beyond simple disruption of families, the night shift was creating health problems, especially for women. The 10 per cent who did not react badly to the night shift were said to be young workers who wanted the money that the small night shift premium brought. The union then demanded the end of the night shift, but adopted the tactic of demanding additions to the night shift premium so that eventually it would become uneconomic and the management would abolish it. For the time being, the night shift continued to exist.

Conclusion

This chapter has brought together a number of themes which are central to our argument and demonstrated that they combine to produce particular organizational trajectories of development. Although we have argued the centrality of the relationship between FDI, privatization and the role of the state in determining the general pattern of Poland's development, in this chapter we have demonstrated that this does not determine an inevitable and monochromatic pattern to that development as it unfolds in emerging organizations. The path of development of any organization is driven by a dialectical relationship between structural forces, on the one hand, and the actions of individuals and groups, on the other. The action of the individual and groups is limited by the parameters laid down by the structural forces at play. It is equally important to realize that actions taken by individuals and groups reshape the structure of those forces themselves. In the case of Wawel and ZPT Krakow then, the action of groups such as management are important as we have seen, but crucial to the development of the labour process is the form and function of workplace Solidarity organization. In particular, the policy of desperately seeking Polish capitalism determined attitudes not only to privatization *per se* but also to the form of privatization deemed to be acceptable, and thus crucially to FDI.

So far this accords with the emphasis on global–local relationships, however this fails to take account of one crucial player – the state. Firstly, TNCs have had to negotiate directly with the state, seeking to obtain agreement before making overtures to individual Polish companies. Equally, individual Polish firms seek to influence the terms and nature of their transformation by dealing directly with the state. In the case of Wawel, many trips to Warsaw were necessary to negotiate and finalize the terms of their worker/management buyout. Under the pact on state owned enterprises, particular enterprises have six months to agree between themselves and the ministry a programme for transformation and privatization. Failure to find an agreement within six months means that a solution can simply be imposed. This is a short time-scale given the two years it took Wawel to reach an agreement. By contrast, the state may come directly to negotiate with individual enterprises, as evidenced by a visit from a committee of the Sejm to ZPT Krakow in an attempt to persuade them to accept the Philip Morris proposals for investment.

Although we have argued that there is nothing inevitable or predetermined about organizational outcomes in the process of transformation, we do believe that different outcomes are of crucial importance in determining the future survival chances of these firms. This is best illustrated by examining the situation of Wawel. Although the form of the firm has changed from being state owned to a quasi management buyout, the production process has not. There is an understanding that issues such as marketing, distribution, advertising and quality are crucial to competing in the market. There is, however, little evidence of significant moves to transform these, nor is there evidence of resources sufficient to finance such a restructuring. By way of contrast, PepsiCo's involvement with Wedel (Wawel's main competitor) brings with it not only resources and expertise in underdeveloped areas such as marketing, but also brings new products and access to new markets. Although it would appear that Wawel's competition is still with companies such as Wedel, Wedel is no longer the competitor that it used to be, it is now part of a TNC which is concerned with dominating and shaping markets.

Similarly, the TNC involvement in ZPT Krakow exhibits similar tactics, taking over the production of traditional Polish goods with a reputation and a market, but at the same time importing the production of goods that have well-established brand names from the West. What Philip Morris will gradually take over is an organization that produces Marlboro as well as two of the better known brands of Polish cigarettes. The 40 per cent share of the Polish cigarette market that ZPT Krakow currently possess has the potential to give the company a solidity and stability in the market, giving them the luxury of time to determine and develop their strategy. In the short term, we suggest that this means that ZPT Krakow has a better chance of survival than Wawel. However, the survival of both Wedel and ZPT Krakow will not be decided in Krakow or indeed in Poland, but in the headquarters of PepsiCo and Philip Morris, in Europe or the US. Furthermore, the future of both plants may have little to do with their position in the Polish market and much more to do with their position in the global production systems of their parent TNCs. As we have seen in the case of Europe, the implications of rationalization and restructuring of cigarette production are drastic and cross national boundaries. In the case of Central and Eastern Europe the survival of any particular plant will be dependent not only on what happens in that region, but crucially on the declining markets in the US and the growing markets of Central Asia.

Our analysis also brings together an explanation for the apparent lack of job loss in major organizations in the Krakow region. It is not only the case that Wawel, ZPT Krakow, as well as HTS, the steel works, have political importance, but also the forces at play to date have not had sufficient weight to bring about fundamental restructuring. However, our analysis would suggest that this situation will change in the near future. This has a number of implications: the first, and most obvious, is that unemployment is set to rise rapidly in those urban industrial regions that, hitherto, have been relatively unaffected by unemployment. The second effect might be on the structure and activity of Solidarity itself. Its major concentrations of membership are in precisely the sort of organization that will be increasingly under threat. Furthermore, both the non-active recruitment policy, and the policy of desperately seeking Polish capitalism will be put under severe strain. If the perceived connection between 'good' management, investment, effort and employment is broken, then organization and activity within plants such as Wawel and ZPT Krakow may take on a very different hue from their current colouration.

Solidarity is thus faced with a number of serious problems, some of its own making. However, Solidarity has, until recently, largely uncritically supported the process of restructuring, which alongside a policy of non-active recruitment, contributed to the union's problems. As the initial euphoria of 1989 collapsed in the face of unemployment and poverty, Solidarity policy has shifted from outright support for free market policies to a belief in a mixed economy. This, now allied to a nationalistic streak, produces an approach which we characterize as 'desperately seeking Polish capitalism'. This reflects the fact that most Solidarity workplace organization still believes that capitalism in general, and human resource management in particular, rewards hard work and good workers. It is unlikely that this faith will survive the full force of restructuring that will sweep through the heartland of Solidarity organization in the coming period. We have already described Solidarity workplace organization as being Janus-like, promoting both workplace trade-union organization and acting as principal agent of restructuring. This highly unstable balancing act cannot last, at least not in its present form, for a number of reasons: firstly, because the union's own members are threatened by poverty and unemployment, and show increasing signs of anger and resentment; secondly, many of the major bases of Solidarity membership, the large state owned enterprises (SOEs), have not as yet undergone fundamental restructuring. This process is only in its early stages, but as the 1994 strike in the Huta Warsawa steel works has demonstrated, when the full effects of restructuring become clear, then resentment can boil over into outright opposition; thirdly, the reality of restructuring may lead to a more critical examination of the rhetoric of HRM. At the moment, the language of empowerment and involvement still corresponds to the image of capitalism that the West has sold. However, the reality of 'downsizing' and management by stress will call this symbiosis into question. Solidarity, and the other unions, will continue to play a vital role in conditioning the pattern and pace of restructuring, particularly in the cases of FDI and privatization. However, the role of the unions in general, and Solidarity in particular, will itself undergo a process of transformation, echoing the process of change that they confront.

SECTION IV CONCLUSION

10 A DIFFERENT KIND OF FEAR

Although we have taken an extremely critical view of both free market panaceas and those that prescribe a progressive role for the state as a means of transforming Central and East European economies, it is important to stress that we are not inviting a return to the old regime. We cannot be apologists for a system that we never took to be socialist. Although for two decades the old regime appeared to be capable of delivering rising standards of living, from the 1970s onwards the cracks were beginning to deepen and working-class people were increasingly paying the price. By the 1980s, in Poland basic goods could only be obtained by queuing, by bribery or through exorbitant black market prices. Life expectancy was falling, health was deteriorating and pollution was rife. It is difficult to overstate the repressive nature of the old regime. One evening, late in 1994, we went out for something to eat with two of the Solidarity activists from the Krakow tobacco factory. We asked about the rising crime rate and whether people felt more insecure, more scared than they had been. The answer came back slowly. Yes, people were more scared now of being burgled, for example, but remember people had always been scared under the old regime. You were never sure that someone wasn't listening to you. You didn't dare say what you thought, and you lived under the constant fear of being taken away and locked up. Driving out to the cigarette factory our translators always pointed out a largely anonymous building, set back slightly from the road and resembling a 1960s electronics plant in the UK. This, they point out, usually accompanied by some gesture, was the police headquarters in the old days. Their voices still betray a mixture of defiance and fear.

Back in Solidarity's office, in 1994, we talk about the union's demands. They want the introduction of performance-related pay, training in the enterprise culture for their members, and the creation of proper personnel and sales departments. Earlier in the year we had been on a Solidarity demonstration in Warsaw when the major complaint of most people on the demonstration was that the introduction of proper capitalism was being held up by the red bourgeoisie. For two British socialists and trade unionists this caused problems. For us capitalism is Western multinationals ignoring the labour code; it is poverty, increasingly obvious inequality, unemployment and the utter waste of human lives. We were forever finding ourselves pointing out the obvious and gross horrors that capitalism is heir to. For our hosts, usually Solidarity activists, this obviously caused a degree of pain and upset. This is hardly surprising given that, at one level, we appeared to be suggesting that their struggle against the old regime, often involving dangerous and illegal underground activity, was a waste of time. This, as we pointed out in the introduction, is not our contention at all. However, as socialists, we are deeply sceptical of the material gains that the majority of the population will derive from a more market-orientated economy. In this final chapter, we draw together the threads of our argument and examine the implications of our analysis for the future development of Poland in general and Krakow in particular, and that of our case study factories, and most importantly, the Polish working class.

From State Monopoly Capitalism to Transnational Capitalism

The latter stages of the twentieth century have witnessed a series of profound changes in the world economy. The long post-war boom ran out of steam and the Western economies entered a period of prolonged recession. This was exacerbated by the oil crisis of the early 1970s. At the same time the economies of Central and Eastern Europe entered a spiral of decline, culminating in the collapse of the late 1980s. The same period witnessed the emergence of the Newly Industrialized Countries (NICs) as significant actors on the economic stage, and latterly China emerged as a powerful force in the rapidly developing markets of South East Asia.

These are not isolated historical phenomena. Each, in their different way, are symptomatic of a more general phenomenon, that being the rise to pre-eminence and subsequent decline of a dominant form of capitalist development. The essential characteristics of this form are a central role for the state as owner, ally or regulator of large national capitals, allied to some degree of overt or covert protectionism. The increasing success with which large capital, both private and public and states traded with each other helped fuel the motor of competition, accelerating the forces bringing about internationalization of the world economy. The increasingly international nature of economic development also crucially undermined the viability of semi-protected, autarchic development. The state monopoly capitalisms of Central and Eastern Europe, being extreme forms of this pattern of development, were increasingly sucked into a world that demanded a change in the form of capitalist development.

The new internationalization of production which had overtaken trade in importance as a way of integrating economies, was increasingly driven by foreign direct investment (FDI), mostly through transnational corporations (TNCs). However, internationalization of production does not lead unproblematically to globalization. There are countervailing forces, particularly the tendency towards balkanization of the world economy through the emergence of trade blocs such as NAFTA for the Americas, the European Union (EU) and less clearly the Pacific Basin. Though the model of late industrialization is now in decline, the state, both local and national, retains an important though transformed role. In essence we are suggesting that the decline of an old form of development is being replaced by a confused phase which manifests itself in political contradictions and often competing interests and explains continued state support, to different degrees, for national champions.

Poland had started a conscious, though contradictory process of closer integration into the world economy long before 1989. However, it did so just as the sclerosis in its own economy, and the level of resistance to the previous pattern of rule, was proving to be terminal, but also, crucially, just as the world economy sank into a series of prolonged crises. Furthermore, the character of the world economy was changing, giving an increasingly privileged position to TNCs. The interplay of all these forces would effectively determine the pattern of the new form of capitalist development that Poland was undertaking. These tendencies, confused and contradictory though they may be, are manifested in two interrelated phenomena that are central to our analysis of the dynamics of change in Poland – FDI and privatization.

At a very concrete level, given the relative backwardness of productive capacity and the lack of domestic capital, there is an inextricable link between FDI, privatization and the transformation of these economies. The literature on transformation has been obsessed with the mechanics of privatization, but has failed to locate privatization in a global context. The continued existence of state ownership or regulation of the means of production, distribution or exchange in an era increasingly characterized by trans-state capitals and capitalism, is increasingly at odds with the demands of some sections of capital who are demanding the opening up of national markets. This would explain the elimination of non-tariff barriers through the Single European Market, however, a more overt manifestation would be American tobacco companies, in alliance with the US government, forcing open markets in the East under the threat of trade sanctions.

Although large companies have driven deregulation, they have been aided and abetted by the Bretton Woods institutions, such as the World Bank and IMF, which, through conditionality, have imposed privatization, deregulation and 'structural adjustment' on governments whether willing or not. However, we are not trying to suggest that all governments have had to be forced to move in this direction. The collapse of the Keynesian consensus and the associated rise of the New Right has promoted the death knell of the late industrialization model with state ownership increasingly viewed as a block to economic development. The role of the state is now viewed as providing the appropriate support structures to attract sections of mobile capital. This is not an uncontradictory phenomenon in so far as even right-wing governments will still protect national champions. However, the dominant tendency is for states (both local and national) to compete with each other. As Dunford (1994: 110) concludes:

> What results is a one to many game which major investors can exploit to their advantage, playing off against one another, and using concessions agreed in one place to exact yet greater concessions from rival locations. At the same time national states create structures that enable them to play this game more effectively but that reinforce its logic.

The position in which countries such as Poland find themselves will then depend on their relationship to emerging blocs (such as the EU) and international trajectories of development in sectors under transformation. More particularly, the state can take the decision to privatize, but the outcomes of privatization will be significantly affected by the participation of transnational corporations. The state can negotiate with these organizations over the terms of entry, but in the final analysis, though states can bribe and cajole TNCs, they have little influence over decisions to locate or invest.

An important element of the role of the state in attracting mobile capital is now taken to be the provision of appropriate human capital. In essence, this means that a skilled, flexible and acquiescent labour force is supposed to be a key competitive advantage. The state is well aware of the importance of the objective nature of labour in so far as economic development packages usually incorporate a large element of training. However, the state is usually also well aware of the subjective, and potentially oppositional, nature of labour. This explains why the process of transformation since 1989 has been characterized by both compromise and confrontation: compromise in the form of formal powers given to workers' councils, and the allocation of shares to workers, free or otherwise, as part of the privatization programme; confrontation in the sense of the abolition of workers' councils at the point of privatization, although the government has usually preferred more roundabout, if not underhand, methods.

Poland and the European Union

For Poland, the implications of its peripheral status with the EU are far from straightforward. Despite well-publicized moves to liberalize trade via the Association Agreements, Poland faces restrictions, to some degree, on the export of goods that constitute a significant proportion of trade with Europe, such as steel, agriculture and textiles. In addition, the rules of origin militate against its ability to attract foreign investment on the basis of assembly for export to the EU. There is no doubt that EU membership would open up access to major markets, however; at the same time it would mean an increase in competition, as any form of protecting vulnerable industries would become increasingly difficult. It might also be the case that membership of the EU could lead to closure of productive capacity in Poland, as the removal of barriers to entry allows for the Polish market to be served from production facilities within another member state.

As we have seen in Chapter 2, exposure to the chill winds of competition has meant the demise of whole industries, particularly those characterized as 'high tech'. We have emphasized the crucial role played by foreign investment in determining which sectors will become competitive. Further, we have pointed to the fact that FDI has been concentrated in a small number of firms in a small number of sectors, leaving vast swathes untouched. Despite attempts at soft industrial policy (sectoral privatization) the potential for competitiveness of Polish firms has been largely determined by the arrival, or otherwise, of FDI. Where FDI has arrived, the result is that the strategic decision-making regarding the future of that unit no longer takes place within Polish borders. Furthermore, the survival of any particular unit may be determined by actions that take place far away from Poland itself, and have little to do with either the nature of the Polish market or the particular productive unit in question. The image of decentralized TNC control structures is belied by the reality of increasing central control. In fact, the growing sophistication of central monitoring systems allows for the appearance of localness whilst simultaneously increasing the degree of centralized control. We are witnessing the emergence of the chameleon corporation, remaining essentially unchanged, but adopting the superficial hue of the locality.

Krakow

It has been argued in some quarters that Poland will be locked into the emerging international division of labour as supplier of raw materials and semi-processed goods. At best, it is suggested that FDI will bring only simple assembly operations. This will leave Poland as peripheral to, but dependent on, the European Union. This picture, however, fails to capture the process of uneven development that has taken place within Poland, particularly since 1989 both in terms of regions and sectors.

Uneven development manifests itself both within and between sectors. We have already noted that some areas of so-called high technology industry have been virtually eliminated, although there are pockets of relative excellence that may survive. At a more general level, within all sectors development has not been even. Organizations have developed and adapted at different rates, leaving some firms with a greater chance of attracting the FDI that will lock them directly into world markets. Unevenness also has a regional dimension, leaving some areas unlikely to attain even peripheral status. Within Poland, regions and organizations will be combined with, and lock into, the international division of labour in an uneven fashion. Therefore, within overall junior and peripheral status, there will be examples of relative success, however, for some regions and organizations within sectors the future threatens exclusion.

For Krakow then, the picture appears to be mixed. Unemployment in 1995 was below the national average, and the region appears to have some advantages, particularly the level of education of the local population, and the potential for developing tourism. However, the region and its institutions are entering for the first time into the dog-eat-dog game of local economic development which will pit them not just against relatively backward regions of Poland, but against regions and localities that have been involved in this competition for a long time. It is acknowledged within the locality that the local institutional framework is not sufficiently developed to compete with more 'mature' regions. However, our argument goes further, in that our analysis suggests that even if a more developed institutional framework existed it would still only have limited powers to affect the trajectory of development of the local economy. Furthermore, Dunford's criticism of national economic development policy applies just as strongly to the actions of the local state. Both 'bootstraps' and the new localism distil down, as we have seen, to little more than infrastructural development, support for SMEs and attempts to attract FDI. In other words, both policies attempt to create the conditions and institutions that will lock localities into the deadly competitive logic of the local economic development game. Further, the idea of local control appears somewhat hollow when policy is aimed at making localities subservient to the wishes of large capital.

We do accept that there will be fundamental changes in the structure of the local economy, and that this will come about through more than just the restructuring of large firms. There is, and will continue to be, significant growth in the number of small firms in the local economy. However, as we have pointed out, this is not a simple or unproblematic phenomenon. The emergence of small firms should not be equated with the emergence of a dynamic and competitive local economy. As Alice Amsden and her colleagues (1994: 92) have pointed out, the problem with many Polish companies is that they are too small to compete on the international stage. Furthermore, the emergence of a flea market, rather than the myth of the free market, is no basis on which to build successful local economic development. Small firms, important in themselves, will not be the prime motors of local economic development. Large firms in the locality and their future restructuring will have a critical impact on the shape of the local economy and the future of Krakow's population.

However, the forms of large firm organization that have emerged depart radically from orthodox Western models. The interplay of the forces we have prioritized mean that ownership of emerging company structures exhibits a complex mix of local and national state, local, national and international capital and management and worker interests. We would, however, expect these complex structures to dominate for the foreseeable future, with some of these forms being more transient than others.

Firms in the Process of Transformation

The majority of confectionery plants have significant levels of foreign investment, with little prompting necessary from the state. However, in Wawel the active choice to resist FDI and take the worker/management buyout route is being undermined by the terms of the lease imposed by the regional government. Resources are tied in to repaying the terms of the lease, leaving very little possibility for generating funds to finance either investment or marketing. Whilst Wawel appears to still be competing with Wedel, a renowned Polish chocolate firm, significant investment by PepsiCo in Wedel has transformed the nature of competition. The major form of competition in oligopolistic markets is product differentiation, which requires access to extensive know how and resources. Wawel simply does not have access to either of these. The problems that this situation raises threatens not only to undermine the worker/management buyout status of the organization but also to push the firm in the direction of FDI as a source of funds. The worker/ management buyout, as we have seen, was weighted in favour of management from the outset; however, it would appear that the necessity of generating external funds was driving the organization in the direction of more common capitalist forms. The only apparent source of finance was foreign partners, and thus the independence of the worker/management buyout was in question. Even if Wawel is successful in finding a foreign partner, then significant investment, as we have seen, would lead to large numbers of redundancies in areas such as wrapping, packaging and packing.

Interviews with senior officials in the ministry of privatization would seem to suggest that the experience of Wawel is not unusual. The possibility of worker/management buyouts on leasing arrangements from voivodes was put into the legislation almost as an afterthought and as a concession to the power of organized labour, echoing a tradition of worker self-management deeply embedded in Polish history. This eased the process of privatization, but was fundamentally flawed. The terms of the leasing arrangements restricted the possibility of further internally generated investment. Shareholding, as we have seen, rapidly became concentrated in management's hands and more usual forms of capitalist organization, more open to foreign investment began to emerge. On this reading, worker/management buyouts were little more than transitional forms, easing the path towards foreign direct investment and conventional capitalist structures.

Like confectionery. the majority of major cigarette companies in Poland have witnessed the presence of foreign direct investment. In the case of ZPT Krakow, Philip Morris have had a long-standing relationship concerning the production of Marlboro. However, the case of ZPT Krakow demonstrates that the story is not one of a simple and uncontested march to domination by foreign firms. Successive governments have vacillated over the question of transforming this sector. Monopoly considerations and concerns over damage to tax revenues gave way, on the change of government, to concern for Polish tobacco growers, particularly pertinent for a government that included the Peasant Party.

The Solidarity organization in the plant also had a vital role to play. Whilst never opposed to Philip Morris gaining increased ownership, the union was initially opposed to majority ownership. A subcommittee of the lower house of parliament (Sejm) visited Krakow in an attempt to persuade the union to change its mind. This the union eventually did, but it came about for a number of reasons. Firstly, as we have seen,

Solidarity at workplace level faces two ways at once, being in the forefront of the demands for restructuring but also increasingly having to act as a union defending the material interests of its members. In ZPT Krakow, Solidarity saw the Philip Morris management as a source of management expertise that they believed to be vital for their future existence. However, Philip Morris could only be allowed an increased share in the plant under two conditions. Firstly, a business plan had to be agreed which included guaranteed levels of investment and employment; and secondly, the government retained what the union described as a 'golden share' in the organization. Thus Philip Morris could only increase its level of ownership if certain guarantees were fulfilled, and the state retained an important element of ownership. It remains to be seen just how much protection the golden share provides, and the experience of FDI in other sectors suggests that employment and investment guarantees are not always fireproof.

It is somewhat ironic that the global steel industry in general, and the European sector in particular, more closely resembles central planning than a free market. The degree of protection afforded to their home industries by European states suggests that increased access to the EU market is unlikely for the Polish industry. This also reinforces our argument that the state remains a significant actor on the global economic stage. Overproduction in the industry as a whole means that there is little drive to acquire further production assets, and this is reflected in the limited forays across national boundaries. The implication is that the likelihood of significant FDI in Poland is limited.

The principal aim of the restructuring of HTS, the steelworks, was to hive off the core element of continuous casting, which has already received significant investment in order that the new independent company would be free of the debts and liabilities of the old HTS, both in terms of resources and traditions. This was viewed as a precondition for attracting the necessary foreign investment in the longer run. The new unit, employing around 10 000 people, although initially still serving protected home markets would be geared up for the expected international competition.

The shell of the old HTS would remain a principal shareholder in the spinoffs. Separated from, though still bound to their parent organization, the spinoffs are increasingly open to competition. For many of the spin offs it is questionable as to how long HTS will remain a market at all, as they are increasingly forced to tender for work in other markets.

If successful, organizations that have previously been anonymous within the bulk of HTS will now have a visibility that profitability brings, opening up the possibility of cherry picking by foreign investors. Thus, for both the new streamlined steel plant and the spun off former satellites, the future lies in the effects of being locked into (or out of) international markets and competition.

Once again, the role of labour is crucial. The decline in direct employment from 23 000 to 17 000 was partly achieved by offering 51 per cent of the shares in the spinoffs to workers. Equally importantly, the union's acceptance of the necessity of restructuring saw both Solidarity and the OPZZ (the official Federation) union take shares in particular spinoffs. Furthermore both unions accepted the necessity of further job loss as the new structure emerged. Small firms were seen as the answer to redundancy by both union and management, and the new East Krakow Development Agency had been set up to create new employment on the HTS site. However, strikes in 1994 in both Huta Katowice and Huta Warszawa demonstrated how fragile this peace could be. If redundancies become a reality and small firms fail to become the hoped for job creating panacea, as we expect, then the current consensus could collapse.

Work and Unemployment

Two interrelated factors are combining to affect crucially the way that working people we talked to view the changes that are taking place both inside and outside of work. These factors are the increased uncertainty of existence and the unevenness and inequalities engendered by the process of change. In effect we are witnessing the effects of a transition from a low work intensity, mass underemployment system to one that will increasingly be characterized by highly intensive work practices and mass unemployment. This has important implications for those both in and out of work. The transition to a new form of labour process is being driven by the shift from semi-protected autarchic development to increased integration into a world economy, with the increased levels of competition that is attendant on such a shift. Protection, such as continued state subsidies and import restrictions, continues to exist and reduces the pressure to change. However, those sectors and firms that have been opened up to world markets, principally through FDI, have witnessed simultaneously an increased pressure to change, but also have acquired Western management tools designed to aid that adaptation. However, for the workforces concerned, adaptation translates into either unemployment or increased intensity of work.

We have already pointed to the extreme unevenness of the benefits of the market economy. The proliferation of Mercedes in Warsaw and the burgeoning billboards advertising Western goods belies the fact that for the majority of people the reality is poverty and declining standards of living. Although people no longer have to queue to get basic goods, rising prices mean that basics now consume an increasing proportion of people's wages, and luxuries are largely out of reach. The transformation has brought about a growing disparity in earnings between those at the top and the bottom of the wage ladder. Furthermore, rising unemployment, hitherto virtually unknown, has added a further twist to the spiral of rising poverty. Combined, these two phenomena produce around 50 per cent of the population who are now existing on or below the poverty line. The certainty of low wages, low intensity of work and high surveillance, has been replaced by uncertainty, poverty and unemployment. Rampant inequalities existed under the old regime, the *nomenklatura* benefiting from the privileges of constituting a favoured class; however, the transformation has brought more extreme and more visible inequalities. Furthermore, in many instances it is exactly the same people who continue to occupy privileged class locations. However, for most of the Polish working class there is a tension arising from the image of capitalism that people had, and therefore the high expectations of transformation confronting the realities of life in Poland in the mid-1990s. As Jacqueline Hayden (1994: 18–19) has pointed out, for many Poles, including Solidarity activists in the 1980s, the dream was for an American life style. Capitalist democracy meant dollars, Coke and Levis; and proliferating billboards and advertisements on the TV after 1989 have done little to dispel the image. However, by 1995, it was becoming painfully clear that capitalism did not bring automatic membership of the consumer society.

At a very general level there is a move in the direction away from the collective provision of a range of goods and services accessed either directly or indirectly through the status of employee. This reduction in the social wage needs further exploration. However, we wish to dispel the myth that widespread and equal provision of basic goods and services existed under the old regime. As we saw in the case of Wawel, access to facilities such as childcare provision was often limited to those in relatively privileged positions. Nevertheless, it was the case that a wide range of welfare benefits was provided through work, and provision extended beyond the individual worker and encompassed families. For example, workers in HTS were entitled to subsidized meals not only for themselves but also for up to four other members of their family.

The trend is away from the collective provision of welfare benefits towards the individualized and atomized acquisition of such provision, based on the ability to purchase them. However, this process is uneven and being driven by a number of forces. Driven by a budget deficit, the state has retreated to a position whereby welfare provision consists of little more than a low level safety net, and, furthermore, the state sees no role for itself in stopping people falling into that safety net. A principle of subsidiarity reigns, whereby the state will only provide that which the private sector will not. As we have seen in the case of HTS, firms that are privatized, or those in the process of preparing themselves for privatization, concentrate on what are deemed to be their core activities, with welfare provision being peripheral at best and expendable at worst. In ZPT Krakow for example, new flats had been built on the factory site, but were being sold at market rates that were well above that which most workers could afford. Anecdotal evidence suggests that in some cases firms in receipt of significant FDI have accelerated this process through the wholesale ditching of old benefits packages, now thought to be inappropriate to the 'mission' of the firm, whilst adopting incentive based payments.

The commodification of welfare provision had a number of implications, particularly for women workers. As we have seen, women are bearing the brunt of rising unemployment. However, as the women we talked to in both Wawel and ZPT Krakow stressed, two incomes (at least) were an absolute necessity for a family unit, simply to provide for a minimum level of existence. Women were being pulled in two directions. On the one hand, the re-emergence of traditional and highly reactionary images of the family were putting pressure on women to return to the home and this has been echoed in higher unemployment rates for women and low rates of return from the unemployment register. On the other hand, as necessities swallow up an ever larger proportion of family incomes, there is no real choice about staying in work. Hanging on to a job becomes an absolute necessity. The biggest fear, for the people we talked to, was the threat of unemployment for themselves or their partner. This is unlikely to diminish in the future in Krakow, or indeed other areas of Poland as restructuring gets fully under way.

There is an assumption that the arrival of foreign investment will at best increase levels of employment or at worst simply maintain the status quo. However, as regional Solidarity officials pointed out, there are already examples of FDI arriving with job guarantees, which are then undermined by attractive voluntary redundancy packages which lead to a significant reduction in jobs. Furthermore, as we have seen in the case of Wawel, any significant levels of investment would inevitably lead to significant job loss caused by more advanced production systems. As it is unlikely that companies such as Wawel could find any significant productive use for the labour that would be displaced, unemployment would seem to be inevitable. In all our case-study workplaces, including HTS, increased levels of investment though securing jobs for some would seem to lead either directly or indirectly to unemployment for large numbers of the current workforce. Therefore, the fear of unemployment, already apparent, can only grow as the process of restructuring unwinds.

If the arrival of new Western production techniques is accompanied, in some distorted shape or form, by management techniques such as Human Resource Management or Total Quality Management, then current levels of concern will rise. The language of 'empowerment' may at first sight appear to be seductive but the reality of 'management by stress' will soon dawn. The fear of unemployment will be compounded by increased pressure in work itself. This is what we mean by the transition from a low work intensity mass underemployment system to one characterized by highly intensive work practices and mass unemployment. At present, when we visit factories work tends to grind to a halt as people look to see who has arrived, or talk to their colleagues about the visitors. This is a 'luxury' that is unlikely to survive Western management practices.

We would suggest that these emerging pressures will increasingly raise questions over the already fragile consensus over restructuring. Solidarity, as we have seen, has tended to be Janus-like, acting both as agent of restructuring and workplace trade-union organization. Increased pressure on workers brought about by redundancies and increased intensity of working practices will pull the union more in the direction of 'orthodox' workplace trade-union organization. The women we talked to stressed that one of the major gains that transformation had brought was the freedom to speak out, complain and organize at work. The future of workers, in the short term in the sense of the number and nature of jobs that are available, as well as in the longer-term questions of control over their own working lives, will depend crucially on the organization and activity of workers themselves.

Overall, we are pessimistic about the general prospects for the standards of living of a large proportion of the Polish population. Transformation has brought poverty and unemployment for some and insecurity for many, although the process of combined and uneven development will mean that some regions, particular workplaces and some segments of the working population will undoubtedly benefit, if only in a relative sense. None of the orthodox theoretical approaches informing policy at local or national level (for example bootstraps and flexible specialization) are going to fundamentally alter this picture. More optimistically, one of the undoubted gains to emerge from the collapse of the old regimes is the potential to free the theory and practice of socialism from the poisonous influence of Stalinism. Furthermore, the Polish working class has a long and rich tradition of organization, opposition and struggle. Our optimism regarding the future is based on a belief that a growing disillusionment with the process of marketization will combine with emerging forms of organization and be informed by a liberatory language of socialism to raise fundamental questions about a system that, for many, has produced little more than a different kind of fear.

BIBLIOGRAPHY

Note - The authors regret that it has not been possible to provide the page numbers for articles in journals or chapters contributed to edited volumes.

Adam, J. (1994) The transition to a market economy in Poland. *Cambridge Journal of Economics*, 18.

Alexander, G.S and Skapska, G. (1994) *A Fourth Way? Privatisation, Property and the Emergence of New Market Economies.* London: Routledge.

Amin, A. (1988) The flexible firm in Italy. Paper presented to conference on Restructuring Work and Employment, University of Warwick.

Amin, A. and Dietrich, M. (1990) From hierarchy to hierarchy. Paper presented to European Association for Evolutionary Political Economy Conference.

Amin, A. and Malmberg, M. (1991) *Competing Structures of Structural and Institutional Change in the European Production System.* mimeo, Centre for Urban and Regional Development Studies, University of Newcastle upon Tyne.

Amsden, A., Kochanowicz, J., and Taylor, L. (1994) *The Market Meets Its Match.* Cambridge: Harvard University Press.

Ash, T. and Hare, P. (1994) Privatisation in the Russian Federation: changing enterprise behaviour in the transition period. *Cambridge Journal of Economics*, 18.

Atkins, W.S (1993) *Krakow Labour Market Strategy Project: Final Report.* Krakow: W.S. Atkins Management Consultants

Barker, C. and Weber, K. (1982) Solidarnosc: from Gdansk to military repression. *International Socialism*, 15.

Barker, C. (1986) *Festival of the Oppressed.* London: Bookmarks.

Barker, C. (1991) A note on the theory of capitalist states. In Clarke, S. (ed.) *The State Debate.* London: Macmillan.

Bednarczyk, M., Jaworski, J., and Kot, J. (1992) *Private Enterprise Development and the Economic and Political Restructuring of the Krakow Region in Poland.* Krakow Academy of Economics, Central Europe Working Paper, 10.

Berg, A. and Sachs, J. (1992) Structural adjustment and international trade in eastern Europe. *Economic Policy: A European Forum. Eastern Europe,* 14.

Bim, A. (1993), Hybrid forms of enterprise organisation in the former USSR and Russian Federation. Paper presented at American Social Sciences Association meeting, Anaheim.

Blanchard, O., Dornbusch, R., Krugman, P., Layard, R., and Sumner, L. (1991) *Reform in Eastern Europe.* London: MIT Press.

Blanchard, O. (1994) Transition in Poland. *Economic Journal,* 104.

Blanchard, O. and Layard, R. (1991) How To privatise, Discussion Paper 50, Centre for Economic Performance, London School of Economics.

Bloch, A. (1989) Entrepreneurialism in Poland and Hungary. *Telos,* 79.

Bluszkowski, J. (1993) *Economic Conditions of the Operation of Joint Ventures in Poland.* Warsaw: Friedrich Ebert Stiftung/PAIZ.

Bos, D. (1992) Privatisation in Europe: a comparison of approaches. *Oxford Review of Economic Policy,* 9 (1).

Bovaird, A. (1995) Urban governance and quality of life marketing. Paper presented to European Regional Studies Association conference, Gothenburg.

Brada, J.C. (1993) The transformation from communism to capitalism: how far? how fast? *Post Soviet Affairs,* 9 (2).

Buck, T., Thomson S., and Wright M. (1992), Post communist privatisation and the United Kingdom experience. *Public Enterprise,* 11 (2–3).

Budd, L. (1995) Territorial competition and globalisation. Paper presented to European Regional Studies Association conference, Gothenburg.

Caley, K., Chell, E., Chittendon, F., and Mason, C. (eds) (1992) *Small Enterprise Development.* London: Paul Chapman Publishing.

Callinicos, A. (1989) *Making History.* London: Polity Press.

Callinicos, A. (1991) *The Revenge of History.* London: Polity Press.

Calvo, G.A and Corricelli, F. (1992) Stabilising a previously planned economy in Poland. *Economic Policy: A European Forum. Eastern Europe,* 14.

Casson, M. (1993) *Enterprise Culture and Institutional Change in Eastern Europe,* University of Reading, Discussion Papers in Economy Series 6 (274).

Cecchini, P. (1988) *The European Challenge 1992.* Aldershot: Wildwood House.

Chang, H.-J. (1993) The political economy of industrial policy in Korea. *Cambridge Journal of Economics,* 17.

Chang, H.-J (1995) Return to Europe? In Chang, H.-J. and Nolan, P. *The Transformation of the Communist Economies.* Basingstoke: St Martin's Press.

Cieochinska, M. (1992) The development of the private sector in Poland 1989–1990. *Communist Economies in Transition,* 4(2).

Clarke, S. (ed.) (1991) *The State Debate.* London: Macmillan.

Clarke, S., Fairbrother, P., and Borisov, V., (1993) *What About the Workers?* London: Verso.

Cochrane, A. (1993) *Whatever Happened to Local Government?* Milton Keynes: Open University Press.

Collins, R. (1993) Sony in Poland: a case study. *European Management Journal,* 11 (1).

Commission of the European Communities (1993) *Trade and Foreign Investment in the Community's Regions: The Impact of Economic Reform in Central and Eastern Europe.* Brussels: European Commission.

Cooke, P. (1988) Municipal enterprise, growth coalitions and social justice. *Local Economy,* 3 (3).

Cooke, P. and Imrie, R. (1989) Little victories. *Entrepreneurship and Regional Development,* 1 (1).

Coopers and Lybrand (1992) *Hertfordshire TEC: Promoting Hertfordshire.* London: Coopers And Lybrand.

Cowling, K (1992) Reflections on the privatisation issue. Paper presented to Alternative Approach to the Transformation of the former Centrally Planned Economies, Cambridge.

Cowling, K. and Sugden, R. (1987) *Transnational Monopoly Capitalism.* Sussex: Wheatsheaf Books.

Cowling, K. and Sugden, R. (1994) *Beyond Capitalism.* London: Pinter Publishers.

Curran, J. and Blackburn, R. (1994) *Small Firms and Local Economic Networks.* London: Paul Chapman Publishing.

Dobosiewicz, Z. (1992) *Foreign Investment in Eastern Europe.* London: Routeledge.

Donges, J.B. (1992) Foreign investment in Eastern Europe. Paper presented at the International Economics Study Group Conference on International Investment, University of Nottingham.

Dornbusch, R. (1992) The case for trade liberalisation in developing countries. *Journal of Economic Perspectives*, 1 (1).

Dubois, P. and Linhart, D. (1992) *From Local Networks to a Territory Network*. Final report for European Union, Future of Industry in Europe programme, Gelsenkirchen.

Dunford, M (1994) Winners and losers. *European Urban and Regional Studies*, 1 (2).

Dunning, J.H. (1993) *The Globalisation of Business*. London: Routledge.

Dzwonczyk, J. and Sobczyk, A. (1993) *The System of Interest Representation in Poland*. mimeo, Krakow Academy of Economics.

Earle, J.S., Frydman, R., and Rapaczynski, A. (eds) (1993) *Privatisation in the Transition to a Market Economy*. London: Central European Press.

Economist Intelligence Unit (1994) *Country Report, Poland*.

Economist Intelligence Unit (1995) *Country Report, Poland*.

Eisenchitz, A. and Gough, J. (1993) *The Politics of Local Economic Policy*. London: Macmillan.

Elger, T. and Smith, C. (1994) Global Japanisation? In Elger, T. and Smith, C. (eds) *Global Japanisation*. London: Routledge.

Elson, D. (1986) The new international division of labour in the textile and garment industry. *International Journal of Social Policy*, 6 (2).

Elson, D. and Pearson, R. (1981) Nimble fingers make cheap workers: an analysis of women's employment in third world export manufacturing. *Feminist Review*, 7.

Estrin, S. (ed) (1994) *Privatisation in Central and Eastern Europe*. Harlow: Longman.

European Bank for Reconstruction and Development, (1992) *Annual Report*.

European Committee of Food, Catering and Allied Workers' Unions (1993) *L'Industrie Europeene du Tabac*. Conference du SETA–UITA pour le Secteur du Tabac, Seville.

Fevre, R. (1989) *Wales is Closed*. Nottingham: Spokesman Books.

Financial Times (1994) *Survey: Poland*. March 18.

Financial Times (1993) *Survey: International Telecommunications*. October 28.

Flecker, J. and Scheinstock, G. (1992) All collaboration and no control? Paper presented to International Labour Process Conference, University of Aston.

Foreman–Peck, J. (1985) Seedcorn or chaff. *Economic History Review*, 8 (3).

Froebel, F., Heinrichs, J., and Kreye, D., (1981) *The New International Division of Labour*. Cambridge: Cambridge University Press.

Frydman, R. and Rapaczynski, A. (1994) *Privatization in Eastern Europe: Is the State Withering Away?* Central European Press, Budapest.

Gardawski, J. and Zukowski, T. (1993) What the Polish workers think. *Labour Focus on Eastern Europe*, 45.

Garton Ash, T. (1991) *The Polish Revolution*. London: Granta Books.

Gomulka, S. (1992) Polish economic reform, 1990–91: principles, policies, outcomes. *Cambridge Journal of Economics*, 16.

Gomulka, S. (1993) Poland: glass half full. In Portes, R. (ed.) *Economic Transformation in Central Europe: A Progress Report*. London: Centre for Economic Performance and Research.

Gomulka, S. and Jasinki, P. (1994) Privatisation in Poland, 1989–1993: policies, methods and results. In Estrin, S (ed.) *Privatisation in Central and Eastern Europe*. Harlow: Longman.

Gora, M. Kotowska, I., Porek, T., and Podgorski, J. (1993) Poland: labour market trends and policies. In Fischer, G. and Standing, G. (eds) *Structural Change in Central and Eastern Europe*. Geneva: Organization for Economic Cooperation and Development (OECD).

Gora, M. and Lehmann, H. (1993) Flow and stock analysis of Polish unemployment. *Labour*, 6 (2).

Grabher, G. (1992) Eastern conquista. In Ernste, H. and Meier, V. (eds) *Regional Development and the Contemporary Industrial Restructuring*, London: Belhaven Press.

Guerrieri, P. (1992) Patterns of trade and integration of eastern Europe into the European Community. In Blass, W. and Foster, J. (eds) *Mixed Economies in Europe*. Aldershot: Edward Elgar.

Hamilton, C.B. and Winters, A.L. (1991) Opening up international trade with eastern Europe. *Economic Policy: A European Forum. Eastern Europe*, 14.

Hankiss, E. (1990) quoted in A. Gresh, Les sentiers escarpés du passage a la démocratie. *Le Monde Diplomatique*, February.

Hardy, J. (1994) Eastern promise? Foreign investment in Poland. *European Business Review*, 94 (5).

Hardy, J. and Rainnie, A. (1993) *Privatisation and Foreign Direct Investment: The Polish Experience.* University of Hertfordshire Business School Working Paper, Series UHBS 1993: 8.

Hardy, J. and Rainnie, A. (1994) Poland's economic transformation. *Labour Focus on Eastern Europe,* 47.

Harman, C. (1990) The storm breaks. *International Socialism,* 46.

Harman, C. (1991) The state and capitalism today. *International Socialism,* 51.

Harrison, B. (1989) *The Big Firms Are Coming Out of the Corner.* Working Paper 89–39, School of Urban and Public Affairs, Carnegie Mellon University.

Hausner, J. (1993) Developments in social security in Poland. In Hausner, J. and Mosur, G. (eds) *Transformation Processes in Eastern Europe,* Warsaw: Polish Academy of Sciences.

Hausner, J. and Mosur, G. (1993) *Transformation Processes in Eastern Europe,* Warsaw: Institute of Political Studies, Polish Academy of Sciences.

Hausner, J. and Morawski, W. (1994) Tripartism in Poland. Paper presented to Institute of Labour Research, Budapest.

Hausner, J. and Wojtyna, A. (1992), Privatisation as a restructuring device. Paper presented at the European Association for Evolutionary Political Economy conference, Paris.

Hausner, J. and Wojtyna, A. (1994) Institutional preconditions of collective wage bargaining in the socialist and post socialist economy: the case of Poland. Paper presented to European Association for Evolutionary Political Economy conference, Copenhagen.

Hausner, J., Kosek-Wojnar, M., Sosenko, B., and Surowka, K. (1995) Social welfare policy in Poland. In Pestoff, V. (ed.) *Reforming Social Services in Central and Eastern Europe.* Krakow: Krakow Academy of Economics/Friedrich Ebert Stiftung.

Hayden, J. (1994) *Poles Apart.* Dublin: Irish Academic Press.

Hayek, F. (1944) *The Road to Serfdom.* Chicago: University of Chicago Press.

Haynes, M. (1987) Understanding the soviet crisis. *International Socialism.* 34.

Haynes, M. (1992a) Class and crisis. *International Socialism.* 54.

Haynes, M. (1992b) State and market and the transition crisis in eastern Europe. Paper given at Realism and Human Sciences Conference, St Catherines College, Oxford.

Haynes, M. (1994) The wrong road on Russia. *International Socialism.* 64.

Hilbert, J., Sperling, H-J., and Rainnie, A. (1993) *SMEs at the Crossroads?* Report prepared for European Commission Future of Industry in Europe (FINE) Programme, Gelsenkirchen.

Hindley, B. (1992) Exports from eastern and central Europe and contingent protection. In Flemming, J. and Rollo, J.M.C (eds) *Trade, Payments and Adjustments in Central and Eastern Europe*. London: Royal Institute of International Affairs.

Hirst, P. (1989) The politics of industrial policy. In Hirst, P and Zeitlin, J (eds) *Reversing Industrial Decline*, London: Berg.

Hirst, P. and Thompson, G. (1992) The problem of 'globalisation': international economic relations, national economic management and the formation of trading blocs. *Economy and Society*, 21 (4).

Hirst, P. and Thompson, G. (1995) Globalisation and the future of the nation state. *Economy and Society* 24 (3).

Hirst, P. and Zeitlin, J. (1989) *Reversing Industrial Decline*, Oxford: Berg.

Hirst, P. and Zeitlin, J. (1991) Flexible specialisation versus post fordism. *Economy and Society*, 20 (1).

Hudson, R. (1992) *Restructuring the West European Steel Industry*. Centre for European Studies Working Paper No 3, University of Durham.

Hudson, R. (1995) Regional futures: industrial restructuring, new production concepts and spatial development strategies in the new Europe. Paper presented to European Regional Studies Association conference, Gothenburg.

Hughes, G. and Hare, P. (1991) Trade policy and restructuring in eastern europe in Flemming, J. and Rollo, J.M.C. (eds) *Trade Payments and Adjustment in Central and Eastern Europe* London: Royal Institute of International Affairs.

Hughes, G. and Hare, P. (1992) Industrial restructuring in eastern Europe. *European Economics Review*, 36.

Hunya, G. (1992) Foreign direct investment and privatisation in central and eastern Europe. *Communist Economies in Transformation*, 4 (4).

ILO (1995) *World Employment 1995*. Geneva: International Labour Office.

Institute for Market Economy Research (1993) A ranking of Eastern European countries and Polish sectors and regions. In *Gazeta Bankowa*, 40.

Jackson, M. (1992) Constraints on systematic transformation and their policy implications. *Oxford Review of Economic Policy*, 7 (4).

Jedrzejczak, G.T. (1992) The Polish capital markets 1991: instruments, institutions, perspectives. *Public Enterprise*, 11 (2–3).

Jenkins, R. (1991) The political economy of industrialisation: a comparison of Latin America and East Asian newly industrialised countries. *Development and Change*, 22.

Jenkins, S.R. (1984) Divisions over the international division of labour. *Capital and Class*, 22.

Jensen, H. and Plum, V. (1993) From centralised state to local government. *Environment and Planning D*, 11.

Jessop, B. (1994) International competitiveness, regional economic strategies, and the post-socialist economies: constraints, dilemmas, and prospects. Paper presented to conference on Transforming Post-Socialist Societies. Krakow: Friedrich Ebert Stiftung and Krakow Academy of Economics.

Johnson, S. and Loveman, G. (1993) The implications of the Polish economic reform for small business. In Acs, Z. and Audretsch, D. (eds) *Small Firms and Entrepreneurship: An East-West Perspective.* Cambridge: Cambridge University Press.

Jolly, A. (1992) East Europe's top investment prospect. *CBI News*, March.

Karwinska, A. (1992), *Challenges for Poland of the 1990s.* Krakow Academy of Economics, Seminar Paper No. 12.

Kennedy, M. (1991) *Professionals, Power and Solidarity.* Cambridge: Cambridge University Press.

Kierzkowski, J., Okolski, M., and Wellisz, S. (eds) (1993) *Stabilisation and Structural Adjustment in Poland.* London: Routledge.

Kloc, K. (1992), Polish labour in transition, *Telos*, 92.

Kloc, K. (1993) Trade unions and economic transformation in Poland. *Journal of Communist Studies*, 9 (4).

Knell, M. and Rider, C. (eds.) (1992) *Socialist Economies in Transition.* Aldershot: Edward Elgar.

Kolankiewicz, G. (1982) Employee self management and socialist trade unionism. In Woodall, J. (ed.) *Policy and Politics in Contemporary Poland.* London: Frances Pinter.

Kolarska-Bobimska, L. (1993) *Social Interests and their Political Representation in Poland.* Mimeo, Krakow Academy of Economics.

Kolvereid, L. and Krzysztof, O. (1994) Entrepreneurship in emerging versus mature economies. *International Small Business Journal*, 12 (4).

Kondratowicz, A. and Okolski, M. (1993) The Polish economy on the eve of the Solidarity take-over. In Kierzkowski, J., Okolski, M., and Wellisz, S. (eds) *Stabilisation and Structural Adjustment in Poland.* London: Routledge.

Kornai, J. (1990a) *The Road To Freedom.* New York: W.W. Norton.

Kornai, J. (1990b) *Vision, Reality and State.* Hemel Hempstead: Harvester Wheatsheaf.

Kosek-Wojnar, K. (1995) The reform of self government and financial policy in Poland. *Emergo*, 2 (1).

Kot, J., Dziura, M., Piasecka, E., Bednarczyk, M., Hardy, J., and Rainnie, A. (1995) Restructuring the Cracow Region. Paper presented to European Regional Studies Association conference, Gothenburg.

Kowalik, A. (1993) Steel makers must change plant, management and mentality. *British and American Embassies Economic Review*, 71–93.

Kowalik, T. (1994) A reply to Maurice Glasman. *New Left Review*, 206.

Kozminski, A. (1992) The main issues of industrial policy for Poland. *Communist Economies and Economic Transformation*, 4 (2).

Ksiezopolski, M. (1991) The labour market in transition and the growth of poverty in Poland. *Labour and Society*, 16 (2).

Ksiezopolski, M. (1992) The prospects for social policy development in Poland. In Deacon, B. (ed.) *Social Policy and Social Justice and Citizenship in Eastern Europe*. London: Sage.

Kuron, J. and Modzelewski, K. (1982) *Solidarnosc: The Missing Link*. London: Bookmarks.

Kurski, J. (1993) *Lech Walesa: Democrat or Dictator?* Boulder: Westview.

Laba, R. (1991) *The Roots of Solidarity*. Princeton: Princeton University Press.

Lane, C. (1991) Industrial reorganisation in Europe. *Work, Employment and Society*, 5 (4).

Levcik, F. and Stankovsky, J. (1979) *Industrial Cooperation between East and West*. London: Macmillan.

Levitas, A. and Strzalkowski, P. (1992) What does 'uwlaszczemie nomenklatury' (propertisation of the nomenklatura) really mean? *Communist Economies and Economic Transformation*, 2 (3).

Lewis, P. (1994) *Central Europe Since 1945*. Harlow: Longman.

Lewis, P. (1995) Political institutionalisation and party development in post communist Poland. *Europe-Asia Studies*, 46 (5).

Lipton, D. and Sachs, J. (1990) Creating A Market Economy in Poland. *Brooking Papers on Economic Activity* 1., Washington: Brookings Institution.

Lo, D. (1995) Economic theory and the transformation of the soviet-type system. In Chang, H.-J. and Nolan, P., *The Transformation of the Communist Economies*. Basingstoke: St Martins Press.

Lowy, M. (1981) *Combined and Uneven Development*. London: Verso.

McDermott, G.A. (1993) Rethinking the ties that bind. The limits of privatisation in the Czech republic. Paper presented to conference on the Social Embeddedness of the Economic Transformation in Central and Eastern Europe, Social Science Research Centre Berlin (WZB).

MacDonald, R. (1992) Runners, fallers and plodders. In Caley, K., Chell, E., Chittendon, F., and Mason, C. *Small Enterprise Development,* London: Paul Chapman Publishing.

McDonald, K.R., (1993) Why privatisation is not enough, *Harvard Business Review,* May–June.

McKinnon, R. (1991) Liberalising foreign trade in socialist economies. In Williamson, J. (ed.) *Currency Convertibility in Eastern Europe,* Washington: Institute for International Economics.

McMichael, P. and Myhre, D. (1991) Global regulation versus the nation state. *Capital and Class,* 43.

MacShane, D. (1981) *Solidarity,* Nottingham: Spokesman Books.

Maddison, A. (1991) *Dynamic Forces in Capitalist Development: A Long Run Comparative View,* Oxford: Oxford University Press.

Major, I. (1993) *Privatisation in Eastern Europe,* Aldershot: Edward Elgar.

Marginson, P. (1994) Multinational Britain: employment and work in an internationalised economy. *Human Resource Management Journal,* 4 (4).

Martin, B. (1993) *In the Public Interest,* London: Zed Publishers.

Martinos, H. (1988) Identifying local economic development research priorities. In Bennett, R. (ed.) *Local Economic Development.* London: Economic and Social Research Council.

Maxcy, G. (1981) *Multinational Motor Industry.* London: Croom Helm.

Messerlin, P. (1992) The association agreement between the EC and central Europe: trade liberalisation or constitutional failure. In Flemming, J. and Rollo, J.M.C. (eds) *Trade, Payments and Adjustment in Central and Eastern Europe.* London: The Royal Institute of Economic Affairs.

Messerlin, P. (1995) Trade relations of the eastern European countries. In Saunders, C. (ed.) *Eastern Europe in Crisis and the Way Out.* London: Macmillan.

Michalski, J. (1991) The privatisation process in Poland: legal aspects. *Communist Economies and Economic Transformation,* 3 (3).

Morawski, W. (1987) Self management and economic reform. In Kovalewicz, J. (ed.) *Crisis and Transition,* Oxford: Berg.

Morawski, W. (nd) Trade unions in Poland. Mimeo, Institute of Sociology, Warsaw University.

Mujzel, J. (1993) Privatisation: the Polish experience. In Hausner, J. and Mosur, G. (eds) *Transformation Processes in Eastern Europe.* Warsaw: Polish Academy of Sciences.

Mujzel, J. (nd) *State Owned Enterprises in Transition.* Mimeo, Krakow Academy of Economics.

Mulgen, G. (1991) *Communication and Control.* London: Polity Press.

Murrell, P. (1992) Evolution in economics and in economic reform of centrally planned economies. In Clague, C. and Rausser, G. (eds) *The Emergence of Market Economies in Europe.* Oxford: Basil Blackwell.

Murrell, P. (1993) What is shock therapy? What did it do in Poland and Russia? *Post Soviet Affairs,* 9 (2).

Myant, M. (1993) *Transforming Socialist Economies.* Aldershot: Edward Elgar.

Nell, E. (1992), The failure of demand management in socialist economies. In Knell, M. and Rider, C. (eds) *Socialist Economies in Transition.* Aldershot: Edward Elgar.

Nuti, D. (1990) Market socialism: the model that might have been but never was. In Aslund, A. (ed.) *Market Socialism or the Restoration of Capitalism.* Cambridge: Cambridge University Press.

Nuti, D.M. (1982) The Polish crisis: economic factors and constraints. In Drewnowski, J. (ed.) *Crisis in the East European Economy.* London: Croom Helm.

Ohmae, K. (1990) *The Borderless World.* London: Collins.

Ost, D. (1989) The transformation of Solidarity, *Telos,* 79.

Ost, D. (1992) Shock therapy and its discontents, *Telos,* 92.

Ost, D. (1993) *Labor, Class and Democracy.* mimeo, Krakow Academy of Economics.

PAIZ (1993) *Economic Conditions for the Operation of Joint Ventures in Poland.* Warsaw: PAIZ/Friedrich Ebert Stiftung.

Paliwoda, S.J. (1981) *Joint East/West Marketing and Production Ventures.* Aldershot: Gower.

Pankow, W. (1987) The Solidarity movement, management and the political system in Poland. In Kowalewicz, J. (ed.) *Crisis and Transition.* Oxford: Berg.

Pankow, W. (1993) *Work Institutions in Transformation.* Warsaw: Friedrich Ebert Stiftung.

Parker, D. (1993) International aspects of privatisation: A critical assessment of business restructuring in the UK, Czechoslovakia and Malaysia. University of Hertfordshire, Business School Working Paper.

Pickel, A. (1992) Jump starting a market economy: a critique of the radical strategy for economic reform in the light of the East German experience. *Studies in Comparative Communism*, 25 (2).

Pinot, B. (1992) Transitional state enterprises in Poland. World Bank Working Paper.

Piore, M. and Sabel, C. (1984) *The Second Industrial Divide*. New York: Basic Books

Pitelis, C. (1991) *Market and Non-market Hierarchies*. Oxford: Blackwell.

Pitelis, C. and Sugden, R. (eds) (1991) *The Nature of the Transnational Firm*. London: Routledge.

Polak, J. (1991) Convertibility: an indispensable element in the transition process in Eastern Europe. In Williamson, J. (ed.) *Currency Convertibility in Eastern Europe*. Washington: Institute for International Economics.

Polanyi, K. (1944) *The Great Transformation*. Boston: Beacon Press.

Pounds, N., Dziewonski, K., Kortus, B., and Vlassenbroeck, W. (1981) The growth of Krakow and Nowa Huta. In Cochrane, A., Hamnett, C., and McDowell, L. (eds) *City, Economy and Society*. London: Harper & Row.

Poznanski, K. (1993) Restructuring property rights in Poland, *Eastern European Politics and Societies*, 7 (3).

Radice, H. (1993) Global integration, national disintegration? Foreign capital in the reconstruction of central and eastern Europe. University of Leeds, School of Business and Economic Studies Discussion Paper, E93/09.

Radice, H. (1994a) Organising markets in central and eastern Europe: competition, governance and the role of foreign capital. Paper for European Management and Organisations in Transition Workshop on Processes of Industrial Transformation, Nurnberg.

Radice, H. (1994a) The role of foreign investment in the transformation of eastern Europe. In Chang H-J. (ed.) *Economic Reform in Centrally Planned Economies*. London: Macmillan.

Rainnie, A. (1989) *Industrial Relations in Small Firms*. London: Routledge.

Rainnie, A. (1991a) Small firms: between the enterprise culture and new times. In Burrows, R. (ed.) *Deciphering the Enterprise Culture*. London: Routledge.

Rainnie, A. (1991b) Flexible specialisation: new times or old hat? In Blyton, P. and Morris J. (eds) *A Flexible Future?* Berlin: De Gruyter.

Rainnie, A. (1993) The reorganisation of large firms subcontracting. *Capital and Class*, 49.

Rodrik, D. (1992) The limits of trade policy reform in developing countries. *Journal of Economic Perspectives*, 6 (1).

Rosati, D. (1990) *The Polish Road To Capitalism: A Critique of the Balcerowicz Plan.* London: Thames Occasional Paper, Thames Polytechnic.

Rosati, D. (1993) Poland: glass half full. In Portes, R. (ed.) *Economic Transformation in Central Europe.* London: Centre for Economic Policy and Research.

Rosati, D. (1992) Problems of post-CMEA trade and payments. In Flemming, J. and Rollo, J.M.C. (eds) *Trade, Payments and Adjustments in Central and Eastern Europe.* London: Royal Institute of International Affairs.

Rostowski, J. (1993) The implications of rapid private sector growth in Poland. London School of Economics, Centre for Economic Performance, Discussion Paper No. 159.

Roszkovski, W. (1992) Reconstruction of the government and state apparatus. In Latawski, P. (ed.) *The Reconstruction of Poland, 1914–23.* London: Macmillan.

Ryder, A. (1992) Urban planning in post war Poland with reference to Cracow. *Cities*, August.

Schaffer, M. (1992) The economy of Poland. London School of Economics, Centre for Economic Performance, Discussion Paper.

Scott, A. (1988) Flexible production systems and regional development. *International Journal of Urban and Regional Research*, 12 (2).

Scott, A. and Storper, M. (1991) Industrialisation and regional development. In Storper, M. and Scott, A. (eds) *Pathways to Industrialisation and Regional Development,* London: Routledge.

Simatupang, B. (1994) *The Polish Economic Crisis; Background, Causes and Aftermath.* London: Routledge.

Skalmati, F. (1992) On the Selected Problems of Wages in the Transformation of the Polish Economy. Krakow Academy of Economics, Seminar Paper No. 13.

Smith, N. (1990) *Uneven Development.* Oxford: Basil Blackwell.

Smith, N. and Rebne, D. (1992) FDI in Poland, the Czech and Slovak Republics and Hungary: the centrality of the joint entry mode. *The Mid Atlantic Journal of Business*, 28 (3).

Staniszkis, J. (1990) Patterns of change in eastern Europe. *Eastern European Politics and Societies*, 4 (1).

Stark, D. (1990) Path dependence and privatisation strategy. *East European Politics and Society*, 6 (1).

Stark, D. (1993) Not by design: recombinant property in eastern European capitalism. Paper presented to Transforming Post Socialist Societies Conference, Krakow.

Stopford, J. and Strange, S. (1991) *Rival States, Rival Firms*. Cambridge: Cambridge University Press.

Storey, D. and Johnson, S. (1987) *Job Generation and Labour Market Change*. London: Macmillan.

Storey, D. and Strange, A. (1992) New players in the enterprise culture? in Caley, K., Chell, E., Chittendon, F., and Mason, C. (eds) *Small Enterprise Development*. London: Paul Chapman Publishing.

Storey, D. (1994) *Understanding the Small Business Sector*. London: Routledge.

Storper, M. and Scott, A.J. (1992) *Pathways to Industrialisation and Regional Development*. London: Routledge.

Stryjakiewicz, T. (1995) Regional differences in the process of transformation of the Polish economy. Paper presented at the European Regional Studies Association conference, Gothenburg.

Sugden, R. and Cowling, K. (1987) *Transnational Monopoly Capitalism*. London: Wheatsheaf Books.

Supinska, J. (1995) Social costs and social goals of transformation policy. In Saunders C. (ed.) *Eastern Europe in Crisis and the Way Out*. London: Macmillan.

Syzmanski, A. (1984) Class struggle in socialist Poland. *Insurgent Sociologist*, 4.

Thirkell, J., Scase, R., and Vickerstaff, S. (1994) Labour relations in transition in eastern Europe. *Industrial Relations Journal*, 25 (2).

Tittenbrun, J. (1993) *The Collapse of Real Socialism in Poland*. London: Janus Publishing.

Tittenbrun, J. (1995) The managerial revolution revisited: the case of privatisation in Poland. *Capital and Class*, 55.

Totterdill, P. (1989) Local economic strategies as economic policies. *Economy & Society*, 58 (4).

United Nations Centre on Transnational Corporations, (1981) *Transnational Corporations in Food and Beverage Processing*. New York: United Nations.

United Nations (1992) *Statistical Survey of Recent Trends in Foreign Investment in Eastern European Countries*. New York: United Nations.

United Nations World Investment Report (1993) *Transnational Corporations and Integrated International Production.* New York: United Nations.

Van Brabant, J.M. (1989) *Economic Integration in Eastern Europe.* London: Harvester Wheatsheaf.

Van Brabant, J.M. (1992) Convertibility in eastern Europe through a payments union. In Williamson, J. (ed.) *Currency Convertibility in Eastern Europe.* Washington: Institute for International Economics.

Voslensky, M. (1984) *Nomenklatura.* London: Bodley Head.

Wade, R. (1991) *Governing the Market: Economic Theory and the Role of Government in East Asian Industrialisation.* Princeton: Princeton University Press.

Walsh, J. (1989) Capital restructuring and technological change. In Tailby S. and Whitson C. (eds) *Manufacturing Change.* Oxford: Basil Blackwell.

Walters, A. (1992) The transition to a market economy. In Clague, C. and Rausser, G. (eds) *The Emergence of Market Economies in Eastern Europe.* Oxford: Basil Blackwell.

Warsaw Voice (1994) Women's rights: privilege or prejudice. *Warsaw Voice*, 45 (315).

Watson, P. (1993) Eastern Europes silent revolution: gender. *Sociology*, 27 (3).

Weinstein, M. (1994) From cogovernance to ungovernability. Paper presented to Industrial Relations Research Seminar, Massachusetts Institute of Technology.

Weiskopff, T.E. (1992) Alternative approaches to privatisation in post communist societies. Paper presented to Economic and Social Research Council, Political Economy Group, London.

WERI (1993) *Transforming The Polish Economy.* World Economy Research Institute (Warsaw) & International Centre for Economic Growth (San Francisco).

WERI (1994a) *Transforming The Polish Economy II.* World Economy Research Institute (Warsaw) & International Centre for Economic Growth (San Francisco).

WERI (1994b) *Poland: International Economic Report.* Warsaw: World Economy Research Institute.

Whitfield, D. (1992) *The Welfare State.* London: Pluto Press.

Williams, K., Cutler, T., Williams, J., and Haslam, C. (1987) The end of mass production? *Economy & Society*, 16.

Wilson, E.J. (1991) The third phase of the Polish revolution: property rights. *Public Enterprise*, 11 (2–3).

Winieckie, J. (1992) The Polish transition under threat. *Communist Economies in Transition*, 4 (2).

Wisniewski, F. (nd) The ways and development of small and medium enterprises in Poland under system transformation. Mimeo, Department of Economics, University of Poznan.

Wojtyna, A. (1993) Institutional framework for industrial restructuring and policy in Poland. Paper presented to European Association for Evolutionary Political Economy Conference, Barcelona.

Zielinski, M. (1993) Polish survey. In Winiecki, J. and Kondratowicz, A. (eds) *The Macroeconomics of Transition: Developments in East Central Europe*. London: Routledge.

van Zon, H. (1992) Towards Regional Innovation Systems in Central Europe. Report for the Institute of Work and Technology, Gelsenkirchen.

Zubek, V. (1993) The fragmentation of Poland's political party system. *Communist and Post-Communist Studies*, 26 (1).

Zukowski, R. (1993) Stabilisation and recession in a transitional economy: the case of Poland. *World Development*, 21 (7).

Index